A HISTORY
OF
INDIAN PHILOSOPHY

A HISTORY

OF

INDIAN PHILOSOPHY

BY THE LATE
SURENDRANATH DASGUPTA

VOLUME V

SOUTHERN SCHOOLS OF ŚAIVISM

CAMBRIDGE
AT THE UNIVERSITY PRESS
1955

PUBLISHED BY
THE SYNDICS OF THE CAMBRIDGE UNIVERSITY PRESS

London Office: Bentley House, N.W. 1
American Branch: New York

Agents for Canada, India, and Pakistan: Macmillan

Printed in Great Britain at the University Press, Cambridge
(Brooke Crutchley, University Printer)

SURENDRANATH DASGUPTA
A MEMOIR

THE late Surendranath Dasgupta was born in Kusthia, a subdivision of Bengal, in October 1885 (10th of Āśvina). He came from a well-known family in Goila, District Barishal, East Bengal. This family was particularly known for its great tradition of Sanskrit learning and culture. His great-grandfather was a distinguished scholar and also a Vaidya (physician of the Ayurvedic school of medicine). He was known by his title "Kavīndra", and was running a Sanskrit institution known as "Kavīndra College", which continued in existence up to the time of the partition of India in 1947. This institution maintained about 150 students with free board and lodging, and taught Kāvya, Grammar, Nyāya, Vedānta and Āyurveda in traditional Indian style. Professor Dasgupta's father, Kaliprasanna Dasgupta, was the only member of the family who learnt English and took up the job of a surveyor.

In his early years, between five and eight, while he did not know any Sanskrit, he showed certain remarkable gifts of answering philosophical and religious questions in a very easy and spontaneous manner. He could demonstrate the various Yogic postures (*āsanas*); and used to pass easily into trance states, while looking at the river Ganges or listening to some Kirtan song. He was visited by hundreds of learned men and pious saints at his father's residence at Kalighat and was styled "Khoka Bhagawan" (Child God). Mention may particularly be made of Srimat Bijay Krishna Goswami, Prabhu Jagat Bandhu and Sivanarayan Paramhansa. He was sometimes taken to the Theosophical Society, Calcutta, where a big audience used to assemble, and the boy was put on the table and questioned on religious and theological matters. The answers that he gave were published in the Bengali and English newspapers along with the questions. Some of these are still preserved.

He was educated at Diamond Harbour for a time, and then for seven years in the Krishnagar Collegiate School and College. He was interested in Sanskrit and science alike, and surprised the professor of chemistry by his proficiency in the subject so much that he never taught in the class unless his favourite pupil was present. He took his M.A. degree from Sanskrit College, Calcutta, in 1908. His fellow-students noticed with interest his habits and peculiarities. He took no care of his clothes and hair; he studied on a mat with a pillow for his table; and his place was littered with books and papers. Though he did not talk very much, he already had a reputation for scholarship when he was an M.A. student at the Sanskrit College. His scholarship in Pāṇini was so great that when even his teachers had differences of opinion about a grammatical matter, he was called out of his class to solve it. His first research work on Nyāya, which was written while he was in the Sanskrit College, was read out before the Pandits, and was very highly appreciated by them and the then Principal, the late Mahamahopadhyaya H. P. Sastri. Incidentally it may be noted that Nyāya was not one of the subjects of his M.A. curriculum. After his childhood, both as a student and as a young man, he had many striking religious and spiritual experiences, which were known to a group of his intimate friends and admirers.

One of the peculiar traits of Dasgupta was that he seldom wished to learn anything from others. He had an inner pride that led him to learn everything by his own efforts. He never wanted any stimulus from outside. Whenever he took up any work, he threw his whole soul and being into it. He passed his M.A. in Philosophy in 1910, as a private candidate, summarising all the prescribed books in his own way. He was twice offered a state scholarship to study Sanskrit in a scientific manner in Europe, but as he was the only child of his parents, he refused out of consideration for their feelings. He began his service at Rajshahi College as an officiating lecturer in Sanskrit. He was soon provided with a permanent professorship at Chittagong College, where he worked from 1911 to 1920 and from 1922 to 1924.

Chittagong was to him like a place of banishment, being far away from the great libraries of Calcutta. The College was newly started and had none of the facilities that it possesses now. But Dasgupta had taken the resolution that he would dedicate himself to the study of the Indian "Śāstras" in their entirety. For him to take a resolution was to accomplish it, and while many of his colleagues enjoyed club life in an easy-going manner, he continued his studies for fourteen hours or more a day, in spite of the teasing of his friends. At this time Maharaja Manindra Chandra Nandi of

Cassimbazar made an offer of 300 rupees a month for Dasgupta to start his library; this is now one of the best of its kind, containing many unpublished manuscripts and over 15,000 printed books. It was given by him as a gift to the Benares Hindu University on his retirement from the Calcutta University. Love of knowledge seems to have been the guiding passion of the professor's life. He never sought position or honour, though they were showered upon him in quick succession in his later days. He had a unique sincerity of purpose and expression, and the light that came from his soul impressed kindred souls.

When Lord Ronaldshay, the Governor of Bengal, came to visit Chittagong College, he had a long talk with Professor Dasgupta in his classroom, and was so much impressed by it that he expressed the desire that the first volume of the *History of Indian Philosophy* might be dedicated to him. Originally Dasgupta's plan was to write out the history of Indian systems of thought in one volume. Therefore he tried to condense the materials available within the compass of one book. But as he went on collecting materials from all parts of India, a huge mass of published and unpublished texts came to light, and the plan of the work enlarged more and more as he tried to utilise them. As a matter of fact, his was the first and only attempt to write out in a systematic manner a history of Indian thought directly from the original sources in Sanskrit, Pali and Prakrit. In a work of the fourteenth century A.D., the *Sarva-darśana-saṃgraha* of Mādhavācārya, we find a minor attempt to give a survey of the different philosophical schools of India. But the account given there is very brief, and the work does not give an exhaustive survey of all the different systems of philosophy. In the present series the author traced, in a historical and critical manner, the development of Indian thought in its different branches from various sources, a considerable portion of which lies in unpublished manuscripts. He spared no pains and underwent a tremendous amount of drudgery in order to unearth the sacred, buried treasures of Indian thought. He revised his original plan of writing only one volume and thought of completing the task in five consecutive volumes constituting a series. He shouldered this gigantic task all alone, with the sincerest devotion and unparalleled enthusiasm and zeal.

Dasgupta had taken the Griffith Prize in 1916 and his doctorate in Indian Philosophy in 1920. Maharaja Sir Manindra Chandra Nandi now urged him to go to Europe to study European philosophy at its sources, and generously bore all the expenses of his research tour (1920–22). Dasgupta went to England and distinguished himself at Cambridge as a research student in philosophy under Dr McTaggart. During this time the Cambridge University Press published the first volume of the *History of Indian Philosophy* (1921). He was also appointed lecturer at Cambridge, and nominated to represent Cambridge University at the International Congress of Philosophy in Paris. His participation in the debates of the Aristotelian Society, London, the leading philosophical society of England, and of the Moral Science Club, Cambridge, earned for him the reputation of being an almost invincible controversialist. Great teachers of philosophy like Ward and McTaggart, under whom he studied, looked upon him not as their pupil but as their colleague. He received his Cambridge doctorate for an elaborate thesis on contemporary European philosophy. The impressions that he had made by his speeches and in the debates at the Paris Congress secured for him an invitation to the International Congress at Naples in 1924, where he was sent as a representative of the Bengal Education Department and of the University of Calcutta; later on, he was sent on deputation by the Government of Bengal to the International Congress at Harvard in 1926. In that connection he delivered the Harris Foundation lectures at Chicago, besides a series of lectures at about a dozen other Universities of the United States and at Vienna, where he was presented with an illuminated address and a bronze bust of himself. He was invited in 1925 to the second centenary of the Academy of Science, Leningrad, but he could not attend for lack of Government sanction. In 1935, 1936 and 1939 he was invited as visiting professor to Rome, Milan, Breslau, Königsberg, Berlin, Bonn, Cologne, Zürich, Paris, Warsaw and England.

While in Rome he delivered at the International Congress of Science in 1936 an address on the Science of Ancient India with such success that shouts of "Grand' uomo" cheered him through the session of the day. This led eventually to the conferment of the Honorary D.Litt. upon him by the University of Rome in 1939. He was on that occasion a state guest in Rome and military honours were accorded to him. At this time he read out before many cultured societies English translations of his own Bengali verses called *Vanishing Lines*. The appreciation that these verses received secured for him a special reception and banquet at the Poets' Club. Before this, only two other Indian poets had been accorded this reception: Tagore and Mrs Naidu. Laurence Binyon spoke of his poems in the following terms: "I am impressed by the richness of imagination which pervades the poems and the glow of mystic faith and fervent emotion—reminding me of one of William Blake's sayings: 'Exuberance is beauty'. It would be a great pity if the poems are not published in English."

The University of Warsaw made him an honorary Fellow of the Academy of Sciences. He was elected Fellow of the Royal Society of Literature. The Société des Amis du Monde of Paris offered him a special reception, and M. Renou, Professor of Sanskrit in the University of Paris, wrote to him afterwards: "While you were amongst us, we felt as if a Śaṅkara or a Patañjali was born again and moved amongst us." Kind and simple and gentle as he was, Dasgupta was always undaunted in challenging scholars and philosophers. In the second International Congress of Philosophy in Naples, the thesis of his paper was that Croce's philosophy had been largely anticipated by some forms of Buddhism, and that where Croce differed he was himself in error. On account of internal differences Croce had no mind to join the Congress, but the fact that Dasgupta was going to challenge his philosophy and prove it to be second-hand in open congress, induced him to do so. In the same way he challenged Vallée Poussein, the great Buddhist scholar, before a little assembly presided over by McTaggart. In the meetings of the Aristotelian Society he was a terror to his opponents, his method of approach being always to point out their errors. He inflicted this treatment on many other scholars, particularly Steherbatsky and Levy.

Disinterested love of learning and scientific accuracy were his watchwords. He had to make a most painstaking tour of South India to collect materials for his great *History*. Though he was well known as a scholar of Sanskrit and philosophy, his studies in other subjects, such as physics, biology, anthropology, history, economics, political philosophy, etc. are very considerable. Above all, he developed a new system of thought which was entirely his own. A brief account of this appeared in *Contemporary Indian Philosophy* edited by Radhakrishnan and Muirhead and published by Allen and Unwin.

In 1924, as a mark of recognition of his scholarship, he was admitted to I.E.S. service in Calcutta Presidency College and was posted as Head of the Department of Philosophy. In 1931 he became Principal of the Government Sanskrit College, Calcutta, and *ex-officio* Secretary of the Bengal Sanskrit Association. In the latter capacity he had to arrange about 218 papers in Sanskrit for Sanskrit Title Examinations for about ten thousand candidates coming from all parts of India. During the eleven years of his principalship in Sanskrit College he had worked in various ways for the advancement of Sanskrit learning and culture in India.

In 1942 he retired from Sanskrit College and was appointed King George V Professor of Mental and Moral Science in the University of Calcutta. He worked there for three years and delivered the Stephanos Nirmalendu lectures on the history of religions. He had been suffering from heart trouble since 1940, but was still carrying on his various activities and research work. In 1945 he retired from the Calcutta University and was offered the Professorship of Sanskrit at Edinburgh which had fallen vacant after the death of Professor Keith. The doctors also advised a trip to England. On his arrival in England he fell ill again. In November 1945 he delivered his last public lecture on Hinduism in Trinity College, Cambridge. Since then he was confined to bed with acute heart trouble. He stayed in England for five years (1945–50). Even then he published the fourth volume of his *History of Indian Philosophy* at the Cambridge University Press, the *History of Sanskrit Literature* at Calcutta University, *Rabindranath the Poet and Philosopher* with his Calcutta publishers, and a book on aesthetics in Bengali. In 1950 he returned to Lucknow.

In 1951, through friendly help given by Pandit Jawaharlal Nehru, he started writing the fifth and final volume of the *History of Indian Philosophy*. He had also planned to write out his own system of philosophy in two volumes. His friends and students requested him several times to complete the writing of his own thought first. But he looked upon his work on Indian philosophy as the sacred mission of his life, and thought himself to be committed to that purpose. His love of his mother country and all that is best in it always had precedence over his personal aspirations.

With strong determination and unwavering devotion he brought his life's mission very near its completion. Till the last day of his life he was working for this, and completed one full section just a few hours before his passing away, on 18 December 1952. Even on this last day of his life, he worked in the morning and afternoon on the last chapter of the section of Southern Śaivism. He passed away peacefully at eight in the evening while discussing problems of modern psychology. All his life he never took rest voluntarily and till his end he was burning like a fire, full of zeal and a rare brightness of spirit for the quest of knowledge.

His plan of the fifth volume was as follows:

(1) Southern Schools of Śaivism.
(2) Northern Schools of Śaivism.
(3) Philosophy of Grammar.
(4) Philosophy of some of the Selected Tantras.

Of these the first was to be the largest section and covers more than a third of the proposed work according to his own estimate. He collected manuscripts from various sources from Southern India and completed his survey of the different schools of Southern Śaivism. This is now being published by the Cambridge University Press.

Another aspect of his life, which showed itself in trances and in deep unswerving devotion and faith in his Lord, never left him. These were manifest in him even as a child, and continued all through his life. In trials and troubles and sorrows he was fearless and undaunted. In difficulties he had his indomitable will to conquer; he bore all his sufferings with patience and fortitude. His faith in God sustained him with an unusual brightness and cheerfulness of spirit. He never prayed, as he thought there was no need of it since his dearest Lord was shining in his heart with sweetness, love and assurance. That is why in different critical stages of his illness he never gave up hope, and tried to cheer up his worried wife and attending doctors. It was through sheer determination and unshaken faith that he carried out his life's mission nearly to completion when God took him away—maybe for some purpose known to him alone.

It now remains to thank the Syndics of the Cambridge University Press for the very kind interest that they have shown in the publication of this fifth volume of the *History of Indian Philosophy* by my husband. The Indian Government have permitted me to complete the remaining portion of the work as planned by the author. It is a great task and a very sacred obligation that I owe to my husband, both as his disciple and wife, and I do not know how far I shall be able to fulfil it. It all depends on God's will. But the work as it stands now is self-complete and will serve the need of enquiring minds about the different important schools of Śaivism from the beginning of the Christian era. The references to texts and manuscripts have been duly checked. I beg the forgiveness of readers for any mistake that might remain.

SURAMA DASGUPTA

University of Lucknow, India
19 *June* 1954

CONTENTS

CHAPTER XXXIV

LITERATURE OF SOUTHERN ŚAIVISM

CHAPTER XXXV

VĪRA-ŚAIVISM

CHAPTER XXXVI

PHILOSOPHY OF ŚRĪKAṆṬHA

CHAPTER XXXVII

THE ŚAIVA PHILOSOPHY IN THE PURĀṆAS

CHAPTER XXXVIII

ŚAIVA PHILOSOPHY IN SOME OF THE IMPORTANT TEXTS

CHAPTER XXXIV

LITERATURE OF SOUTHERN ŚAIVISM

The Literature and History of Southern Śaivism.

THE earliest Sanskrit philosophical literature in which we find a reference to Śaivism is a *bhāṣya* of Śaṅkara (eighth century) on *Brahma-sūtra* II. 2. 37. In the commentary on this *śūtra*, Śaṅkara refers to the doctrines of the Siddhāntas as having been written by Lord Maheśvara. The peculiarity of the teachings of the Siddhāntas was that they regarded God as being only the instrumental cause of the world. Here and elsewhere Śaṅkara has called the upholders of this view Īśvara-kāraṇins. If Śiva or God was regarded as both the instrumental and the material cause of the world, according to the different Siddhānta schools of thought, then there would be no point in introducing the *sūtra* under reference, for according to Śaṅkara also, God is both the instrumental and the material cause of the world. Śaṅkara seems to refer here to the Pāśupata system which deals with the five categories, such as the cause (*kāraṇa*), effect (*kārya*), communion (*yoga*), rules of conduct (*vidhi*) and dissolution of sorrow (*duḥkhānta*)[1]. According to him it also holds that Pāśupati (God) is the instrumental cause of the world. In this view the Naiyāyikas and the Vaiśeṣikas also attribute the same kind of causality to God, and offer the same kind of arguments, i.e. the inference of the cause from the effect.

Vācaspati Miśra (A.D. 840), in commenting on the *bhāṣya* of Śaṅkara, says that the Maheśvaras consist of the Śaivas, Pāśupatas, the Kāruṇika-siddhāntins and the Kāpālikas. Mādhava of the fourteenth century mentions the Śaivas as being Nakulīśa-pāśupatas who have been elsewhere mentioned as Lākulīśa-pāśupatas or Lakulīśa-pāśupatas, and they have been discussed in another section of the present work. Mādhava also mentions the *Śaiva-darśana* in which he formulates the philosophical doctrines found in the *Śaivāgamas* and their cognate literature. In addition to this he devotes a section to *pratyabhijñā-darśana*, commonly

[1] The skeleton of this system has already been dealt with in another section as *Pāśupata-śāstras*.

called Kāśmīr Śaivism. This system will also be dealt with in the present volume. Vācaspati mentions the Kāruṇika-siddhāntins and the Kāpālikas. Rāmānuja in his *bhāṣya* on *Brahma-sūtra* II. 2. 37 mentions the name of Kāpālikas and Kālamukhas as being Śaiva sects of an anti-Vedic character. But in spite of my best efforts, I have been unable to discover any texts, published or unpublished, which deal with the special features of their systems of thought. We find some references to the Kāpālikas in literature like the *Mālatī-mādhava* of Bhavabhūti (A.D. 700–800) and also in some of the Purāṇas. Ānandagiri, a contemporary of Śaṅkara and a biographer, speaks of various sects of Śaivas with various marks and signs on their bodies and with different kinds of robes to distinguish themselves from one another. He also speaks of two schools of Kāpālikas, one Brahmanic and the other non-Brahmanic. In the Atharva-veda we hear of the Vrātyas who were devotees of Rudra. The Vrātyas evidently did not observe the caste-rules and customs. But the Vrātyas of the Atharva-veda were otherwise held in high esteem. But the Kāpālikas, whether they were Brahmanic or non-Brahmanic, indulged in horrid practices of drinking and indulging in sex-appetite and living in an unclean manner. It is doubtful whether there is any kind of proper philosophy, excepting the fact that they were worshippers of Bhairava the destroyer, who also created the world and maintained it. They did not believe in *karma*. They thought that there are minor divinities who perform various functions in world creation and maintenance according to the will of Bhairava. The Śūdra Kāpālikas did not believe also in the caste-system and all these Kāpālikas ate meat and drank wine in skulls as part of their rituals. Sir R. G. Bhandarkar thinks on the authority of *Śiva-mahāpurāṇa* that the Kālamukhas were the same as the Mahāvratadharas. But the present author has not been able to trace any such passage in the *Śiva-mahāpurāṇa*, and Bhandarkar does not give any exact reference to the *Śiva-mahā-purāṇa* containing this identification. The *Mahāvrata*, meaning the great vow, consists in eating food placed in a human skull and smearing the body with the ashes of human carcasses and others, which are attributed to the Kālamukhas by Rāmānuja. Bhandarkar also refers to the commentary of Jagaddhara on the *Mālatī-mādhava*, where the *Kāpālika-vrata* is called *Mahāvrata*. Bhandarkar further points out that the ascetics dwelling in the temple of

Kāpāleśvara near Nasik are called the Mahāvratins[1]. Be that as it may, we have no proof that the Kāpālikas and Kālamukhas had any distinct philosophical views which could be treated separately. Members of their sects bruised themselves in performing particular kinds of rituals, and could be distinguished from other Śaivas by their indulgence in wines, women, and meat and even human meat. Somehow these rituals passed into Tāntric forms of worship, and some parts of these kinds of worship are found among the adherents of the Tāntric form of worship even to this day. Tāntric initiation is thus different from the Vedic initiation.

Frazer in his article on Śaivism in the *Encyclopaedia of Religion and Ethics* says that, in some well-known temples in South India, the ancient blood-rites and drunken orgies are permitted to be revived yearly as a compromise with the aboriginal worshippers, whose primitive shrines were annexed by Brahmin priests acting under the protection of local chieftains. These chieftains, in return for their patronage and countenance, obtained a rank as Kṣatriyas with spurious pedigrees. Frazer further gives some instances in the same article in which non-Brahmins and outcastes performed the worship of Śiva and also offered human sacrifices, and one of the places he mentions is Śrīśaila, the Kāpālika centre referred to by Bhavabhūti. These outcaste worshippers were ousted from the temple by some of the Buddhists, and thereafter the Buddhists were thrown out by the Brahmins. By the time of Śaṅkara, the Kāpālikas developed a strong centre in Ujjain. We, of course, do not know whether the South Indian cult of blood-rites as performed by Brahmins and non-Brahmins could be identified with the Kāpālikas and Kālamukhas; but it is quite possible that they were the same people, for Śriśaila, mentioned by Bhavabūti, which is described as an important Kāpālika centre, is also known to us as a centre of bloody rites from the *Sthala-māhātmya* records of that place as mentioned by Frazer. The Kāpālikas and Kālamukhas were anti-Vedic according to the statement of Rāmānuja in *Brahma-sūtra* II. 2. 37. Śaṅkara also, according to Ānandagiri, did not hold any discussion with the Kāpālikas, as their views were professedly anti-Vedic. He simply had them chastised and whipped. The Kāpālikas, however, continued in their primitive

[1] *Vaiṣṇavism, Śaivism and Minor Religious Systems*, by Sir R. G. Bhandarkar (1913), p. 128.

form and some of them were living even in Bengal, as is known to the present writer. The habit of smearing the body with ashes is probably very old in Śaivism, since we find the practice described in the *Pāśupata-sūtra* and in the *bhāṣya* of Kauṇḍinya.

The Kāruṇika-siddhāntins mentioned by Vācaspati have not been referred to by Mādhava (fourteenth century) in his *Sarva-darśana-saṃgraha*, and we do not find a reference to these in any of the *Śaivāgamas*. But from the statement of Śaiva philosophy in the *Vāyavīya-saṃhitā* of the *Śiva-mahāpurāṇa*, as discussed in another section (pp. 106–29), it is not difficult for us to reconstruct the reasons which might have led to the formation of a special school of Śaivism. We find that the doctrine of grace or *karuṇā* is not always found in the same sense in all the Āgamas, or in the *Vāyavīya-saṃhitā*, which was in all probability based on the Āgamas. Ordinarily the idea of grace or *karuṇā* would simply imply the extension of kindness or favour to one in distress. But in the *Śaivāgamas* there is a distinct line of thought where *karuṇā* or grace is interpreted as a divine creative movement for supplying all souls with fields of experience in which they may enjoy pleasures and suffer from painful experiences. The *karuṇā* of God reveals the world to us in just the same manner as we ought to experience it. Grace, therefore, is not a work of favour in a general sense, but it is a movement in favour of our getting the right desires in accordance with our *karma*. Creative action of the world takes place in consonance with our good and bad deeds, in accordance with which the various types of experience unfold themselves to us. In this sense, grace may be compared with the view of Yoga philosophy, which admits of a permanent will of God operating in the orderliness of the evolutionary creation (*pariṇāmakrama-niyama*) for the protection of the world, and supplying it as the basis of human experience in accordance with their individual *karmas*. It is again different from the doctrine of *karuṇā* of the Rāmānuja Vaiṣṇavas, who introduce the concept of Mahālakṣmī, one who intercedes on behalf of the sinners and persuades Nārāyaṇa to extend His grace for the good of the devotees.

The word '*śiva*' is supposed to have been derived irregularly from the root '*vaś kāntan*'. This would mean that Śiva always fulfils the desires of His devotees. This aspect of Śiva as a merciful Lord who is always prepared to grant any boons for which prayers are offered to Him is very well depicted in the *Mahābhārata* and many other Purāṇas. This aspect of Śiva is to be distinguished from the aspect of Śiva as *rudra* or *śarva* or the god of destruction.

We have seen that we know practically nothing of any importance about the Kāpālikas and the Kālamukhas. The other doctrines of Śaivism of the South are those of the Pāśupatas, the Śaiva doctrines derived from the Āgamas and the Vaiṣṇavas. The other schools of Śaivism that developed in Kāśmīr in the ninth and tenth centuries will be separately discussed. The *Pāśupata-sūtra* with the *Pañcārtha bhāṣya* of Kauṇḍinya was first published from Trivandrum in 1940, edited by Anantakriṣṇa Śāstri. This *bhāṣya* of Kauṇḍinya is probably the same as the *Rāśīkara-bhāṣya* referred to by Mādhava in his treatment of *Nakulīśa-pāśupata-darśana* in *Sarva-darśana-saṃgraha.* Some of the lines found in Kauṇḍinya's *bhāṣya* have been identified by the present writer with the lines attributed to Rāśīkara by Mādhava in his treatment of the Nakulīśa-pāśupata system. Nakulīśa was the founder of the Pāśupata system. Aufrect in the *Catalogus Catalogorum* mentions the *Pāśupata-sūtra*[1]. The *Vāyavīya-saṃhitā* II. 24. 169, also mentions the *Pāśupata-śāstra* as the *Pañcārtha-vidyā*[2]. Bhandarkar notes that in an inscription in the temple of Harṣanātha which exists in the Śikar principality of the Jaipur State, a person of the name of Viśvarūpa is mentioned as the teacher of the *Pañcārtha-lākulāmnāya.* The inscription is dated V.E. 1013 = A.D. 957. From this Bhandarkar infers that the Pāśupata system was attributed to a human author named Lakulin and that the work composed by him was called *Pañcārtha.* This inference is not justifiable. We can only infer that in the middle of the tenth century Lakuliśa's doctrines were being taught by a teacher called Viśvarūpa, who was well reputed in Jaipur, and that Lakulīśa's teachings had attained such an authoritative position as to be called *āmnāya*, a term used to mean the Vedas.

In the *Pāśupata-sūtra* published in the Trivandrum series, the first *sūtra* as quoted by Kauṇḍinya is *athātaḥ paśupateh paśupataṃ*

[1] Bhandarkar notes it in his section on the Pāśupatas, *op. cit.* p. 121 n.

[2] The present writer could not find any such verse in the edition of *Śiva-mahāpurāṇa* printed by the Venkateśvara Press, as II. 24 contains only seventy-two stanzas.

yogavidhiṃ vyākhyāsyāmaḥ. Here the *yoga-vidhi* is attributed to Paśupati or Śiva. In the *Sūtasaṃhitā* IV. 43. 17, we hear of a place called Nakula and the Śiva there is called Nakulīśa. The editor of the *Pāśupata-sūtra* mentions the names of eighteen teachers beginning with Nakulīśa[1]. These names are (1) Nakulīśa, (2) Kauśika, (3) Gārgya, (4) Maitreya, (5) Kauruṣa, (6) Īśāna, (7) Paragārgya, (8) Kapilāṇḍa, (9) Manuṣyaka, (10) Kuśika, (11) Atri, (12) Piṅgalākṣa, (13) Puṣpaka, (14) Bṛhadārya, (15) Agasti, (16) Santāna, (17) Kauṇḍinya or Rāśīkara, (18) Vidyāguru. The present writer is in agreement with the view of the editor of the *Pāśupata-sūtra*, that Kauṇḍinya the *bhāṣyakāra* lived somewhere from the fourth to the sixth century A.D. The style of the *bhāṣya* is quite archaic, and no references to the later system of thought can be found in Kauṇḍinya's *bhāṣya*. We have already seen that according to the *Śiva-mahāpurāṇa* there were twenty-eight yogācāryas and that each of them had four disciples so that there were 112 yogācāryas. Out of these twenty-eight yogācāryas the most prominent were Lokākṣī, Jaigīṣavya, Ṛṣabha, Bhṛgu, Atri and Gautama. The last and the twenty-eighth ācārya was Lakulīśa, born at Kāyā-vatarana-tīrtha. Among the 112 yogācāryas, Sanaka, Sanandana, Sanātana, Kapila, Āsuri, Pañcaśikha, Parāśara, Garga, Bhārgava, Aṅgira, Śuka, Vaśiṣṭha, Bṛhaspati, Kuṇi, Vāmadeva, Śvetaketu, Devala, Śālihotra, Agniveśa, Akṣapāda, Kaṇāda, Kumāra and Ruru are the most prominent[2].

[1] These names are taken from Rājaśekhara's *Ṣaḍdarśana-samuccaya* composed during the middle of the fourteenth century. Almost the same names with slight variations are found in Guṇaratna's commentary on *Ṣaḍdarśana-samuccaya*.

[2] See *Śiva-mahāpurāṇa*, *Vāyavīya Saṃhitā* II. 9, and also *Kūrma-purāna* I. 53. The *Vāyu-purāṇa* describes in the twenty-third chapter the names of the four disciples of each of the twenty-eight *ācāryas*. Viśuddha Muni mentions the name of Lakulīśa in his work called *Atma-samarpaṇa*. See also Introduction to the *Pāśupata-sūtra*, p. 3n.

The list of twenty-eight teachers given in the *Śiva-mahāpurāṇa* does not always tally with the list collected by other scholars, or with that which is found in the *Ātma samarpaṇa* by Viśuddha Muni. It seems therefore that some of these names are quite mythical, and as their works are not available, their names are not much used. Viśuddha Muni summarises the main items of self-control, *yama*, from the *Pāśupata-śāstra*, which are more or less of the same nature as the *yamas* or measures of self-control as found in the *Yogaśāstra* introduced by Patañjali. It is not out of place here to mention that the concept of God in *Yogaśāstra* is of the same pattern as that of the Paśupati in the *Pāśupata-sūtra* and *bhāṣya*.

Mr Dalal in his introduction to *Gaṇakārikā* says that the *Lākulīśa-pāśupata-darśana* is so called from Lakulīśa, who originated the system. *Lakulīśa* means "a lord of those bearing a staff". Lakulīśa is often regarded as an incarnation of God Śiva with a citron in the right hand and a staff in the left. The place of the incarnation is Kāyārohaṇa in Bhṛgu-kṣetra which is the same as Kāravaṇa, a town in the Dabhoi Taluka of the Baroda State. In the *Kāravaṇa-māhātmya* it is said that a son of a Brahmin in the village Ulkāpurī appeared as Lakulīśa and explained the methods and merits of worshipping and tying a silken cloth to the image of the God Lakulīśa. This work is divided into four chapters; the first is from the *Vāyu-purāṇa*, the remaining three are from the *Śiva-mahāpurāṇa*. At the commencement of the work, there is obeisance to Maheśvara, who incarnated himself as Lakuṭa-pāṇīśa. There is a dialogue there between Śiva and Pārvatī, in which the latter asks Śiva of the merits of tying a silken cloth. Śiva then relates the story of his incarnation between the Kali and Dvāpara yugas as a Brahmin named Viśvarāja in the family of the sage Atri. His mother was Sudarśana. Some miraculous myths relating to this child, who was an incarnation of Śiva, are narrated in the *Kāravaṇa Māhātmya*, but they may well be ignored here.

We have already mentioned the name of Atri as being one of the important teachers of the Pāśupata school. But according to the account of these teachers as given above, Nakulīśa should be regarded as the first founder of the system. We have seen also that by the middle of the tenth century there was a teacher of the *Pañcārtha-lākulāmnāya*, which must be the same as the doctrine propounded in the *Pāśupata-sūtra*. It is difficult to say how early the concept of Paśupati might have evolved. From the Mohenjo-daro excavations we have a statuette in which Śiva is carved as sitting on a bull, with snakes and other animals surrounding Him. This is the representation in art of the concept of the lord of *paśus* or *paśupati*, which is found in pre-Vedic times. The concept of Śiva may be traced through the Vedas and also through the Upaniṣads and particularly so in the Śvetāśvatara Upaniṣad. The same idea can be traced in the *Mahābhārata* and many other Purāṇas. The religious cult of Śiva, which defines the concept of Śiva in its various mythological bearings, has to be given up here, as the interest of the present work is definitely restricted to philosophical ideas and the ethical and social attitude of the followers of Śiva[1].

It must, however, be said that the Śaiva philosophy and the worship of Śiva had spread itself far and wide throughout the whole of the peninsula long before the eighth century A.D. We have the most sacred temples of Śiva in the north in Badrikāśrama, in Nepal (Paśupati-nātha), in Kāśmīr, in Prabhāsa, in Kathiawar (the temple of Somanātha), in Benaras (the temple of Viśvanātha), the Nakulīśvara temple in Calcutta, and the temple of Rāmeśvaram in extreme South India. This is only to mention some of the most important places of Śiva-worship. As a matter of fact, the worship of Śiva is found prevalent almost in every part of India, and in most of the cities we find the temples of Śiva either in ruins or as actual places of worship. Śiva is worshipped generally in the form of the phallic symbol and generally men of every caste and women also may touch the symbol and offer worship. The Śaiva forms of initiation and the Tāntric forms of initiation are to be distinguished from the Vedic forms of initiation, which latter is reserved only for the three higher castes. But as the present work is intended to deal with the philosophy of Śaivism and Tāntricism, all relevant allusions to rituals and forms of worship will be dropped as far as possible.

The Jaina writer Rājaśekhara of the middle of the fourteenth century mentions the name of Śaiva philosophy in his *Ṣaḍ-darśana-samuccaya* and calls it a *yoga-mata*[2]. He describes the Śaiva ascetics as holding staves in their hands and wearing long loin cloths (*prauḍha-kaupīna-paridhāyinaḥ*). They had also blankets for covering their bodies, matted locks of hair, and their bodies were smeared with ashes. They ate dry fruits, bore a vessel of gourd (*tumbaka*), and generally lived in forests. Some of them had wives, while others lived a lonely life. Rājaśekhara further says that the Śaivas admitted eighteen incarnations of Śiva, the Over-lord, who creates and destroys the world. We have already mentioned the names of the teachers that are found in *Ṣaḍdarśana-samuccaya*. These teachers were particularly adored and among

[1] Those who are interested in the study of the evolution of the different aspects of God Śiva, may consult Bhandarkar's *Vaiṣṇavism and Śaivism*, and also the article on Śaivism by Frazer in the *Encyclopaedia of Religion and Ethics*.

[2] *atha yoga-mataṃ brumaḥ, śaivam-ity-aparā-bhidham.* Rājaśekhara's *Ṣaḍ-darśana-samuccaya*, p. 8 (2nd edition, Benares).

them it was Akṣapāda who enunciated a system of logic in which he discussed the *pramāṇas*, perception, inference, analogy and testimony and also described the sixteen categories that are found in the *Nyāya-sūtra* of Gautama or Akṣapāda. Rājaśekhara mentions the names of Jayanta, Udayana, and Bhāsarvajña. Thus according to Rājaśekhara the Naiyāyikas were regarded as Śaivas. It does not seem that Rājaśekhara had made any definite study of the Nyāya system, but based his remarks on the tradition of the time[1]. He also regards the Vaiśeṣikas as Pāśupatas. The Vaiśeṣika saints wore the same kind of dress and the marks as the Naiyāyikas and admitted the same teachers, but they held that the perception and inference were the only two *pramāṇas* and that the other *pramāṇas* were included within them. He also mentions the six categories that we find in the *Vaiśeṣika-sūtra*. Rājaśekhara calls the Naiyayikas Yaugas. The Vaiśeṣika and the Nyāya are more or less of the same nature and both of them regard the dissolution of sorrow as ultimate liberation. Guṇaratna, the commentator of Haribhadra Suri's *Ṣaḍdarśana-samuccaya* was a Jaina writer like Rājaśekhara and he was in all probability a later contemporary of him. Many of his descriptions of the Naiyāyikas or Yaugas seem to have been taken from Rājaśekhara's work, or it may also have been that Rājaśekhara borrowed it from Guṇaratna, the descriptions being the same in many places. Guṇaratna says that there were found kinds of Śaivas such as the Śaivas, Pāśupatas, Mahāvratadharas and the Kālamukhas[2]. In addition to these both Guṇaratna and Rājaśekhara speak of those who take the vow (*vratins*) of service to Śiva and they are called Bharaṭas and Bhaktas. Men of any caste

[1] *śrutānusārataḥ proktam naiyāyika-matam mayā. Ibid.* p. 10.

[2] *śaivaḥ pāśupataścaiva mahāvrata-dharas tathā,*
turyāḥ kālamukhā mukhyā bhedā ete tapasvinām.

Guṇaratna's commentary on Haribhadra's *Ṣaḍdarśana-samuccaya*, p. 51 (Suali's edition, Calcutta, 1905).

According to Guṇaratna, therefore, the Mahāvratadharas and the Kālamukhas are entirely different. The Kāpālikas are not mentioned by Guṇaratna. These four classes of Śaivas were originally Brahmins and they had the sacred thread. Their difference was largely due to their different kinds of rituals and behaviour (*ācāra*):

ādhāra-bhasma-kaupīna-jaṭā-yajñopavītinaḥ,
sva-svācārādi-bhedena caturdhā syus tapasvinaḥ.

Rāmānuja mentions the names of Kāpālikas and Kālamukhas as being outside the pale of the Vedas (*veda-bāhya*). In *Śaṅkara-vijaya* of Ānandagiri also the Kāpālikas are represented as being outside the pale of the Vedas. But the Kālamukhas are not mentioned there.

could be included in the class of Bharaṭas (servants) and Bhaktas (devotees) of Śiva. The Naiyāyikas were always regarded as devotees of Śiva and they were called Śaivas. The Vaiśeṣika philosophy was called Pāśupata[1]. Haribhadra also says that the Vaiśeṣikas admitted the same divinity as the Naiyāyikas[2].

Excluding the Kāpālikas and the Kālamukhas, about whom we know very little except the traditional imputations against their rituals and non-Vedic conduct, we have the text of the Pāśupata system and the Śaiva philosophy as described in the Śaiva Āgamas. We have also the *Pāśupata-śāstra* as described in the *Vāyavīya saṃhitā*, the Śaiva philosophy of Śrīkaṇṭha as elaborated by Appaya Dīkṣita, and the Śaiva philosophy as expounded by King Bhoja of Dhāra in his *Tattva-prakāśa* as explained by Śrīkumāra and Aghora-śivācārya. We have also the Vīra-śaivism which evolved at a later date and was explained in a commentary on *Brahma-sūtra* by Śrīpati Paṇḍita who is generally placed in the fourteenth century[3]. Śrīpati Paṇḍita was posterior to the Pāśupatas and Rāmānuja, and also to Ekorāma and the five ācāryas of the Vīra-śaiva religion. Śrīpati was also posterior to Mādhavācārya. But it is curious that Madhava seems to know nothing either of Vīraśaivism or of Śrīpati Paṇḍita. He was of course posterior to Basava of the twelfth century, who is generally regarded as being the founder of Vīra-śaivism. As Hayavadana Rao points out, Śrīpati was posterior to Śrīkaṇṭha, who wrote a *bhāṣya* on the *Brahma-sūtra*[4]. We have treated in a separate section the philosophy of Śrīkaṇṭha. Śrīkaṇṭha lived somewhere in the eleventh century and may have been a junior contemporary of Rāmānuja. Śrīkaṇṭha in his treatment of *Brahma-sūtra* III. 3. 27–30, criticises the views of Rāmānuja and Nimbārka. Hayavadana Rao thinks on inscriptional grounds that Śrīkaṇṭha was living in A.D. 1122[5].

Meykaṇḍadeva, the most famous author of the Tamil translation of the Sanskrit work *Śiva-jñāna-bodha* belonged to Tiru-

[1] See Guṇaratna's commentary, p. 51.

[2] *devatā-viṣayo bhedo nāsti naiyāyikaiḥ samam,*
vaiśeṣikāṇām tattve tu vidyate'sau nidarśyate.
Haribhadra's *Ṣaḍdarśana-samuccaya*, p. 266.

[3] C. Hayavadana Rao's *Śrīkara-bhāṣya*, Vol. I, p. 31.

[4] *Ibid.* p. 36.

[5] *Ibid.* p. 41.

venneyllur near the South Arcot district. There is an inscription in the sixteenth year of the Chola King Rājarāja III (A.D. 1216–48) which records a gift of land to an image set up by Meykaṇda. This fixes the date of Meykaṇḍadeva, the disciple of Parañjoti muni to about the middle of the thirteenth century. Hayvadana Rao after a long discussion comes to the view that Meykaṇḍa actually lived about A.D. 1235, if not a little earlier[1]. From inscriptional sources it has been ascertained that Śrīkaṇṭha, the commentator of *Brahma-sūtra* lived about A.D. 1270. It is quite possible that Meykaṇḍa and Śrīkaṇṭha were contemporaries. The philosophical difference between Meykaṇḍa and Śrīkaṇṭha is quite remarkable, and the two persons cannot therefore be identified as one[2]. Śrīkaṇṭha thinks that the world is a transformation of the *cicchakti* of the Lord. It does not provide for the creation of the material world, does not speak of the *āṇava-mala*, and is apparently not in favour of *jīvan-mukti*. Further Śrīkaṇṭha appears to establish his system on the basis of the *śruti*. Meykaṇḍa, however, tries to establish his system on the basis of inference, and there are many other points of difference as will be easily seen from our treatment of Meykaṇḍa-deva. It does not seem that Śrīkaṇṭha had any relation with Meykaṇḍadeva.

Śrīpati quotes from Haradatta in very reverential terms. Hayvadana Rao refers to an account of the life of Haradatta as given in the *Bhaviṣyottara-purāṇa*, and to the writings of his commentator Śiva-liṅga-bhūpati, which would assign Haradatta to the Kali age 3979, corresponding roughly to A.D. 879. In the *Śiva-rahasya-dīpikā*, however, Kali age 3000 is given as a rough approximation of the date of Haradatta. Professor Shesagiri Śāstrī accepts the former date as a more correct one and identifies the Haradatta quoted in *Sarva-darśana-saṃgraha* as being the same as the author of *Harihara-tāratamya* and the *Caturveda-tātparya-saṃgraha*. As we have mentioned elsewhere, Haradatta was the author of the *Gaṇakārikā*. Mr Dalal in all probability had confused the two in his introduction to the *Gaṇakārikā*, in which he says that Bhāsarvajna was the author of *Gaṇakārikā*. In reality Haradatta wrote only the *Kārikā*, and the Nyāya author Bhāsar-

[1] *Ibid.* p. 48.

[2] *Ibid.* p. 49. The systems of Śrīkaṇṭha and of Meykaṇḍa have been dealt with in separate sections of the present work.

vajña wrote a commentary on it called the *Ratnaṭīkā*[1]. Śrīpati also quotes from *Siddhānta śikhāmaṇi*, a Vīraśaiva work written by Revaṇārya.

It is curious to note that though Vīra-śaivism was founded at least as early as the time of Basava (A.D. 1157–67), Mādhava in the fourteenth century does not know anything of Vīra-śaivism. It is, however, doubtful if Basava was really the founder of Vīra-śaivism in India. We have got some sayings in Canarese known as the *vacanas* of Basava, but we find that his name is seldom mentioned as a teacher of any articles of the Vīra-śaiva faith. There is a semi-mythical account of Basava in a work called *Basava-purāṇa*. It is said there that Śiva asked Nandin to incarnate himself in the world for the propagation of the Vīra-śaiva faith. Basava was this incarnation. He was a native of Bāgevāḍi from where he went to Kalyāṇa where Vijjala or Vijjana was reigning (A.D. 1157–67). His maternal uncle, Baladeva, was the minister, and he himself was raised to that position after his death. Basava's sister was given away to the king. He was in charge of the treasury and spent large sums in supporting and entertaining the Liṅgāyat priests or mendicants called Jaṅgamas. When the king came to know of this, he became angry and sent troops to punish him. Basava collected a small army and defeated these troops. The king brought him back to Kalyāṇa and there was apparently some reconciliation between them. But Basava later on caused the king to be assassinated. This depicts Basava more as a scheming politician than as a propounder of new faith.

Returning to our treatment of the literature of the Pāśupatas, we see that between the Vaiṣṇavas and the monists like the Śaṅkarites we have a system of thought representing the monotheistic point of view. This view appears in diverse forms in which God is sometimes regarded as being established as upholding the universe, but beyond it; sometimes it is held that God is beyond the world and has created it by the material of His own energy; at other times it

[1] The colophon of the *Gaṇakārikā* runs as follows:

ācārya-bhāsarvajña-viracitāyāṃ gaṇakārikāyāṃ
ratnaṭīkā parisamāptā.

This led to the confusion that the *Gaṇakārikā* was the composition of Bhāsarvajña, who only wrote the commentary. This Haradatta must be distinguished from the Haradatta of the *Padamañjarī* on the *Kāśikā-vṛtti*, and also from the commentator of the *Āpastamba-sūtra*.

has been held that God and energy are one and the same. Sometimes it has been held that God has created the world by His mercy or grace and that His grace is the inner dynamic force which follows the course of creation and maintenance. It is in this way that a compromise has been made between the theory of grace and the theory of *karma*. There are others, however, who think that we do not as of necessity have a right to reap the fruits of our actions, but we have to be satisfied with what is given to us by God. The Pāśupatas hold this view, and it is important to notice that the Nyāya which admits the doctrine of *karma* also thinks that we are only entitled to such enjoyments and experiences as are allotted to us by God. The fact that both the Nyāya and the Pāśupatas think that God can be established by inference, and that the grace of God is ultimately responsible for all our experiences, naturally leads us to link together the Nyāya-vaiśeṣika view with the Pāśupata view. The tradition is preserved in the two *Ṣaḍdarśana-samuccayas* of Rājaśekhara and Haribhadra with Guṇaratna, which, as well as the benedictory verses in most Nyāya works until the tenth and eleventh centuries, justify the assumption that the Nyāya-vaiśeṣika was a school of Pāśupatas which paid more emphasis to evolving a system of logic and metaphysics. The Pāśupata system generally accepted the caste-division, and only those belonging to higher castes could claim to attain spiritual liberation. Yet as time rolled on we find that men of all castes could become devotees or servants of God and be regarded as Śaivas. We find the same kind of gradual extension and withdrawal of caste system among the Vaiṣṇavas also. Both in Śaivism and Vaiṣṇavism, *bhakti* or devotion to God came to be regarded as the criterion of the faith.

We have already referred to the statement in the *Kāravaṇa-māhātmya* about how the Lord incarnated Himself as a descendant of Atri. He is said to have walked to Ujjain and taught a Brahmin there called Kuśika who came from Brahmāvarta. These teachings were in the form of the present *sūtras* called the *Pañcārtha*, the main substance of which has already been described. It is generally believed that the original *sūtras*, divided into five chapters (*pañcārtha*), were composed somewhere in the first or the second century A.D. The *bhāṣya* of Kauṇḍinya is probably the same as the *Rāśīkara bhāṣya*. Kauṇḍinya does not mention the name of any writer contemporary to him. He refers to the *Sāṃkhya-yoga* but not to Vedānta or the Upaniṣads. It is interesting to note therefore that this system does not pretend to claim the authority of the Upaniṣads or its support. The authority of the *sūtras* is based on the assumption that they were composed by Paśupati himself. There are many quotations in the work of Kauṇḍinya, but it is not possible to identify their sources. The style of Kauṇḍinya's *bhāṣya* reminds one of the writings of Patañjali the grammarian, who probably lived about 150 B.C. Kauṇḍinya is generally believed to have lived between A.D. 400–600, though I do not know why he could not be placed even a century or two earlier. The date of *Gaṇakārikā* is rather uncertain. But Bhāsarvajña wrote a commentary on it called *Ratnaṭīkā*. He seems to have lived in the middle of the tenth century A.D. It is interesting to note that the temple of Somanātha is also mentioned in the *Kāravaṇa-māhātmya* as one of the most important Pāśupata centres.

In the *Sarva-darśana-saṃgraha* of Mādhava of the fourteenth century, we find a treatment of Nakulīśa-pāśupata system, the Śaiva system and the Pratyabhijñā system of Kāśmīr. The Nakulīśa-pāśupata system is based upon the *Pāśupata-sūtra* and the *bhāṣya* of Kauṇḍinya called also the *Rāśīkara-bhāṣya*. The Śaiva system is based on the various *Śaivāgamas* and also on the *Tattva-prakāśa* of Bhoja. Thus Mādhava mentions about ten Śaiva works which, with many others, have been available to the present writer either in whole manuscripts or in fragments[1]. Śaṅkara, in his *bhāṣya* on the *Brahma-sūtra* II. 2. 37, speaks of the Māheśvaras along with others who regarded God as the instrumental cause, but not the material cause. He does not seem to distinguish the subdivisions of the Maheśvaras. But Vācaspati speaks of four subdivisions of the Maheśvaras. Mādhava, however, treats the two types of the Śaiva school as Nakulīśa-pāśupata and Śaiva in two different sections. From Śaṅkara's *bhāṣya* it appears that he was familiar only with the *Pañcārtha* of the *Pāśupata-sūtra*. But Ānandagiri in his *Śaṅkara-vijaya* refers to six different kinds of Śaiva sects such as Śaiva, Raudra, Ugra, Bhaṭṭa, Jaṅgama and Pāśupata. These different sects bore different kinds of marks on

[1] The works mentioned by Mādhava in his *Sarva-darśana-saṃgraha* are as follows: *Mṛgendrāgama*, *Pauṣkarāgama*, *Tattva-prakāśa* of Bhoja, Somasambhu's *bhāṣya*, Aghora-śivācārya's commentary on *Tattva-prakāśa*, *Kālottarāgama*, Rāmakaṇḍa's commentary on *Kālottarā*, *Kiraṇāgama*, *Saurabheyāgama* and *Jñāna-ratnāvalī*.

their bodies and distinguished themselves from one another by various rituals. But most of their specific religious literature now in all probability has long disappeared. The Pāśupatas have a literature, and the sect is still living. But the external signs of the Pāśupatas as found in *Śaṅkara-vijaya* are entirely different from those which are found in Guṇaratna's commentary. Guṇaratna (fourteenth century) regards the Kāṇādas as Pāśupatas. He also regards the Naiyāyikas, called also the Yaugas, as being Śaivites of the same order as the Kāṇādas, and behaving in the same manner, and bearing the same kind of marks as the Kāṇādas. From the description of the Śaiva sects by Ānandagiri very little can be made out of the doctrines of those Śaiva sects. One can only say that some of those Śaivas believed that God was the instrumental cause (*nimitta kāraṇa*), besides the material cause (*upādāna kāraṇa*). Śaṅkara refuted this type of Śaivism in his commentary on *Brahma-sūtra* II. 2. 37. Both Pāśupatas and the followers of the *Śaivāgama* held the instrumentality of God, while Śaṅkara regarded God as being both the instrumental and material cause. In the *Śaṅkara-vijaya* we also find reference to some schools of Śaivism, the members of which wore the stone phallic symbols on their bodies. They held a doctrine similar to the *ṣaṭ-sthala* doctrine of the Vīra-śaivas, though we find the proper formulation of the Vīra-śaiva system at least five hundred years after Ānandagiri. We have seen that Vācaspati Miśra in his *Bhāmatī* speaks of four types of Śaivas. Mādhava of the fourteenth century describes only two sects of Śaivas as Nakulīśa-pāśupata and the Śaivas of the Āgamas, excluding the separate treatment of the *Pratyabhijñā* system generally known as the Kāśmīr school of Śaivism.

The *Śaivāgamas* or Siddhāntas are supposed to have been originally written by Maheśvara, probably in Sanskrit. But it is said in *Śiva-dharmottara* that these were written in Sanskrit, Prākṛt and the local dialects[1]. This explains the fact that the Āgamas are available both in Sanskrit and some Dravidian languages such as Tamil, Telegu, and Kanarese. It also explains the controversy as to whether the Āgamas or Siddhāntas were originally written in

[1] *saṃskṛtaiḥ prākṛtair vākyair yaśca śiṣyānurūptaḥ*
deśa-bhāṣā-dyupāyaiś ca bodhayet sa guruḥ smṛtaḥ.
Śiva-dharmottara quoted in *Śiva-jñāna-siddhi.* (MS. no. 3726, Oriental Research Institute, Mysore.)

Sanskrit or in the Dravidian tongue. The present writer had the good fortune to collect a large number of the Āgamas either as complete wholes or in fragmentary portions. Many of the manuscripts are in a decaying state and some of them have been completely lost. The Sanskrit manuscripts on which our present attempt is founded are available in the big manuscript libraries at Triplicane, Adyar and Mysore. It is curious to note that Benares, the principal seat of Śaivism, has but few manuscripts of importance. The important Siddhāntas and Āgamas are quite numerous and most of them are in manuscripts mainly in South India[1]. The same works may be found also in many cases in the whole Dravidian language; but the inspiration and the thought are almost always taken from Sanskrit. The essence of Dravidian culture is therefore almost wholly taken from Sanskrit, at least so far as philosophy is concerned.

The study of old Tamil is fairly difficult, and those who had made a lifelong study of Tamil, like Pope or Schomerus, had but little time to dig into Sanskrit to any appreciable extent. The present writer, being unacquainted with the Dravidian languages, had to depend almost wholly on the Sanskrit literature, but has taken good care to ascertain that the works in Dravidian, pertinent to the subject, are well represented in the Sanskrit manuscripts.

It is difficult to ascertain the respective dates of the Āgamas. We only feel that most of the Āgamas mentioned above were completed by the ninth century A.D. Some of them were current in the time of Śaṅkarācārya, who lived some time in the eighth or

[1] Some of the Āgamas are as follows: *Kāmika*, *Yogaja*, *Cintya*, *Kāraṇa*, *Ajita*, *Dīpta*, *Sūkṣma*, *Aṃsumāna*, *Suprabheda*, *Vijaya*, *Niḥśvāsa*, *Svāyaṃbhuva*, *Vīra*, *Raurava*, *Makuta*, *Vimala*, *Candra-jñāna*, *Bimba*, *Lalita*, *Santāna*, *Sarvokta*, *Pārameśvara*, *Kiraṇa*, *Vātula*, *Śiva-jñāna-bodha*, *Anala*, *Prodgīta*.

In the *Śiva-jñāna-siddhi* we find extensive quotations from other Āgamas and Tantras as illustrating the philosophical and religious position of Siddhāntas. The works from which the quotations have been taken are as follows: *Hima-saṃhitā*, *Cintya-viśva*, *Śiva-dharmottara* (*purāṇa*), *Pauṣkara*, *Siddha-tantra*, *Sarva-matopanyāsa*, *Parā*, *Ratna-traya*, *Nivāsa*, *Mṛgendra*, *Jñāna-kārikā*, *Nāda-kārikā*, *Kālottara*, *Viśva-sārottara*, *Vāyavya*, *Mātaṅga*, *Śuddha*, *Sarva-jñānottara*, *Siddhānta-rahasya*, *Jñāna-ratnāvalī*, *Meru-tantra*, *Svacchanda* and *Devī-kālottara*.

Most of the above Āgamas are written in Sanskrit characters in about half a dozen Dravidian languages, such as Tamil, Telegu, Kanarese, Grantha and Nandi-nāgri. Several Tantras based on these Āgamas are also found as Sanskrit compositions in Dravidian scripts. So far as the knowledge of the present writer goes, there is hardly anything of philosophical value or systematic thought which is available in Dravidian, and not available in Sanskrit.

ninth century A.D. Some of the Purāṇas also mention the names of some of the Āgamas referred to above. The *bhāṣya* of Kauṇḍinya on the *Pāśupata-sūtras* has many untraceable quotations, but there is no mention of the names of the Āgamas referred to above, though one might have expected reference to the names of some of these Āgamas, as they carry on the same faith in different fashions. On the other hand, the Āgamas do not mention the name of the *Pāśupata-sūtras* or the *bhāṣya* of Kauṇḍinya. It seems, therefore, that though later writers sometimes mixed up the Pāśupata and the Āgamic systems, as for example the *Vāyavīya-saṃhitā*, or in later times Appayadīkṣita, Śaṅkara himself speaks only of the Siddhāntas written by Maheśvara. Vācaspati refers to four schools of Śaivism, and Mādhava refers to two schools of southern Śaivism, Nakulīśa-pāśupata and the Śaivas. In still later times, in the Jaina tradition as kept by Rājaśekhara and Guṇaratna, we find the names of a long list of teachers of the Pāśupata school. We find also the names of twenty-eight yogācāryas, each having four disciples, in the *Vāyavīya-saṃhitā*.

We have already discussed in a separate section the essence of the Āgamic system as preserved in the *Tattva-prakāśa* of Bhoja with the commentary of Śrīkumāra and Aghora-śivācārya. Mādhava in his *Sarva-darśana-saṃgraha* also mentions the names of some of the Āgamas and Āgamic writers referred to above.

Schomerus in his *Der Śaiva Siddhānta*, in which he describes the particular form of Śaiva monism, speaks of the names of various other schools of Śaivism as he picks them up on a commentary on *Śiva-jñāna-bodha*[1]. The Śaiva-siddhānta view dealt with by Schomerus is one of the many trends of Śaiva thought that was prevalent in the country. Schomerus thinks that they are more or less the same except the Pāśupata, the Vīraśaiva and the Pratyabhijñā. Schomerus does not seem to utilise the texts of the Āgamas and to show in what way they proceeded with the subject. We have, however, in our treatment of Āgamic Śaivism, tried to utilise the materials of the Āgamas that are still available as complete wholes or in fragments. But a large part of the Āgamas deals

[1] He puts them in two groups: (i) Pāśupata, Māvrata-vāda (possibly Mahāvrata), Kāpālika, Vāma, Bhairava, Aikya-vāda; (ii) Ūrdha-śaiva, Anādi-śaiva, Ādi-śaiva, Mahā-śaiva, Bheda-śaiva, Abheda-śaiva, Antara-śaiva, Guṇa-śaiva, Nirguṇa-śaiva, Adhvan-śaiva, Yoga-śaiva, Jñāna-śaiva, Aṇu-śaiva, Kriyā-śaiva, Nālu-pāda-śaiva, Śuddha-śaiva.

with rituals, forms of worship, construction of the places of worship and *mantras*, and the like. These have no philosophical value and could not, therefore, be taken account of and had simply to be ignored.

The Āgamic Śaivism belongs principally to the Tamil country, the Pāśupata to Gujarat and Pratyabhijñā to Kāśmīr and the northern parts of India. The Vīra-śaiva is found mostly among the Kanarese-speaking countries. Schomerus points out that it is sometimes claimed that the Āgamas were written in the Dravidian languages in prehistoric times, and that they owe their origin to revelation by Śiva, to Nandiperuman in the form of Śrīkaṇṭha-rudra in the Mahendra Parbata in Tinivelly District. Owing to a great flood much of these twenty-eight Āgamas were lost. The rest is now available in the Sanskrit translations and even the Dravidian texts abound with Sanskrit words. But this claim cannot be substantiated in any way. The reference to the Āgamas is found in the *Vāyavīya-saṃhitā* of the *Śiva-mahāpurāṇa* and the *Sūta-saṃhitā*[1]. The references show that the *Kāmika* and other Āgamas were written in Sanskrit, as they formed a cognate literature with the Vedas. Portions of the *Kāmika* in Sanskrit quotations have been available to the present writer; similarly *Mṛgendra*, which formed a part of the *Kāmika*, is wholly available in Sanskrit. In the section on the Āgamic Śaivism the present writer has drawn his materials from these Āgamas. It has already been noted that there is a definite text in the *Svāyaṃbhuvāgama* that these Sanskrit works were translated into Prākṛt and other local dialects. We are, therefore, forced to think that the assertion that these Āgamas were originally written in Dravidian and then translated into Sanskrit, seems only to be a mythical patriotic belief of the Tamil people.

Schomerus mentions the names of twenty-eight *Śaivāgamas*, though he sometimes spells them wrongly[2]. He further mentions

[1] In *Sūta-saṃhitā*, part I, ch. 2, we find that the Vedas, Dharmaśāstras, Purāṇas, Mahābhārata, Vedāṅgas, Upavedas, the Āgamas such as *Kāmika*, etc. the *Kāpāla* and the *Lākula*, the *Pāśupata*, the *Soma* and the *Bhairavāgamas* and such other Āgamas are mentioned in the same breath as forming a cognate literature. *Sūta-saṃhitā* is generally regarded as a work of the sixth century A.D.

[2] *Kāmika*, *Yogaja*, *Cintya*, *Kāraṇa*, *Ajita*, *Dīpta*, *Sūkṣma*, *Sāhasraka*, *Aṇsumān*, *Suprabheda*, *Vijaya*, *Niḥśvāsa*, *Svāyaṃbhuva*, *Anila*, *Vīra*, *Raurava*, *Makuṭa*, *Vimala*, *Candrahāsa*, *Mukha-jug-bimba* or *Bimba*, *Udgīta* or *Prodgīta*, *Lalita*, *Siddha*, *Santāna*, *Nārasiṃha*, *Pārameśvara*, *Kiraṇa* and *Vātula*. Most of these have been already mentioned by the present writer and some of them are in his possession. Schomerus says that these names are found in Śrīkaṇṭha's *bhāṣya*, but the present writer is definite that they are not to be found there.

the names of fourteen canonical texts forming the materials of the *Śaiva-siddhānta Śāstra*. They are written in Tamil and the present writer only has the privilege of having the Sanskrit texts of the most important of them called the *Śiva-jñāna-bodha* of Meykaṇḍa-deva[1].

Meykaṇḍadeva's *Śiva-jñāna-bodha* is a brief summary in twelve verses of an argumentative character taken from *Rauravāgama*. These twelve verses have also commentaries called *Vārtika* and a number of other sub-commentaries. Meykaṇḍadeva's real name was Svetabana, and there are a number of mythical statements about him. A great scholar Aruḷ-nanti Śivācārya became the disciple of Meykaṇḍadeva. Namaḥ-śivāya-deśika was the fifth disciple in succession of Meykaṇḍadeva, and Umāpati, who was the third successor of Meykaṇḍadeva, lived in A.D. 1313. It is held, therefore, that Meykaṇḍa lived in the first third of the thirteenth century. Umāpati was also the author of the *Pauṣkarāgama*.

The earliest Tamil author of Śaiva-siddhānata is Tirumular, who probably lived in the first century A.D. Only a part of his writings has been translated in the *Siddhānta-dīpikā* by N. Pillai. The later four Ācāryas of Śaiva-siddhānta are Māṇikka-vāchakar, Appar, Jñāna-sambandha and Sundara, who flourished probably in the eighth century. Later on we have two important Śaiva-siddhānta writers, Nampiyāṇdār and Sekkilar. The former has a collection of works which passed by the name of *Tamil-veda*. He flourished probably towards the end of the eleventh century.

This Tamil-veda is even now recited in Śaivite temples of the south. It consists of eleven books; the first seven are of the nature of hymns. Of three Ācāryas, *Appar*, *Jñāna-sambandha* and *Sundara*, the eighth book is *Tiru-vāchaka*, the ninth again consists of hymns. In the tenth book we find again some hymns of Tirumular. A part of the eleventh book contains mythological legends which form the groundwork of *Periya-purāṇa*, the basis of the most important Tamil legends of the Tamil saints. The book was completed by the eleventh century. The Śaiva-siddhānta

[1] The Tamil works referred to by Schomerus as forming the group of the *Śaiva-siddhānta Śāstra* are as follows: *Śiva-jñāna-bodha*, *Śiva-jñāna-siddhi*, *Irupavirupathu*, *Tiruvuntiyar*, *Tirukkalirrupadiyar*, *Unmaivilakka*, *Śiva-prakāśa*, *Tiruvarudpayan*, *Vinā-veṇba*, *Poṟṟipakrodai*, *Kodikkavi*, *Nencuvidutūtu*, *Uṇmaineṟivilakka* and *Saṅkalpa-nirākaraṇa*. The *Śiva-jñāna-bodha* of twelve verses is supposed to be a purport of the *Rauravāgama* and it has eight commentaries.

school sprang forth as a school of Śaivism in the thirteenth century with Meykaṇḍadeva and his pupils Aruḷnanti and Umāpati.

The account of Śaivism, as can be gathered from the Tamil sources, may be found in Pope's translation of *Tiru-vāchaka*, *Der Śaiva-siddhānta* by Schomerus, and in the writings of N. Pillai. The present writer is unfamiliar with the Tamil language and he has collected his account from original Sanskrit manuscripts of the Āgamas of which the Tamil treatment is only a replica.

The Āgama Literature and its Philosophical Perspective.

The philosophical views that are found in the Āgama literature had been briefly summarised in the *Sarva-darśana-saṃgraha* under Śaivism and have also been treated fairly elaborately in some of the sections of the present work. The Āgama literature is pretty extensive, but its philosophical achievement is rather poor. The Āgamas contain some elements of philosophical thought, but their interest is more on religious details of the cult of Śaivism. We find therefore a good deal of ritualism, discussion of the architectural techniques for the foundation of temples, and *mantras* and details of worship connected with the setting up of the phallic symbol of Śiva. Yet in most of the Āgamas there is a separate section called the *Vidyā-pāda* in which the general philosophical view underlying the cult is enunciated. There are slight differences in the enunciation of these views as we pass on from one Āgama to another. Most of these Āgamas still lie unpublished, and yet they form the religious kernel of Śaivism as practised by millions of people in different parts of India. There may thus be a natural inquiry as to what may be the essential tenets of these Āgamas. This, however, cannot be given without continual repetitions of the same kind of dogmatic thought. The present work is, of course, mainly concerned with the study of philosophy, but as the study of Śaiva or Śākta thought cannot be separated from the religious dogmas with which they are inseparably connected, we can only take a few specimens of the Āgamas and discuss the nature of thought that may be discovered there. In doing this we may be charged with indulging in repetitions, but we have to risk it in order to be able to give at least a rapid survey of the contents of some of the most important Āgamas. In what follows, the reader will have the opportunity of judging the literary contents of the philosophical aspects of some of the important Āgamas, thereby getting a comprehensive view of the internal relation of Śaivism to other branches of Indian philosophy.

The *Mṛgendrāgama* has often been quoted in the *Sarva-darśana-saṃgraha*. This work is said to be a subsidiary part of *Kāmikāgama*, supposed to be one of the oldest of the Āgamas, and has been referred to in the *Sūta-saṃhitā* which is regarded as a work of the sixth century. The *Sūta-saṃhitā* refers to the *Kami-kāgama* with the reverence that is due to very old texts.

Mṛgendrāgama[1] opens the discussion of how the old Vedic forms of worship became superseded by the Śaiva cult. It was pointed out that the Vedic deities were not concrete substantial objects, but their reality consisted of the *mantras* with which they were welcomed and worshipped, and consequently Vedic worship cannot be regarded as a concrete form of worship existing in time and space. But devotion to Śiva may be regarded as a definite and concrete form of worship which could, therefore, supersede the Vedic practices. In the second chapter of the work, Śiva is described as being devoid of all impurities. He is omniscient and the instrumental agent of all things. He already knows how the individual souls are going to behave and associates and dissociates all beings with knots of bondage in accordance with that.

The *Śaivāgama* discusses the main problem of the production, maintenance, destruction, veiling up of the truth and liberation. These are all done by the instrumental agent, God Śiva. In such a view the creation of the world, its maintenance and destruction are naturally designed by the supreme Lord in the beginning, yet things unfold in the natural course. The changes in the world of our experiences are not arranged by the later actions of beings. But yet the attainment of liberation is so planned that it cannot take place without individual effort.

Consciousness is of the nature of intuitive knowledge and spontaneous action (*caitanyaṃ dṛk-kriyā-rūpam*). This conscious-

[1] Since writing this section on the basis of the original manuscript the present writer has come across a printed text of the *Vidyā* and *Yogapāda* of *Mṛgendrāgama* published in 1928 by K. M. Subrahmaṇya Śāstri, with a commentary by Bhaṭṭa-nārāyaṇa Kaṇṭha called *Mṛgendra-vṛtti*, and a sub-commentary by Aghora-śivācārya called *Mṛgendra-vṛtti-dīpikā*.

ness always abides in the soul, and some of the categories for the application of this consciousness are discussed along with the various religio-moral conducts called *caryā*. There is also a brief criticism for refuting Vedānta, Sāṃkhya, Vaiśeṣika, Buddhism and Jainism.

The *Śaivāgama* holds that, from perceiving our bodies and other embodied things, we naturally infer that there is some instrumental agent who must be premised as the cause of the world. A difference of effects naturally presumes a difference in the cause and its nature. Effects are accomplished through particular instruments. These instruments are all of a spiritual nature. They are also of the nature of energy. In the case of inference the concomitance is generally perceived in some instances. But in the case of attributing creation to Śiva we have no datum of actual experience, as Śiva is bodyless. But it is held that one can conceive the body of Śiva as being constituted of certain *mantras*. When anyone is to be liberated, the quality of *tamas* as veiling the consciousness of the individual is removed by God. Those whose *tamas* is removed naturally ripen forth for the ultimate goal of liberation. They have not to wait any longer for Śiva to manifest their special qualities. We have already seen that Śiva is the manifesting agent or *abhivyañjaka* of all our activities.

The source of all bondage is *māheśvarī śakti* which helps all people to develop and grow in their own pattern (*sarvānugrāhikā*). Though there may be many cases in which we suffer pain, yet the *māheśvarī śakti* is regarded as being of universal service. The explanation is to be found in the view that often it is only through the way of suffering that we can attain our good. Śiva is always directing the *śakti* for our own good, even though we may seem to suffer in the intervening period (*dharmiṇo'nugraho nāma yattaddharmānuvartanam*). All actions of the Lord are for the sake of the individual souls, that is, for making them wise and act forward, so that ultimately they may be purged of their *malas*.

The different causal chains manifest different kinds of chains in the effects. The Śaiva view accepts *sat-kārya-vāda* and so admits that all the effects are there. It is only in the manner in which the causal chains manifest that different kinds of chains are effected. Thus the same *malas* appear in diverse forms to different kinds of persons and indicate different stages of progress. The *mala* is regarded as the unholy seed that pervades the whole world and manifests through it and is ultimately destroyed. It is through these manifestations that one can infer the existence of God, the instrumental cause (*kartā'-numīyate yena jagad-dharmeṇa hetunā*). This *mala* is inanimate, for such a theory suits the nature of effects. It is easier to assume preferably one cause of *mala* than many. The cloth is manifested by the action of the weaving spindles. The substance of the cloth would have been manifested in other forms according to the action of the various accessories, for all the effects are there, though they can only be manifested through the operation of accessories. It is difficult to imagine the concept of productive power. It is better to assume that the things are already there and are revealed to us by the action of the different kinds of causes[1].

The individual souls are all-pervasive and they possess eternal power by the Power of God. The only trouble is that on account of the veils of *mala* they are not always conscious of their nature. It is through the action of Śiva that these veils are so far removed that the individual souls may find themselves interested in their experiences. This is done by associating the individual minds with the thirty-six *kalās* produced from the disturbance of *māyā*. We have already discussed the nature of these thirty-six *tattvas* or categories in our treatment of the philosophy of *Tattva-prakāśikā* of Bhoja. It is through these categories that the veils are torn asunder and the individual becomes interested in his experiences. *Kalā* means that which moves anybody (*prasāraṇaṃ preraṇam sā kurvati tamasaḥ kalā*). The individual soul has to await the grace of God for being associated with these *kalās* for all his experiences, as he is himself unable to do so on his own account. The *karma* done by a man also remains embedded in Prakṛti and produces effects by the category of *niyati*.

[1] *sānvaya-vyatirekābhyāṃ ruḍhito vā 'vasīyate,*
tadvyakti-jananaṃ nāma tat-kāraka-samāśrayāt.
tena tantu-gatākāraṃ paṭākārā'barodhakaṃ,
vemādinā 'panīyātha paṭavyaktiḥ prakāśyate.

Ninth *paṭala*.

Śiva-jñāna-bodha.

By Meykaṇḍadeva

This is a brief work of twelve *kārikās* (sometimes called *sūtras*), and taken from *Rauravāgama*, as has already been pointed out. It has a number of commentaries. Its Tamil translation forms the basic work of the *Śiva-jñāna-siddhi* school of thought, and has been elaborated by many capable writers. The general argument of the *Śiva-jñāna-siddhi* is as follows:

This world, consisting of males, females and other neutral objects, must have a cause. This cause is not perceivable, but has to be inferred. Since it has come into being in time, it may be presumed that it has a creator. Moreover the world does not move of itself and it may, therefore, be presumed that there must be an agent behind it.

The world is destroyed by God and is re-created by Him to afford proper facilities to the *malas* for their proper expression. The position, therefore, is that though the material cause (*upādāna*) is already present, yet there must be a *nimitta-kāraṇa* or instrumental agent for the creation and the maintenance of the world. At the time of dissolution the world-appearance becomes dissolved in the impurities or *malas*. After a period, the world again reappears through the instrumentality of Śiva. Śiva thus on the one hand creates the world, and on the other hand destroys it. It is said that as in the summer all roots dry up and in the rains they shoot up again into new plants, so though the world is destroyed the impressions of the old *malas* remain inlaid in the *prakṛti*, and when the proper time comes they begin to show themselves in diverse forms of world creation according to the will of God. The creation has to take a definite order in accordance with the good and bad deeds of persons. This creation cannot take place spontaneously by compounding the four elements.

God is the instrumental agent through which the functions of creation, maintenance and destruction take place. The Śaiva view of Meykaṇḍadeva is entirely opposed to the purely monistic theory of Śaṅkara. The *jīva* cannot be regarded as identical with Brahman. It is true that in the Upaniṣads the individual soul (or *jīva*) and Brahman are both regarded as self-luminous and inner-controlled, but that does not mean that the self and the Brahman are identical.

The instrumental agent is one. The individual souls being bound by bondage or *pāśa* cannot be regarded as being identical with the ultimate agent or Brahman.

The deeds of a person do not automatically produce effects. The effects are associated with the person in accordance with the will of God. The deeds themselves are inanimate and they cannot therefore produce effects spontaneously. All effectuation is due to God, though it does not imply any change of state in the nature of God. An analogy is taken to illustrate how changes can be produced without any effort or change in the changeless. Thus the sun shines far away in the sky and yet without any interference on its part, the lotus blooms in the lake on the earth. So God rests in His self-shiningness, and the changes in the world are produced apparently in a spontaneous manner. God lives and moves in and through all beings. It is only in this sense that the world is one with God and dependent on Him.

The very denial of the different assertions that the self is this or that proves the existence of the self through our self-consciousness. We thereby assume the existence of an unconditioned self, because such a self cannot be particularised. It is easily seen that such a self is not the same as any of the visible organs or internal organs or the *manas*.

The self is different from the inner organs, the mind and the senses; but yet they can be taken as forming a joint view of reality, as in the case of the sea. The waves and billows and the foam and the wind form one whole, though in reality they are different from one another. The *malas* which are supposed to be mainly embedded in the *māyā*, naturally stick to our bodies which are the products of *māyā*, and being there they pollute the right perspective as well as the right vision of all things. The commentator, whose name is untraceable, adduces the example of the magnet and iron filings to explain the action of God on the world without undergoing any change. It is the power of Śiva working in and through us by which we can act or reap the fruits of our action according to our deeds.

Śiva is to be known through inference as the cause which is neither visible nor invisible. His existence thus can only be known by inference. The *acit* or unconscious material passes before Śiva, but does not affect it, so that Śiva is quite unconscious of the world-appearance. It is only the *jīvas* that can know both the world and Śiva[1]. When a saint becomes free from impurities of three kinds, the *āṇava*, *māyika* and *kārmaṇa-mala*, the world appearance vanishes from before his eyes, and he becomes one with the pure illumination.

Suradantācārya in his *Vyākhyāna-kārikā* repeats the above ideas, but holds that Śiva through His omniscience knows all about the world and the experiences of all beings, but He is not affected by them[2]. Another fragmentary commentary of an unknown author, who had written a commentary on *Mṛgendra* called *Mṛgendra-vṛtti-dīpikā*, which sometimes refers to the *Svāyambhuvāgama* and the *Mātaṅga-parameśvara-āgama*, discusses some of the main topics of *Śiva-jñāna-bodha* in the work called *Paśupati-pāśa-vicāra-prakaraṇa*.

Paśu is defined as pure consciousness (*cinmātra*) covered with impurities. The *paśu* goes through the cycle of birth and rebirth, and it goes also by the name *ātman*. It is all-pervading in space and time. The pure consciousness is of the nature of *jñāna* and *kriyā*. The Āgamas do not believe that the soul is one. It is pure consciousness that appears as distinct from one another by their association of different kinds of *mala* which are integrated with them from beginningless time[3].

Its body consists of all the categories, beginning with *kalā* and running up to gross matter. The soul is called *anīśvara* because it may have a subtle body, but not the gross one, so that it is unable to enjoy its desire. The soul is regarded as *akriya* or devoid of action. Even when through knowledge and renunciation it avoids all action, the body may go on by the successive impulses of previous actions (*tiṣṭhati saṃskāra-vaśāt cakra-bhramavad-dhṛta-śarīrah*). Though there are many souls, they are spoken of in the singular number as *paśu* in the universal sense.

The *mala* is regarded as being included within *pāśa*. It is not therefore a different category. The pure self-consciousness is entirely different from the impurity or *mala*. How can then the *mala* affect the purity of the pure consciousness? To this the reply

1 *nācit-cit sannidhau kintu na vittas te ubhe mithaḥ,*
prapañca-śivayor vettā yaḥ sa ātmā tayoḥ pṛthak.

2 *. . . śivo jānāti viśvakam,*
sva-bhogyatvena tu paraṃ naiva jānāti kiñcana.

3 *anena mala-yukto vijñāna-kevala uktaḥ. saṃmūḍha ityanena pralayena kalāder upasaṃhṛtatvāt samyak mūḍhaḥ. Paśupati-pāśa-vicāra-prakaraṇa* (Adyar Library manuscript).

is that as pure gold may be associated with dross without affecting its nature, so the pure consciousness that constitutes the Śiva within us may remain pure, even though it may be covered with *mala* from beginningless time. The *mala* thus does not affect the nature of the self as Śiva.

It is by the grace of Śiva, attained through proper initiation in Śaivism by a proper preceptor, that the impurities can be removed, and not by mere knowledge as such. The *mala* being the nature of substance, it can be removed only by an action on the part of God. Mere knowledge cannot destroy it. The *malas* being beginningless are not many but one. According to different kinds of *karma*, the *malas* have distinct and different kinds of bondage. The different distinctive powers and obscurations made by the *mala* serve to differentiate the different selves, which basically are all Śiva. Liberation does not mean any transformation, but only the removal of particular *malas* with reference to which different individual entities as *jīvas* were passing through the cycle of birth and rebirth. This removal is effected by Śiva when the Śaiva initiation is taken with the help of proper preceptors[1].

The *malas* consist of *dharma* and *adharma*, and may be due to *karma* or *māyā*; they also constitute the bondage or the *pāśas*. This Āgama refers to *Mṛgendrāgama*, the doctrines of which it follows in describing the nature of *pāśa*, *mala*, etc. The *pāśa* is really the *tirodhānaśakti* of Śiva. The *pāśas* are threefold: (1) *sahaja*, those *malas* with which we are associated from beginningless time and which stay on until liberation; (2) *āgantuka*, meaning all our senses and sense-objects; and (3) *sūṃsargika*, that is those which are produced by the intercourse of *sahaja* and the *āgantuka mala*.

The creation and the manifestation of our experiences take place in accordance with our *karma* as revealed by God. Just as a field sown with seeds does not produce the same kind of crop for every peasant, so in spite of same kinds of actions we may have different kinds of results manifested to us by God. The *karmas* and other things are all inanimate, and thus it is only by the will of God that different kinds of results are manifested to us. The Śaiva view thus upholds the *satkārya-vāda* theory and regards God as *abhivyañjaka* or manifestor of all our experiences and *karmas*.

[1] *evañ ca pāśā-panayanad ātmanaḥ sarva-jñatva-sarva-kartṛtvātmaka-śivatvābhivyaktir eva mukti-daśāyām, na tu pariṇāma-svarūpa-vināśaḥ.*

Mātaṅga-parameśvara-tantra.

The *Śaiva śāstra* is described as *ṣaṭ-padārtha* and *catuṣ-pāda* and not as *tri-padārtha* and *catuṣ-pāda*; formerly it was written by Sadā-śiva in ten million verses and Ananta summarised it in one lakh verses, which has been further summarised in 3500 verses. The six categories are (1) *pati*; (2) *śakti*; (3) *triparvā*; (4) *paśu*; (5) *bodha*; and (6) *mantra.*

Śakti or energy is the means by which we can infer *pati*, the possessor of *śakti*. In inference we sometimes infer the possessor of the quality by its quality, and sometimes the cause from the effect or the effect from the cause. Sometimes the existence of a thing is taken for granted on the authority of the Vedas. From the body of Śiva, which is of the nature of *mantras*, the *śakti* emanates downwards in the form of *bindu*, which later on develops into the world[1]. Śiva enters into the *bindu* and unfolds it for various types of creation. The diversity in the world is due to a difference in *karma* and *guṇa* of the individual souls, where the individual souls may be regarded as the container and the *karma* as contained. The individual souls are responsible for their actions and have to enjoy their good or bad fruits. God is the controller of the creation, maintenance and destruction of the world. It is He who is the instrumental cause of the world, and the energies are the material cause and are regarded as the *samavāyi-kāraṇa* of the world. This world is the production of *māyā*. As the rays of the sun or the moon induce the blooming of flowers spontaneously without any actual interference, so the Śiva manifests the world by His mere proximity.

Seven *sahaja-malas* have been enumerated as follows: (1) *moha*, (2) *mada*, (3) *rāga*, (4) *viṣāda*, (5) *śoṣa*, (6) *vaicitta* and (7) *harṣa.*

The *kalās* are produced from *māyā*, and it is in association with *māyā* that they carry on their work, just as paddy seeds can produce shoots in association with the husk in which they are enclosed.

The souls as they are driven through the world, become attached to worldly things through *kalā*. This association is further

[1] It is traditionally believed that the *mantras* or hymns constitute the body of a deity.

tightened by *vāsanā*; so the souls become attached to all enjoyments, and this is called *rāga*. With all attachments there is sorrow, and therefore non-attachment to all sense-pleasures leads to the best attainment of happiness.

The nature of *kāla* and *niyati* are discussed in the same way as in other books of Śaiva-siddhānta.

Māyā comes out from God as an expression of His subtle energy, and from *māyā* there evolves the *pradhāna*, which in its first stage is only pure being or *sattā*. Later on other categories evolve out of it and they supply the materials for the experience of *puruṣa*. The *puruṣa* and the *prakṛti* thus mutually support each other in the development of categories and experience.

The *ahaṅkāra* infuses the self in and through the sense-organs and operates as their functions. The same may be said regarding the application of *ahaṅkāra* in and through the *tanmātras*. The *ahaṅkāra* thus represents the entire psychic state in a unity. The *ahaṅkāra* is present also in dormant state in trees, plants, etc.

Pauṣkarāgama.

In the *Pauṣkarāgama jñāna* is defined as consisting of the energy inherent in Śiva. Six categories described are "*patiḥ kuṇḍalinī māyā paśuḥ pāśaś ca kārakah.*" *Laya*, *bhoga* and *adhikāra* are the three functions of *śakti*. *Māyā* as generated by the actions of men, supplies the elements by which the objects of experience and experience are made. *Paśu* is that which experiences and reacts. The categories beginning from *kalā* to earth (*kṣiti*) are real entities. *Laya* is called bondage and is regarded as the fifth category. The sixth category is equal to *bhukti*, *mukti*, *vyakti*, *phala*, *kriyā* and *dīkṣā* taken together. *Bindu* and *aṇus* are the real entities. When the manifold creation shrinks into the *bindu*, we have that stage in Śiva which is called dissolution (*laya*). In the original state actions of the type of *sadṛśa pariṇāma* go on. Śiva is described as *vispaṣṭa cinmātra* and *vyāpaka*. His energies only can operate, while He remains unmoved. When the energies begin to operate in the *bindu*, the *bindu* becomes fit for being the data of experience. This state of *bindu* with Śiva reflected in it is called the *sadā-śiva*. Even in this stage there is really no change in Śiva. When the energies are in the state of operation, we have the state of creation, and the experience of it is called *bhoga*.

The point arises that if the *bindu* is itself active in creation, then its relation with Śiva becomes redundant. On the other hand, if the *bindu* is moved by Śiva to active operation, Śiva becomes changeable. The reply is that an agent can affect any material in two ways, either by his simple desire or by his organised effort, as in the case of the making of a pot by the potter. Śiva moves the *bindu* simply by His *saṃkalpa*, and therefore He does not suffer any change. In the case of the action of the potter also, it is by the wish of Śiva that the potter can act. Therefore, Śiva is the sole agent of all actions performed by animate beings or by inanimate matter.

It may be said that Śiva is wholly unconditioned, and therefore He can remain the sole agent without undergoing any change. Another tentative answer is that in the presence of Śiva, the *bindu* begins to work without any causal efficiency (compare the movement of *prakṛti* in the presence of *puruṣa*).

The *bindu* has sometimes been described as *śāntyatīta* and other times as the material cause of the creation. This difficulty is explained on the assumption that part of the *bindu* is *śāntyatīta* and the other part is responsible for being the material cause of the world. The third category including the *bindu* and Śiva is called Īśvara. Śiva produces commotion in *bindu* merely by His presence. In this way Śiva is not only the instrumental agent of all happenings in the inanimate, but He also is responsible for all actions of the human body which are seemingly produced by the human will.

Knowledge and activity are in essence identical, and for that reason, when there is action (*vyāpāra*), we may feel as if we are the agents of those actions. The element of action that seems to express itself is thus something more than the action, and it is called the *adhikāra-kriyā*. The action and that which is acted upon is the result of *guṇa-saṃkalpa*. Śiva stands as the *citi-śakti* which makes all energies dynamic, as the sun makes the lotus bloom from a distance without any actual interference.

In further explaining the philosophical situation Śiva says that a part of the *bindu* is in the transcendental (*śāntyatīta*) state, while the other part is responsible for the creative action. This second category, that is, the lower half of the *bindu*, is supposed to be moved by Śiva. The energies are often classified under different names as performing different functions. *Śakti* and *śaktimān* are the same. They are only differently classified according to their diverse functions.

The inanimate world is inoperative without the action or the interference of a conscious being. That conscious being is God Śiva; even the milk in the udder of the cow flows by the active affection of the cow for the calf. The illustration of the magnet drawing the iron filings does not fit in, for there also is the person who brings the magnet near the iron filings.

It cannot, however, be urged that the *puruṣas* themselves could be regarded as active agents, for according to the scriptural texts they are also moved to activity by the will of God[1].

The world-appearance cannot be proved to be false or illusory. It is made up of the stuff of one common object called *māyā*, which is later on conceived as functioning in different ways called *sattva*, *rajas* and *tamas*. The *māyā* stuff is the repository of all *karmas*. But yet not all persons gain the fruits of all their *karmas*. They have to depend upon some other being for the proper fruition of their *karmas*. This is where God comes in as the ultimate bestower of the fruits of *karma*.

Mala or impurity is always associated with all souls. The Āgama tries to refute the epistemological view of other systems of thought like the Cārvāka and the monism of Śaṅkara. The Āgama holds that since the souls are eternal, their knowledge must also be eternal due to eternal unchanging cause. The difference of knowledge in individuals is due to the obscuration of their knowledge by the various veils of *mala*. The original cause of knowledge is all-pervading and is the same in all persons[2].

The self is realised as revealing itself and others. If it is supposed that the self is reflected through *buddhi*, then even *buddhi*

[1] *vivādādhyāsitaṃ viśvaṃ viśva-vit-kartṛ-pūrvakam,*
kāryatvād āvayoḥ siddhaṃ kāryaṃ kumbhādikaṃ yathā.

First *paṭala*.

[2] *tac ceha vibhu-dharmatvān na ca kvācitkam iṣyate,*
nityatvam iva tenātmā sthitaḥ sarvārtha-dṛk-kriyaḥ.
jñātṛtvam api yadyasya kvācitkaṃ vibhutā kutaḥ,
dharmiṇo yāvatī vyāptis tāvad-dharmasya ca sthitiḥ,
yathā paṭa-sthitaṃ śauklyaṃ paṭaṃ vyāpyākhilaṃ sthitam,
sthitaṃ vyāpyaivam ātmānaṃ jñātṛtvam api sarvadā,
na ca nirviṣayaṃ jñānaṃ parāpekṣaṃ svarūpataḥ.

Fourth *paṭala*.

also may be regarded as conscious self. So the idea of explaining the situation as being the reflection of consciousness in *buddhi*, also fails. Again this reflection of consciousness in *buddhi* cannot be regarded as conscious entity. It may also be pointed out that the consciousness as spirit cannot be reflected in *buddhi* which is known as spiritual. The view of mutual reflection of consciousness into *buddhi* and *buddhi* into consciousness is also untenable. It has, therefore, to be admitted that the soul as an eternal being can perceive all things and act as it likes. If the qualities inhere permanently or temporarily in an entity, then that inherence in the entity must be of a permanent or of a temporary nature as the case may be. The consciousness of the soul should, therefore, be regarded as co-extensive with its being. The selves are atomic in size and cannot therefore pervade the whole body. We have already said that the self in revealing itself also reveals other things. We must remember in this connection that an entity like the fire cannot be distinguished from the energy that it has.

Again the objects perceived cannot be regarded as mere ignorance (*ajñāna*), for one cannot deal with mere *ajñāna*, just as one cannot bring water without a pitcher. The things we perceive are real entities. This *ajñāna* cannot be taken in the sense of *prāgabhava*, for then that would imply another origination of knowledge; or it could be explained as wrong knowledge. This wrong knowledge may be regarded as accidental or natural. If it is accidental or natural, then it must be due to some causes and cannot, therefore, be regarded as wrong knowledge. If it is wrong knowledge only arising occasionally, then it cannot contradict right knowledge. Ordinarily one cannot expect the illusoriness of silver to contradict the knowledge of conch-shell[1]. For this reason the self, which is intuitively realised as all-consciousness, cannot be regarded as having only limited knowledge. That appearance of the souls possessing limited knowledge must be due to its association with impurities. The energy of consciousness is eternal, and therefore its nature cannot be disturbed by the association of impurities which may constitute experience, as arising from *dharma* and *adharma*. The *malas* are regarded as sevenfold, and include within them the passions of *mada*, *moha*, etc. These *malas* are

[1] *kiñ caitad anyathā-jñānaṃ na samyag jñāna-bādhakam.*
Fourth *paṭala*.

regarded as being natural to the souls. The *mala* of *moha* appears in various forms, as attachment to wife, son, money, etc.

It is only the spiritual that can contradict the non-spiritual. Two spiritual entities or the non-spiritual entities cannot contradict each other. One soul cannot be contradicted by another soul.

If the association of *malas* with the souls is regarded as beginningless, then how can they veil the nature of the self, and what must be the nature of this veil? It cannot be said that this veiling means the covering of what was already illuminated; for in that case, this obscuration of illumination of an entity, which is of the nature of light, must mean its destruction. The reply is that the energy of consciousness (*cicchakti*) cannot be veiled by the *malas*. The *malas* can only arrest its function.

Śakti is defined as being of the nature of immediate intuition and action. If that is so, the *śakti* is associated with knowable objects. How can then the objects be different from the energy? In reply it is said that the intuitive knowledge and action (*dṛkkriyā*), the *śakti*, as such remains united as *dṛk* and *kriyā*. They are indivisibly connected as one, and it is for us to think of them as divided into *dṛk* and *kriyā*[1]. All words denoting particular objects are for others and are under the veil of *mala*. By the suppression of *mala*, the energy is turned away from sense objects. In this way the *mala* operates against the *cicchakti*, and thereby *malas* obscure the omniscient character of the souls.

In the fifth chapter, the Āgama deals with the different kinds of *pāśas* or bonds. These bonds are *kalā*, *avidyā*, *rāga*, *kāla* and *niyati*. These five categories are regarded as proceeding from *māyā*. The consciousness shows itself through these *kalās*. The consciousness is associated with both intuitive knowledge and the power of work. The *kalās* reflect the consciousness of the soul only partially. This reflection is effected in accordance with one's *karma*.

All experience is due to the functioning of the power of knowledge and of the objects to be known. This is technically called *grāhaka* and *grāhya*. It is by the association of consciousness that the *kalās* appear to be functioning for the apprehension of things. From *kalā* comes *vidyā*. *Kalā* supplies the basis of experience as time and space. Later on other categories of the intellect also

[1] *avibhāgasya bhāgoktau tad-vibhāga upādhitaḥ.*

Fourth *paṭala*.

evolve and we have the concept of *buddhi* as deliberate decision. In this way the different categories such as *ahaṅkāra* or *abhimāna* are produced. They in themselves would not be conscious except through the consciousness which impregnates them.

The *buddhi* manifests itself through diverse forms according to their *vāsanās*. A full enumeration of them is given in the texts, but we omit them as they are not philosophically important. They, however, include the various instinctive tendencies and delusions which are enumerated in Sāṃkhya and other places.

The difficulty is that the *buddhi* and *ahaṅkāra* seem to cover the same ground. How is it then possible to distinguish *buddhi* from *ahaṅkāra*? To this the reply is that when something is deliberately known as this or that, we have the stage of *buddhi*. But in the stage of *ahaṅkāra* we seem to behave as knowers, and all objects that come to our purview are labelled as parts of our knowledge. There is no means by which the ego-consciousness of any individual can be confused with the ego-consciousness of another. They are thus realised as different from one another[1].

The Āgama describes the three kinds of creation as *sāttvika*, *rājasa* and *tāmasa* as proceeding from three kinds of *ahaṅkāra*, and describes the origination of *jñānendriyas*, *karmendriyas*, *tanmātras* and *manas*. When things are perceived by the senses and their value as this or that is attested by an inner function, so that the red can be distinguished from the blue, that inner function is called *manas*[2].

When we perceive an animal having certain peculiarities, then we can extend the use of the word to denote another animal having the same kind of features. The inner function by which this is done is *manas*.

The Āgama gives an elaborate description of the cognitive senses and particularly of the organ of the eye. The mere proximity of consciousness cannot generate the activity. This can only be generated by the association of the consciousness with the sense organs.

The Āgama criticises the Buddhist position and supposes that the Buddhist doctrine of *artha-kriyā-káritā* can hold good only if the entities are not momentary, but have extensive existence.

1 *yady abhinnam ahaṅkṛt syāu devadatto 'pyahaṃ matiḥ,*
anyasyām upajāyeta nātmaikatvaṃ tataḥ sthitam. Sixth *paṭala*.

2 *cakṣuṣā locite hy arthe tamarthaṃ buddhi-gocaram,*
vidadhātīha yad viprās tanmanaḥ paripaṭhyate. Sixth *paṭala*.

Speaking of the *guṇas*, the Āgama refuses to admit their substantive nature. It is only when certain *guṇas* are in a collocated state that we call them *guṇa* reals.

Our senses can only perceive certain objective qualities, but they cannot perceive any substratum behind them. Therefore it is logically incorrect to infer any substratum, which may be called *guṇas* as reals. After a discussion about what may be the original material cause either as partless atoms or as immaterial *prakṛti*, the Āgama decides in favour of the latter. But this *prakṛti* is not the state of equilibrium (*sāmyāvasthā*) of the *guṇas* as the Sāṃkhya holds.

The Āgama discusses the *prāpya-kāritva* and *aprāpya-kāritva* of the different senses. It also says that movement does not belong originally to every atom, but it belongs only to the living atoms, the souls. It cannot also be due to the mere presence of other things.

When the *manas* is associated with *cicchakti*, then it attains the knowledge of all things by the exercise of the internal organs. At the first moment this knowledge is indeterminate. Later on various determinations become associated with it. The perception of things at different times becomes synthetised and concretised, otherwise the various memory images might arise before the mind and prevent the formation of a synthetic image, as we find in the case of a concrete perception.

It is only the ego-consciousness or the *abhimāna* that produces in us the sense agency (*katṛtva*). Without this sense of *abhimāna* there would be no difference between the self and other material objects. From ego-consciousness there proceeds the deliberate consciousness of decision (*niścaya*).

Knowledge of things cannot arise merely from *buddhi*, for the stuff of *buddhi* is material. Consciousness can only arise occasionally in consequence of its relation with *cicchakti*. If the mental states are always changing, then they cannot be perceived as constant, though they may appear to be so, like the flame of a lamp which changes from moment to moment, but yet appears to be the same.

Turning to the doctrine of *artha-kriyā-kāritā* of the Buddhists, the Āgama says that if the doctrine of *artha-kriyā-kāritā* be accepted, then the existence of things cannot properly be explained. The proper view is that of *pariṇāma-vāda*. If the things are momentary, then effects cannot be produced, for a thing must remain for at least two moments in order to produce an effect. If the two moments are separate entities, then one cannot be the cause of the other. The causal change can only be with reference to the existing things, but not with regard to the entities which are momentary. In order that there may be a production, the thing must remain for two moments at least. Things that are existent need not always be productive. The production of an effect may depend on accessory causes. A jug cannot be produced by threads, but the threads may produce a piece of cloth. This shows that the effect is always already in the cause.

It cannot also be held that our mental states are identical with the external objects, for in that case it would be difficult to explain the multiplicity of our cognitive states in accordance with their objects. We would not be able to explain how one entity assumes so many diverse forms. The only course left is to admit some external objects with which our senses come into contact. These objects consist of a conglomeration of *tanmātras*. It is in and through this conglomeration of *tanmātras* that new qualities arise to which we give the names of different *bhūtas*. The difference between *tanmātras* and *bhūtas* is that the former are more subtle and the latter more gross. This view is somewhat different from the Sāṃkhya view, for here the *bhūtas* are not regarded as different categories, but only as a conglomeration of *tanmātras*. The idea that the *guṇas* are certain objective entities is again and again repudiated. It is held that it is the conglomeration of *guṇas* that is regarded by us as substantive entity.

The Āgama then criticises the theory of atoms which are partless. It is held that the partless atoms cannot have sides in which other atoms could be associated. The question is raised that *tanmātras* being formless (*amūrta*) cannot themselves be the causes of all forms. The world of forms thus leads us to infer some material as its cause. To this Śiva replies that the *prakṛti* can be regarded as being endowed with form and also as formless[1].

Śiva in further replying to the questions says that things having form must have other entities endowed with forms as their causes. Therefore one may infer that the atoms are the causes of the world. In that case one cannot deny the fact that the atoms have forms. In further discussing the subject Śiva says that the atoms are many

[1] *māyā tu paramā mūrta nityānityasya kāraṇam,*
ekāneka-vibhāgādhyā vastu-rūpā śivātmikā. Sixth *paṭala*.

and they have parts. So they are of the same type as other effects, such as jug, etc. As such the cause of the world must be regarded as being something which is formless. All effects are *anitya*, dependent on others (*āśrita*), and have parts and are many. The Śaivism, therefore, holds that their cause must be different, it must be one, independent and partless. Therefore it discards the view that the atoms are the material cause of the world[1]. The gross elements gradually evolved from the five *tanmātras*.

The Āgama refutes the view that *ākāśa* is mere vacuity. Had it been a vacuity, it would have been a negation, and a negation always belongs to the positive entity. The Āgama also refutes the possibility of *ākāśa* being regarded as any kind of negation. *Śabda* is regarded as the specific quality of *ākāśa*.

The Āgama says that it admits only four *pramāṇas*: *pratyakṣa*, *anumāna*, *śabda*, and *arthāpatti*. In reality it is pure consciousness devoid of all doubts that constitutes the truth underlying the *pramāṇas*. Doubt arises out of the oscillation of the mind between two poles. Memory refers to objects experienced before. In order that any knowledge may attain to the state of proper validity, it must be devoid of memory and doubt.

Pure consciousness is the real valid part in knowledge. *Buddhi* being itself a material thing cannot be regarded as constituting the valid element of knowledge. It is in and through the *kalās* that the pure consciousness comes into contact with the objective world. This perception may be either *nirvikalpa* or *savikalpa*. In the *nirvikalpa* perception there is no reference in the mind to class concepts or names. By the *nirvikalpa* perception one can perceive things as they are without any association of names, etc.

Perception is of two kinds: (1) as associated with the senses, and (2) as unassociated with the senses as in the case of intuitive knowledge by *yoga*. When associated with senses the perceptive function removes the veil between the objects and the self, so that the objects can be directly perceived. In explaining the nature of perception the Āgama follows the Nyāya technique of *saṃyukta-samavāya*, etc., for explaining the situation. It believes like Nyāya in five types of propositions, namely *pratijñā*, *hetu*, *dṛṣṭānta*, *upanaya* and *nigamana*.

1 *tato na paramāṇūnāṃ hetutvam yuktibhir mataṃ.* Sixth *paṭala*.

Vātulāgama[1].

Vātulāgama from Adyar with commentary seems to be almost identical with the *Vātulāgama* of the Mysore Oriental Research Institute, only with this difference that the *Vātulāgama* of Mysore contains more verses in the concluding tenth chapter in which the Vīra-śaiva doctrine is praised above other Śaiva doctrines. But the original beginning is more or less like the general Śaiva doctrine as may be found in *Tattva-prakāśikā* with Aghora-śivācārya's commentary. There is also the tendency to derive the existence of Śiva as the ultimate reality on the basis of inference, as may be found in the Siddhānta systems of Śaivism, such as the *Mṛgendrāgama* or in the Lākulīśa-Pāśupata system. The supplementary portion of *Vātulāgama* introduces the doctrine of *liṅga-dhāraṇa* of the Vīra-śaivas, but does not say anything about its specific philosophy or about its other doctrines associated with *ṣaṭ-sthala.*

Vātula-tantram[2].

Śiva-tattva is of three kinds: (1) *niṣkala*, (2) *sakala* and (3) *niṣkala-sakala*. Śiva may be distinguished in ten ways: (1) *tattva-bheda*, (2) *varṇa-bheda*, (3) *cakra-bheda*, (4) *varga-bheda*, (5) *mantra-bheda*, (6) *praṇava*, (7) *brahma-bheda*, (8) *aṅga-bheda*, (9) *mantra-jāta*, (10) *kīla*. Though previously it has been said to be of three kinds, it has three forms again: (1) *subrahmaṇya-śiva*, (2) *sadā-śiva* and (3) *maheśa*.

Śiva is called *niṣkala* when all His *kalās*, that is parts or organs or functions, are concentrated in a unity within Him. In further defining the nature of *niṣkalatva*, the author says that when the pure and impure elements that contribute to experience are collected together and merged in the original cause, and remain there as the budding cause of all powers that are to develop the universe, we have the *niṣkala* stage. The commentator supports this idea by quotations from many texts. The *sakala-niṣkala* is that in which the deeds of persons are in a dormant state, and when the time of creation comes it associates itself with the *bindu* state for

[1] Oriental Research Institute, Mysore.
[2] Adyar Library manuscript.

the formation of the world. The *bindu* represents the *māyopādāna* with which Śiva associates Himself for the creation[1]. These different names of *sakala* and *niṣkala* and *sakala-niṣkala* of Śiva are but different moments in Śiva and do not constitute any actual transformation in Him, for He always remains unchanged in Himself. In Śiva, therefore, there is no change. The changes are to be found in the *bindu* and the *anus*[2].

God can only be proved by *anumāna* as being the instrumental cause of the world. This is taking the old Śaiva view of the Siddhānta, like the *Mṛgendrāgama*. The agency of God is to be explained by the supposition that by His desire everything is accomplished. He does not take to any instrument or organs for accomplishing any act. Thus when the potter makes his pot, it is through the infusion of God's power that he can do so. In the case of the potter, the agency is different, because he works with his instruments and organs. Śiva through His energy can know and do all things.

Śiva creates all things by His simple *saṃkalpa* and this creation is called the *śuddhādhva*. The author refers to *Tattva-prakāśika* of Bhoja and the commentary on it by Aghora-śivācārya.

Śakti is the will of God and that is called *bindu*. From that arises *nāda* which is a source of all speech[3].

We have given some analysis of some of the important Āgamas just to show the nature of the subjects that are dealt with in these Āgamas. A more comprehensive account of the Āgamas could easily have been given, but that would have involved only tiresome repetition. Most of the Āgamas deal with the same sort of subjects more or less in the same manner with some incidental variations as

[1] *maheśaḥ sakalaḥ bindu-māyopādāna-janita-tanu-karaṇādibhir ātmānaṃ yadā śuddhāśuddha-bhogaṃ prayacchati tadā śiva-saṅgakaḥ sa eva bhagavān sakala ity ucyate.*

[2] *laya-bhogādhikārāṇāṃ na bhedo vāstavaḥ śive, kintu vindor aṇūnāṃ ca vāstavā eva te matāḥ.*

[3] *śaktir iccheti vijñeyā śabdo jñānam ihocyate, vāgbhavaṃ syāt kriyā-śaktiḥ kalā vai ṣoḍaśa smṛtaḥ. yā parameśvarasya icchā sā śaktir iti jñeyā, śaktestu jāyate śabdaḥ. Yat parameśvarasya jñānaṃ tadeva śabdaḥ. śabdāt jāyate vāgbhavaḥ. yā parameśvarasya kriyā sā tu vāgbhavaḥ. ṣoḍaśa svarāḥ kalā ity ucyante.*

Quoted from *Pauṣkarāgama*:

acetanaṃ jagad viprāś cetana-prerakaṃ vinā,
pravṛttau vā nivṛttau vā na svatantraṃ rathādivat.

regards their emphasis on this or that subject. They also sometimes vary as regards their style and mode of approach. Thus the Āgama called *Śiva-jñāna-siddhi* deals with the various subjects by quotations from a large number of Āgamas. This shows that there was an internal unity among the various Āgamas. From these collective works we can know much of the contents of the different Āgamas. This is important as some of these Āgamas are scarcely available even as a single manuscript.

The date of these Āgamas cannot be definitely fixed. It may be suggested that the earliest of them were written sometime in the second or third century A.D., and these must have been continued till the thirteenth or fourteenth century. In addition to the theological or religious dogmatics, they contain discussions on the nature of the various ducts or *nāḍis* in connection with the directions regarding the performance of *yoga* or mental concentration. There are some slight disputations with rival systems of thought as those of the Buddhists, Jains and the Sāṃkhya. But all this is very slight and may be practically ignored. There is no real contribution to any epistemological thought. We have only the same kind of stereotyped metaphysical dogma and the same kind of argument that leads to the admission of a creator from the creation as of the agent from the effects. Thus apparently the material cause, the *upādāna kāraṇa*, described as *prakṛti* and sometimes atoms, is different from the instrumental cause, God. But in order to maintain the absolute monistic view that Śiva alone is the ultimate reality, this material cause is often regarded as the *śakti* or energy which is identical with God. Sometimes the entire creation is described as having an appearance before the individuals according to their *karma* through God's power of bondage. The individual souls are all infected by various impurities derived from *māyā* or *karma*. These impurities are ultimately destroyed by the grace of God, when the Śaiva initiation is taken.

These Āgamas are also full of directions as regards various religious practices and disciplines, and also of various kinds of rituals, *mantras*, directions for the building of temples or of setting up of various kinds of phallic symbols, which, however, have to be entirely omitted from the present treatment of Śaivism. But it is easy to see that the so-called Śaiva philosophy of the Āgamas is just a metaphysical kernel for upholding the Śaiva religious life and practices. These consist largely in inspiring the devotees to lead an absolutely moral life, wholly dedicated to Śiva, and full of intoxicating fervour of devotion, as one may find in *Tiru-vāchaka* of Māṇikka-vāchakar. This devotion is the devotion of service, of a life entirely dedicated to Lord Śiva.

CHAPTER XXXV

VÍRA-ŚAIVISM

History and Literature of Vīra-śaivism.

THE name 'Vīra-śaiva' as applied to a particular Śaiva sect appears to be of a later date. Mādhava in his *Sarva-darśana-saṃgraha* of the fourteenth century A.D., who mentions the Pāśupatas and the Āgamic Śaivas, does not seem to know anything about the Vīra-śaivas. Śaṅkara and Vācaspati and Ānanda-giri of the eighth and the ninth centuries do not seem to know anything of the Vīra-śaivas. Neither are they alluded to in any of the *Śaivāgamas*. The *Vātula-tantra* seems to have two editions (in manuscript), and in one of them the *ṣaṭ-sthala* doctrine is mentioned in the form of an appendix, which shows that this introduction was of the nature of an apocrypha. The doctrine of *liṅga-dhāraṇa* in the manner in which it is done by the Liṅgāyats of the Vīra-śaivas can hardly be traced in any early works, though later Vīra-śaiva writers like Śrīpati and others have twisted some of the older texts which allude to *liṅga* to mean the specific practices of *liṅga-dhāraṇa* as done by the Liṅgāyats.

There is a general tradition that Basava, a Brahmin, son of Mādirāja and Mādāmba was the founder of the Vīra-śaiva sect. From his native place Bāgevaḍi, he went to Kalyān near Bombay, at a comparatively young age, when Vijjala was reigning there as king (A.D. 1157–67). His maternal uncle Baladeva having resigned on account of illness, Basava was appointed as the minister in complete charge of Vijjala's treasury and other administrative functions. According to another tradition Basava succeeded in deciphering an inscription which disclosed some hidden treasure, and at this, King Vijjala was so pleased that he gave Basava the office of prime minister. According to the *Basava-purāṇa*, which narrates the life of Basava in a mythical purāṇic manner, Basava, on assuming the office, began to distribute gifts to all those who professed themselves to be the devotees of Śiva. This led to much confusion and heart-burning among the other sects, and it so happened that King Vijjala cruelly punished two of the devotees of Śiva. At this, by the instigation of Basava, one of his followers murdered Vijjala. Bhandarkar gives some other details, which the present writer has not been able to trace in the *Basava-purāṇa* (the source, according to Bhandarkar himself)[1].

The *Basava-purāṇa* was written after the time of Śrīpati Paṇḍita. It is said there that at one time Nārada reported to Śiva that, while other religions were flourishing, the Śaiva faith was with few exceptions dying out among the Brahmins, and so it was decaying among other castes also. Lord Śiva then asked Nandi to get himself incarnated for taking the Vīra-śaiva faith in consonance with the *Varṇāśrama* rites[2]. If this remark is of any value, it has to be admitted that even after the time of Śrīpati Paṇḍita the Vīra-śaiva faith had not assumed any importance in the Carnatic region. It also indicates that the Vīra-śaiva faith at this time was not intended to be preached in opposition to the Hindu system of castes and caste duties. It has been contended that Basava introduced social reforms for the removal of castes and caste duties and some other Hindu customs. But this claim cannot be substantiated, as, in most of the Vīra-śaiva works, we find a loyalty to the Hindu caste order. There is, of course, a tendency to create a brotherhood among the followers of Śiva who grouped round Basava, as he was both politically and financially a patron of the followers of Śiva. The *Basava-purāṇa* also says that Basava was taken before the assembly of paṇḍits for the performance of the rite of initiation of the holy thread at the age of eight, according to the custom of compulsory initiation among the Brahmins. Basava, however, at that early age protested against the rite of initiation, on the grounds that the holy thread could purify neither the soul nor body, and that there were many instances in the purāṇic accounts where saints of the highest reputation had not taken the holy thread. We find no account of Basava as preaching a crusade against Hindu customs and manners, or against Brahmanism as such.

Basava's own writings are in Canarese, in the form of sayings or musings, such as is common among the devotees of other sects of Śaivism, Vaiṣṇavism, etc. The present writer had the occasion to go through a large mass of these sayings in their English translations. On the basis of these it can be said that they contain a

[1] See Bhandarkar's *Vaiṣṇavism and Śaivism*, p. 132.

[2] *varṇācārānurodhena śaivācaran pravartaya. Basava-purāṇa*, ch. II, verse 32.

rapturous enthusiasm for the God Śiva, who to Basava appeared as the Lord Kudala Saṅgama. These sayings referred to Śiva as the supreme Lord, and to Basava himself as his servant or slave. They also contain here and there some biographical allusions which cannot be reconstructed satisfactorily without the help of other contemporary evidence. So far as can be judged from the sayings of Basava, it is not possible to give any definite account of Vīra-śaiva thought as having been propounded or systematised by Basava. According to *Basava-purāṇa*, the practice of *liṅga-dhāraṇa* seems to have been in vogue even before Basava. Basava himself does not say anything about the doctrine of *ṣaṭ-sthala*, and these two are the indispensably necessary items by which Vīra-śaivism can be sharply distinguished from the other forms of Śaivism, apart from its philosophical peculiarity. On this also Basava does not seem to indicate any definite line of thought which could be systematised without supplementing it or reconstructing it by the ideas of later Vīra-śaiva writers. Though the kernel of the Vīra-śaiva philosophy may be traced back to the early centuries of the Christian era, and though we find it current in works like *Sūta-saṃhitā* of the sixth century A.D., yet we do not know how the name Vīra-śaiva came to be given to this type of thought.

In the work *Siddhānta-śikhāmaṇi*, written by Revaṇācārya some time between Basava and Śrīpati, we find the name 'Vīra-śaiva' associated with the doctrine of *sthala*, and this is probably the earliest use of the term in available literature. *Siddhānta-śikhāmaṇi* refers to Basava and is itself referred to by Śrīpati. This shows that the book must have been written between the dates of Basava and Śrīpati. The *Siddhānta-śikhāmaṇi* gives a fanciful interpretation of the word, 'vīra' as being composed of 'vi' meaning knowledge of identity with Brahman, and 'ra' as meaning someone who takes pleasure in such knowledge. But such an etymology, accepting it to be correct, would give the form 'vira' and not 'vīra.' No explanation is given as to how 'vi' standing for 'vidyā,' would lengthen its vowel into 'vī.' I therefore find it difficult to accept this etymological interpretation as justifying the application of the word 'vīra' to Vīra-śaiva. Moreover, most systems of Vedāntic thought could be called vīra in such an interpretation, for most types of Vedānta would feel enjoyment and bliss in true knowledge of identity. The word 'vīra' would thus not be a distinctive mark by which we could distinguish Vīra-śaivas from the adherents of other religions. Most of the Āgamic Śaivas also would believe in the ultimate identity of individuals with Brahman or Śiva. I therefore venture to suggest that Vīra-śaivas were called Vīras or heroes for their heroic attitude in an aggressive or defensive manner in support of their faith.

We have at least two instances of religious persecution in the Śaiva context. Thus the Chola King Koluttunga I, a Śaiva, put out the eyes of Mahāpūrṇa and Kureśa, the Vaiṣṇava disciples of Rāmānuja, who refused to be converted to Śaivism. The same sort of story comes in the life of Basava where the eyes of two of his disciples were put out by Vijjala, and Vijjala got himself murdered by Basava's followers. These are but few instances where violence was resorted to for the spread of any religion, or as actions of religious vengeance. I suppose that the militant attitude of some Śaivas, who defied the caste rules and customs and were enthusiasts for the Śaiva faith, gave them the name of Vīra-śaiva or Heroic Śaiva. Even the *Siddhānta-śikhāmaṇi* refers to the view of Basava that those who decried Śiva should be killed[1]. Such a militant attitude in the cause of religion is rarely to be found in the case of other religions or religious sects. In the above context *Siddhānta-śikhāmaṇi* points out in the ninth chapter that, though Vīra-śaivas are prohibited from partaking in the offerings made to a fixed phallic symbol *sthāvara-liṅga*, yet if there is a threat to destroy or disturb such a symbol, a Vīra-śaiva should risk his life in preventing the aggression by violent means.

So far our examination has not proved very fruitful in discovering the actual contribution to Vīra-śaiva philosophy or thought, or even the practice of *ṣaṭ-sthala* and *liṅga-dhāraṇa*, made by Basava. He must have imparted a good deal of emotional enthusiasm to inspire the Śaivas of different types who came into contact with him, either through religious fervour or for his

[1] *atha vīra-bhadrācara-basaveśvaracāraṃ sūcayan bhaktā-cāra-bhedaṃ pratipādayati—*

śiva-nindākaraṃ dṛṣṭvā ghātayed athavā śapet,
sthānaṃ vā tat-parityajya gacched yady-akṣamo bhavet.

Siddhānta-śikhāmaṇi, ch. 9, verse 36.

It is further introduced in the context:

nanu prāṇa-tyāge durmaraṇam kiṃ na syāt,
śivārthaṃ mukta-jīvaś cecchiva-sāyujyam āpnuyāt.

financial and other kinds of patronage. It seems from the *Basava-purāṇa* that his financial assistance to the devotees of Śiva was of rather an indiscriminate character. His money was poured on all Śaivas like showers of rain. This probably made him the most powerful patron of the Śaivas of that time, with the choicest of whom he founded a learned assembly where religious problems were discussed in a living manner, and he himself presided over the meetings.

The present writer is of opinion that the kernel of Vīra-śaiva thought is almost as early as the Upaniṣads, and it may be found in a more or less systematic manner by way of suggestion in the writings of Kālidāsa who lived in the early centuries of the Christian era[1]. The *Sūta-saṃhitā*, a part of the *Skanda-purāṇa*, seems to teach a philosophy which may be interpreted as being of the same type as the Vīra-śaiva philosophy propounded by Śrīpati, though the commentator interprets it in accordance with the philosophy of Śaṅkara. The *Sūta-saṃhitā* gives a high place to the Āgama literature such as the *Kāmika*, and others, which shows that it was closely related with the Āgamic Śaivism[2].

But it is difficult to say at what time the Vīra-śaiva sect was formed and when it had this special designation. Vīra-śaivism differs from the Āgamic Śaivism and the Pāśupata system in its philosophy and its doctrine of *sthala*, the special kind of *liṅga-dhāraṇa* and also in some other ritualistic matters which are not quite relevant for treatment in a work like the present one. It is unfortunate that *Siddhānta-śikhāmaṇi*, a work probably of the thirteenth century, should contain the earliest reference to Vīra-śaivism in literature. A small manuscript called *Vīra-śaiva-guru-paramparā* gives the names of the following teachers in order of priority: (1) Viśveśvara-guru, (2) Ekorāma, (3) Vīreśārādhya, (4) Vīra-bhadra, (5) Viraṇārādhya, (6) Māṇikyārādhya, (7) Buccay-yārādhya, (8) Vīra-malleśvarārādhya, (9) Deśikāradhya, (10) Vṛṣabha, (11) Akṣaka and (12) Mukha-liṅgeśvara. In the *Vīra-śaivāgama*[3], eighth *paṭala*, it is said that in the four *pīṭhas* or pontifical seats, namely *yoga-pīṭha*, *mahā-pīṭha*, *jñāna-pīṭha* and

[1] See author's *A History of Sanskrit Literature*, Vol. I, pp. 728 *et seq.*

[2] *Sūta-saṃhitā*, *yajña-vaibhava-khaṇḍa*, ch. 22, verses 2 and 3. See also ch. 20, verse 22; ch. 39, verse 23.

[3] Madras manuscript.

soma-pīṭha, there were four teachers of different priority, Revaṇa, Marula, Vāmadeva[1], and Paṇḍitārādhya. These names are of a mythical nature, as they are said to be referred to in the different Vedas. But the names that we have quoted above from the *Vīra-śaiva-guru-paramparā* form a succession list of teachers up to the time of the teacher of the author of the manuscript[2]. On studying the succession list of teachers, we find that we know nothing of them either by allusion or by any text ascribed to them, excepting Vīra-bhadra, who has been referred to in the *Siddhānta-śikhāmaṇi*[3]. We cannot say how much earlier Vīra-bhadra was than the author of the *Siddhānta-śikhāmaṇi*. But since Vīra-bhadra is mentioned along with Basava in the same context, we may suppose that this Vīra-bhadra could not have been much earlier than Basava. So if we are safe in supposing that Vīra-bhadra lived somewhere in the twelfth century, we have only to compute the time of the three Ācaryas who lived before Vīra-bhadra. According to ordinary methods of computation we can put a hundred years for the teaching period of the three teachers. This would mean that Vīra-śaivism as a sect started in the eleventh century. It is possible that these teachers wrote or preached in the Dravidian tongue which could be understood by the people among whom they preached. This would explain why no Sanskrit books are found ascribed to them. Basava was probably one of the most intelligent and emotional thinkers, who expressed his effusions in the Kāunāḍa language.

But about our specification of the succession list of Vīra-śaiva teachers much remains yet to be said. It does not explain anything about the other lines of teachers, of whom we hear from stray allusions. Thus we hear of Agastya as being the first propounder of the Śaiva faith. We find also that one Reṇukācārya wrote the work, *Siddhānta-śikhāmaṇi* based upon the verdict of other Vīra-śaiva works and giving us the purport of the mythical dialogue that took place between Reṇuka-siddha and Agastya some time in the past. The Reṇuka-siddha was also called Revaṇa-siddha, and it is supposed that he expounded the Vīra-śaiva Śāstra to Agastya in the beginning of the Kali age. We find at a much later date one Siddha-rāmeśvara, who was impregnated with

[1] Another reading is Rāma-deva (eighth and sixteenth *paṭalas*).

[2] *asmad-ācārya-paryantāṃ bande guru-paramparām.* (Madras manuscript.)

[3] *Siddhānta-śikhāmaṇi. avataraṇikā* of the 36th verse, ch. 9.

the doctrine of Vīra-śaivism; it is in his school of thought that we have a person called Śiva-yogīśvara, who gives us the supposed purport of the dialogue between Raṇuka and Agastya, as it had traditionally come down to him, supplementing it with the teachings of other relevant literature. In the family of Siddharāmeśvara there was born one Mudda-deva, a great teacher. He had a son called Siddha-nātha, who wrote a work called *Śiva-siddhānta-nirṇaya* containing the purport of the Āgamas. The other teachers of the time regarded him as the most prominent of the Vīra-śaiva teachers (*Vīra-śaiva-śikhā-ratna*) and Reṇukācārya, who called himself also Śiva-yogin, wrote the work, *Siddhānta-śikhāmaṇi*. We thus see that there was a long list of Vīra-śaiva teachers before Reṇukācārya, who probably lived somewhere in the thirteenth century. Even if we do not take this into account, Reṇukācārya, the author of *Siddhānta-śikhāmaṇi* says that he had written the work for the elucidation of the nature of Śiva by consulting the Śaiva Tantras beginning from the *Kāmikāgama* to the *Vātulāgama* and also the Purāṇas. He further says that the *Vīra-śaiva Tantra* is the last of the Śaiva Tantras and therefore it is the essence of them all[1].

But what is exactly the content of the Vīra-śaiva philosophy as explained in the *Siddhānta-śikhāmaṇi*? It is said that Brahman is the identity of 'being,' 'bliss' and 'consciousness,' and devoid of any form or differentiation. It is limitless and beyond all ways of knowledge. It is self-luminous and absolutely without any obstruction of knowledge, passion or power. It is in Him that the whole world of the conscious and the unconscious remains, in a potential form untraceable by any of our senses, and it is from Him that the whole world becomes expressed or manifest of itself, without the operation of any other instrument. It implies that when it so pleases God, He expands Himself out of His own joy, and thereby the world appears, just as solid butter expands itself into its liquid state. The qualities of Śiva are of a transcendent nature (*aprākṛta*). The character of being, consciousness and bliss is power (*śakti*). It is curious, however, to note that side by side with this purely ultra-monistic and impersonal view we find God Śiva as being endowed with will by which He creates and destroys the

[1] *Siddhānta-śikhāmaṇi*, ch. I, verses 31–2.

world. As we shall have occasion to notice later on, the whole doctrine of *ṣaṭ-sthala*, which forms the crux of Vīra-śaiva thought, is only an emphasis on the necessity on the part of every individual to look upon him and the world as being sustained in God and being completely identified with God. There are, indeed, many phrases which suggest a sort of *bhedābheda* view, but this *bhedābheda* or difference in unity is not of the nature of the tree and its flowers and fruits, as such a view will suggest a modification or transformation of the nature of Śiva. The idea of *bhedābheda* is to be interpreted with the notion that God, who is transcendent, appears also in the form of the objects that we perceive and also of the nature of our own selves.

The *Siddhānta-śikhāmaṇi* was based on the Āgamas and therefore had the oscillating nature of philosophical outlook as we find in the different Āgamas. Thus in *Siddhānta-śikhāmaṇi*, ch. v, verse 34, it is said that the Brahman is without any form or quality, but it appears to be the individual souls (*jīvas*) by its beginningless association with *avidyā* or nescience. In that sense *jīva* or the individual soul is only a part of God. *Siddhānta-śikhāmaṇi* further says that God is the controller, the mover (*preraka*) of all living beings. In another verse it says that Brahman is both God and the souls of beings at the same time. In pure Śiva there are no qualities as *sattva*, *rajas* and *tamas*[1]. Again *Siddhānta-śikhāmaṇi* oscillates to the Vedānta view that the individual souls, the objects of the world as well as the Supreme Controller, are all but illusory imposition on the pure consciousness or Brahman[2]. The *Siddhānta-śikhāmaṇi* admits both *avidyā* and *māyā* after the fashion of Śaṅkarites. It is in association with *avidyā* that we have the various kinds of souls and it is with the association of *māyā* that Brahman appears as omniscient and omnipotent. It is on account of the *avidyā* that the individual soul cannot realise its identity with Brahman, and thus goes through the cycle of births and rebirths.

Yet there is another point to note. In the *Yoga-sūtra* of Patañjali, it is said that the nature of our birth, the period of life

[1] *guṇa-trayātmikā śaktir brahma-niṣṭhā-sanātanī,*
tad-vaiṣamyāt samutpannā tasmin vastu-trayābhidhā.
Siddhānta-śikhāmaṇi, ch. v, verse 39.

[2] *bhoktā bhojyaṃ prerayitā vastu-trayamidaṃ smṛtam,*
akhaṇḍe brahma-caitanye kalpitaṃ guṇa-bhedataḥ.
Ibid. ch. v, verse 41.

and the nature of our experiences, are determined by our *karma*, and that the law of the distribution of the fruits of *karma* is mysterious. But the effects of *karma* take place automatically. This view is only modified by the Pāśupatas and the Naiyāyikas who belong to their fold. It is interesting to notice that the *Siddhānta-śikhāmaṇi* borrows this idea of *karma* from the Pāśupatas, who hold that the distribution of *karma* is managed and controlled by God. *Siddhānta-śikhāmaṇi* thus seems to present before us an eclectic type of thought which is unstable and still in the state of formation. This explains the author's ill-digested assimilation of elements of thought on Pāśupata doctrine, the varying Āgama doctrines, the influence of Sāṃkhya, and ultimately the Vedānta of the Śaṅkarites. This being so, in the thirteenth century we cannot expect a systematic Vīra-śaiva philosophy in its own individual character as a philosophical system in the time of Basava. It will be easy for us to show that Allama-prabhu, the teacher of Basava, was thoroughly surcharged with the Vedāntism of the Śaṅkara school.

In the *Śaṅkara-vijaya* Ānandagiri, a junior contemporary and a pupil of Śaṅkara gives a long description of the various types of the devotees of Śiva who could be distinguished from one another by their outward marks. Śaṅkara himself only speaks of the Pāśupatas and the Śaivas who followed the Siddhāntas or the Āgamas, in which God Śiva has been described as being the instrumental cause, different from the material cause out of which the world has been made. Vācaspati in his *Bhāmatī*, a commentary on the *bhāṣya* of Śaṅkara on the *Brahma-sūtra* II. 2. 37, speaks of four types of the followers of Śiva. Of these we have found ample literature of the Śaivas and the Pāśupatas, and had ventured to suggest that the Kāruṇika-siddhāntins were also the followers of the Āgamic Śaiva thought. But we could find no literature of the Kāpālikas or of the Kālamukhas referred to in the *bhāṣya* of the same *sūtra* by Rāmānuja. In the *Sūta-saṃhitā* we find the names of the *Kāmika* and other Āgamas, the Kāpālikas, the Lākulas, the Pāśupatas, the Somas, and the Bhairavas, who had also their Āgamas. These Āgamas branched off into a number of sections or schools[1]. In our investigation we have found that the Lākulas and the Pāśupatas were one and the same, and we have the testimony of Mādhava, the author of the *Sarva-darśana-saṃgraha*, to the same effect.

[1] *Sūta-saṃhitā* IV, *Vajña-vaibhava-khaṇḍa*, ch. XXII, verses 2–4.

Sūta-saṃhitā was probably a work of the sixth century A.D., while Mādhava's work was of the fourteenth century. Nevertheless, it seems that the Pāśupatas were earlier than the Lākulas. Neither Śaṅkara nor Vācaspati speaks of the Lākulīśas as being the same as the Pāśupatas. But some time before the fourteenth century the Lākulīśas and Pāśupatas had coalesced and later on they remained as one system, as we find them regarded as one by Appaya Dīkṣita of the sixteenth century in his commentary, *Vedānta-kalpataru-parimala* on *Brahma-sūtra* II. 2. 37. But there can be but little doubt that the Lākulas had their own Āgamas long before the sixth century A.D., which is probably the date of Sūta-saṃhitā. We find references to the Bhairavas, and the name Bhairava is given to Śiva as the presiding male god wherever there is the Śakti deity representing the limbs of Śakti, the consort of Śiva and the daughter of Dakṣa. But we have not been able to secure any Āgamas containing an account of the philosophical doctrine of this creed of Bhairavism, though we have found ritualistic references to Bhairava. The *Sūta-saṃhitā* also refers to the Āgamic *ṛṣis* such as Śveta, etc.; each of these twenty-eight *ṛṣis* had four disciples, thus making the number one hundred and twelve. They are also referred to in the *Sūta-saṃhitā* (Book IV, ch. XXI, verses 2–3), where they are described as smearing their bodies with ashes and wearing the necklaces of *rudrākṣa*. We have noticed before that *Śiva-mahāpurāṇa* also refers to them. The existence of so many Śaiva saints at such an early date naturally implies the great antiquity of Śaivism. These Śaiva saints seem to have been loyal to the *Varṇāśrama dharma* or duties of caste and the stages of life.

A later Āgama probably of the thirteenth century called the *Vīra-śaivāgama* speaks of the four schools of thought, Śaiva, Pāśupata, Vāma and Kula. Śaiva is again divided into Saumya and Raudra. The Saumya is of five kinds including demonology and magic as antidote to poison. The Śaiva school is called Dakṣiṇa, and the cult of Śakti is called Vāma. The two can be mixed together as Vāma and Dakṣiṇa, and regarded as one school. The *Siddhānta śāstra* is called pure Śaiva belonging only to Śiva. There is, however, another sect, or rather three schools of a sect, called Dakṣiṇa, Kālamukha and Mahāvrata[1]. Bhandarkar has suggested that the Kāla-mukhas and the Mahāvratadhārins are

[1] See Rāmānuja's *bhāṣya* (*Śrī-bhāṣya*), II. 2. 37.

one and the same. The Siddhāntas again are divided into three sects: Ādi-śaiva, Mahā-śaiva and Anta-śaiva. These subdivisions of Śaivism have sprung from the Pāśupata-śaivism. The writer of the *Vīra-śaivāgama* says that Śaivism scattered itself into infinite variety of schools of thought or bands of devotees and had a huge literature for supplementing their position[1]. All these sects have now practically vanished with their literature if they had any.

From the testimony of the same Āgama it appears that Vīra-śaivism was not a part of the older Śaivas, but it originated as a doctrinal school which accepted four *liṅgas* in the four pontifical seats, the worship of Śiva as *ṣaṭ-sthala* and their special rites and customs. This view may be correct, as we cannot trace the Vīra-śaiva as a system of thought in any of the earlier works on Śaivism. We have a number of *Vīra-śaivāgamas* such as *Makuṭāgama*, *Suprabhedāgama*, *Vīra-śaivā'-gama* and the like in manuscript. But none of them, excepting the *Basava-rājīya* called also *Vīra-śaiva-sāroddhāra* (manuscript) with the *bhāṣya* of Somanātha, make any reference to Basava or even the Vīra-śaiva philosophy. The *Basava-rājīya* also speaks of Basava as being the incarnation of the bull of Śiva and the patron of Śaivas. But the author of the work does not say anything about the philosophical doctrine of Basava, but only describes the idea of *ṣaṭ-sthala* in an elaborate manner.

Professor Sakhare in his introduction to *Liṅga-dhāraṇa-candrikā* of Nandikeśvara quotes a passage from *Svāyaṃbhuvāgama* in which the mythical origins of Revaṇa-siddha from *Someśa-liṅga*, of Marula-siddha from *Siddheśa-liṅga*, of Paṇḍitārya from *Mallikārjuna-liṅga*, of Ekorāma from *Rāmanātha-liṅga*, and of Viśvārādhya from the *Viśveśa-liṅga*, are described. We have no further evidence of these teachers or the nature of their teachings. We do not even know if they called themselves Vīra-śaivas. This account does not tally with the description found in the *Vīra-śaiva-guru-paramparā*, or with the other Vīra-śaiva texts published or unpublished with which we are familiar.

The *gotras* and the *pravaras* of the Vīra-śaivas, given in the *Suprabhedāgama* as emanating from the unknown past, are quite

[1] *samudra-sikatāsaṃkhyās samayās santi koṭiśaḥ. Vīra-śaivāgama* (Madras manuscript).

fanciful and need not further be discussed. Such a discussion could shed no historical light on the origin and development of the Vīra-śaiva philosophy and dogmatics.

We have seen before that there is a tradition which links Agastya, Reṇuka or Revaṇa-siddha, Siddha-rāma and Reṇukācārya, the author of the *Siddhānta-śikhāmaṇi*. Śrīpati mainly bases his arguments on the Upaniṣads and the Purāṇas, but he also refers to *Agastya-sūtra* and Reṇukācārya. He does not, however, refer to Basava and the contemporaries who were associated with him, such as Allama-prabhu, Cannabasava, Mācaya, Goga, Siddha-rāma and Mahādevī[1]. This seems to show that the Vīra-śaivism had two or more lines of development which later on coalesced and began to be regarded as one system of Vīra-śaiva thought. From Basava's *vacanas* it is difficult to assess the real philosophical value of the faith that was professed by Basava. In the *Prabhu-liṅga-līlā* and the *Basava-purāṇa* we find a system of thought which, in the absence of other corroborating materials, may be accepted as approximately outlining the system of thought which was known as Vīra-śaivism in Basava's time.

We find that the doctrines of *sthala* and *liṅga-dhāraṇa* were known to the author of the *Prabhu-liṅga-līlā*. But though in one place, where instruction was being given to Basava by Allama-prabhu, *ṣaṭ-sthala* is mentioned, yet the entire emphasis throughout the book is on the doctrine of unity of the self with Śiva, the ground of the reality[2]. In the above passage it is held that there are double knots associated with the gross, the subtle and the cause, in accordance with which we have the six *sthalas* in three groups of a pair of each. Thus the two knots associated with the gross go by the name of *bhakta* and *maheśvara*; those with the subtle as associated with *prāṇa* are called *prāṇa* and *prasāda-lingi sthalas*;

[1] Thus it appears from Śrīpati's statement in the *Śrīkara-bhāṣya* II. 2. 37, p. 234, and III. 3. 3, p. 347, that Revaṇa-siddha, Marula-siddha, Rāma-siddha, Udbhaṭārādhya, Vemanārādhya were real teachers who had expressed their views or articles of faith in some distinctive works. But unfortunately no trace of such works can be discovered, nor is it possible to enunciate the actual views propounded by them. Whether Śrīpati had himself seen them or not is merely a matter of conjecture. He does not quote from the works of those teachers, and it is just possible that he is only making statements on the strength of tradition. In another passage (II. 1. 4) Śrīpati mentions the names of Manu, Vāmadeva. Agastya, Durvāsā, Upamanyu, who are quite mythical purāṇic figures along with Revaṇa-siddha and Marula-siddha.

[2] See *Prabhu-liṅga-līlā*, ch. 16, pp. 132–4.

those with the cause are of an emotional nature, and are called *śarana* and *aikya sthalas*. In other works such as *Basava-rājīya*, *Vīra-śaivāgama* and *Siddhānta-śikhāmaṇi* the names of *sthalas* extend to one hundred and one. But in none of those works is the idea of these different *sthalas* explained to show their philosophical importance. In *Prabhu-liṅga-līlā* we hear that Cannabasava knew the mystery of *ṣaṭ-sthala*, but we do not know exactly what that mystery was. In this connection *guru*, *liṅga*, *cara*, *prasāda* and *pādodaka* are also mentioned. The whole emphasis of the book is on the necessity of realising the unity of the self and, indeed, of anything else with Śiva. Allama decries the external ritualism and lays stress on the necessity of realising the ultimate reality of the universe and the self with Śiva. He vehemently decries all forms of injury to animal life, and persuades Goga to give up ploughing the ground, as it would involve the killing of many insects. Allama further advised Goga to surrender the fruits of all his actions to God and carry on his duties without any attachment. As a matter of fact the Vīra-śaiva thought as represented by Allama can hardly be distinguished from the philosophy of Śaṅkara, for Allama accepted one reality which appeared in diverse forms under the condition of *māyā* and *avidyā*. In that sense the whole world would be an illusion. The *bhakti* preached by Allama was also of an intellectual type, as it consisted of a constant and unflinching meditation and realisation of the ultimate reality of all things with Śiva. This view of *bhakti* seems to have influenced Reṇukācārya, the author of *Siddhānta-śikhāmaṇi*, who describes inner devotion (*āntara-bhakti*) in almost the same type of phraseology[1].

In his teachings to Muktāyī, Allama says that just as the sucking babe is gradually weaned from the mother's milk to various kinds of food, so the real teacher teaches the devotee to concentrate his

[1] *liṅge prāṇaṃ samādhāya prāṇe liṅgaṃ tu śāṃbhavam,*
svasthaṃ manas tathā kṛtvā na kiñcic cintayed yadi.
sābhyantarā bhaktir iti procyate śiva-yogibhiḥ,
sā yasmin vartate tasya jīvanaṃ bhraṣṭa-vījavat.
Siddhānta-śikhāmaṇi, ch. 9, verses 8–9.
tataḥ sāvadhānena tat-prāṇa-liṅge,
samīkṛtya kṛtyāni vismṛtya matyā,
mahā-yoga-sāmrājya-paṭṭābhiṣikto,
bhajed ātmano liṅga-tādātmya-siddhim.
Prabhu-liṅga-līlā, ch. 16, verse 63.

mind on external forms of worship and later on makes him give them up, so that he ultimately becomes unattached to all kinds of duties, and attains true knowledge by which all his deeds are destroyed. There is not much use in learning or delivering speeches, but what is necessary, is to realise the unity of all with Śiva[1].

In his conversation with Siddha-rāma and Gorakṣa, he not only demonstrates the non-existence of all things but Śiva, but he also shows his familiarity with a type of magical *yoga*, the details of which are not given and cannot be traced in the *Yogaśāstra* of Patañjali. In the instruction given by Allama to his pupil Basava, the former explains briefly the nature of *bhakti*, *ṣaṭ-sthala* and *yoga*. It seems that the restful passivity that is attained by *yoga* is nothing but complete and steady identification of the ultimate truth, Śiva, with all the variable forms of experience, and our life and experience as a complete person. This *yoga* leading to the apperception of the ultimate unity can be done by arresting all the vital processes in the nervous centres of the body at higher and higher grades, until these energies become one with the supreme reality, God Śiva. It is in this way that the *cakras* are traversed and passed over till the Yogin settle down in Śiva. The entire physical processes being arrested by the peculiar *yoga* method, our mind does not vaccilate or change, but remains in the consciousness of the pure Lord, Śiva.

The teacher of Basava, Allama, says that without a strong effort to make the mind steady by the complete arrest of the vital forces, the *Vāyu*, there can be no *bhakti* and no cessation to bondage. It is by the arrest of these vital forces or *Vāyu*, that the *citta* or the mind of the Vīra-śaiva becomes arrested and merged in the elemental physical constituents of the body, such as fire, water, etc. The *māyā* is a product of *manas*, and *vāyu* also is regarded as a product of *manas*, and this *vāyu* becomes the body through the activity of the *manas*. The existence of the body is possible only by the activity of the vital forces or *vāyu*, which keep us away from realising the unity of all things with Śiva, which is also called *bhakti*. The Vīra-śaiva has, therefore, to take recourse to a process opposite to the normal course of activity of the *vāyus* by concentrating them on one point, and by accepting the mastery of the *vāyus* over the different *cakras* or nerve plexuses (technically

[1] See *Prabhu-liṅga-līlā*, ch. 12, pp. 57–8.

known as the control of the six *cakras*), which would in their own way be regarded as the six stages or stations of the process of the control of the *vāyus*, the *ṣaṭ-sthalas*[1]. It is thus seen that according to the description given in *Prabhu-liṅga-līlā* of the doctrine of *ṣaṭ-sthala*, the process of *ṣaṭ-sthala* is to be regarded as an upward journey through a hierarchy of stations, by which alone the unity with Śiva can be realised. The instruction of this dynamic process of *yoga* is a practical method of a semi-physiological process by which the ultimate identity of God and soul can be realised. In Śaṅkara's monistic philosophy it is said that the realisation of the ultimate identity of the self with Brahman is the highest attainable goal of life. It is, however, said that such an enlightenment can be realised by proper intuition of the significance of the monistic texts such as "thou art that." It refuses to admit any practical utility of any dynamic course of practice which is so strongly advised in the Vīra-śaiva doctrine of *ṣaṭ-sthala* as taught by Allama.

Allama had met Gorakṣa in one of his travels. Gorakṣa, who was also probably a Śaiva, had by his yogic processes attained such miraculous powers that no stroke of any weapon could produce an injury on him. He made a demonstration of it to Allama. Allama in reply asked him to pass a sword through his body. But to Gorakṣa's utter amazement he found that when he ran through Allama's body with his sword, no sound of impact was produced. The sword passed through Allama's body as if it were passing through vacant space. Gorakṣa wanted humbly to know the secret by which Allama could show such miraculous powers. In reply Allama said that the *māyā* becomes frozen, as does the body, and when the body and the *māyā* both become frozen, shadow forms appear as real[2], and the body and the mind appear as one. When the body and the *māyā* are removed in the heart, then the shadow is destroyed. At this, Gorakṣa further implored Allama to initiate him into those powers. Allama touched his body and blessed him, and by that produced an internal conversion. As an effect of this, attachment vanished and with the disappearance of attachment, antipathy, egotism and other vices also disappeared. Allama further said that unless the self could realise that the association with the body was false, and the two were completely separated, one could

[1] *Prabhu-liṅga-līlā*, part III, pp. 6–8 (1st edition).
[2] *Ibid.* p. 25 (1st edition).

not realise the true identity with the Lord Śiva, devotion to whom was the cause of all true knowledge. It is only by the continual meditation of Śiva and by the proper processes of breath control, that it is possible to realise the ultimate unity.

There is a subtle difference between the proper and practical adoption of the dynamic process of *ṣaṭ-sthala* and the realisation of unity as taught by the *Śāṅkara Vedānta.* In the *Śāṅkara Vedānta,* when the mind is properly prepared by suitable accessory processes, the teacher instructs the pupil or the would-be saint about the ultimate knowledge of the unity of the self and the Brahman, and the would-be saint at once perceives the truth of his identity with Brahman as being the only reality. He also at once perceives that all knowledge of duality is false, though he does not actually melt himself into the nothingness of pure consciousness or the Brahman. In the Vīra-śaiva system the scheme of *ṣaṭ-sthala* is a scheme of the performance of yogic processes. By them the vital processes as associated with the various vital forces and the nerve plexuses, are controlled, and by that very means the yogin gets a mastery over his passions and is also introduced to new and advanced stages of knowledge, until his soul becomes so united with the permanent reality, Śiva, that all appearance and duality cease both in fact and in thought. Thus a successful Vīra-śaiva saint should not only perceive his identity with Śiva, but his whole body, which was an appearance or shadow over the reality, would also cease to exist. His apparent body would not be a material fact in the world, and therefore would not be liable to any impact with other physical bodies, though externally they may appear as physical bodies.

A similar philosophical view can be found in the work called *Siddha-siddhānta-paddhati* attributed to Gorakṣa-nāth, who is regarded as a Śaiva saint, an incarnation of Śiva Himself. Many legends are attributed to him and many poems have been composed in vernaculars of Bengali and Hindi, extolling the deeds and miraculous performances of his disciples and of himself. His date seems to be uncertain. References to Gorakṣa are found in the works of writers of the eighth to fifteenth centuries, and his miraculous deeds are described as having taken place in countries ranging from Gujarat, Nepal and Bengal and other parts of northern and western India. One of his well-known disciples was called Matsyendra-nātha. Śiva is called Paśupati, the lord of animals, and the word *gorakṣa* also means the protector of the cattle. In the lexicons the word *go* means the name of a *ṛṣi* and also the name of cattle. There is thus an easy association of the word *gorakṣa* with the word *paśupati*. Gorakṣa's views are also regarded as the views of Siddhānta. This reminds us of the fact that the Śaiva doctrines of the South were regarded as having been propounded by Maheśvara or Śiva in the Siddhāntas, an elaboration of which has elsewhere been made in this work as the Āgama philosophy of the Siddhāntas. Only a few Sanskrit books on the philosophical aspects of the teachings of Gorakṣa-nāth have come down to us. There are, however, quite a number of books in the vernaculars which describe the miraculous powers of the Kānphāṭā Yogis of the school of Gorakṣa-nāth, also called Gorākh-nāth.

One of these Sanskrit works is called *Siddha-siddhānta-paddhati*. It is there that the ultimate reality of the unmoved, and the immovable nature of the pure consciousness which forms the ultimate ground of all our internal and external experiences, are to be sought. It is never produced nor destroyed, and in that sense eternal and always self-luminous. In this way it is different from ordinary knowledge, which is called *buddhi*. Ordinary knowledge rises and fades, but this pure consciousness which is identified as being one with Śiva is beyond all occurrence and beyond all time. It is, therefore, regarded as the ground of all things. It is from this that all effects, for example, the bodies, the instruments or the *karaṇas* (senses, etc.), and the agents, for example, the souls or the *jīvas*, shoot forth. It is by its spontaneity that the so-called God as well as His powers are manifested. In this original state Śiva shows itself as identical with His *śakti*. This is called the *sāmarasya*, that is, both having the same taste. This ultimate nature is the original ego, called also *kula*, which shows itself in various aspects. We should distinguish this ultimate nature of reality, which is changeless, from the reality as associated with class concepts and other distinguishing traits. These distinguishing traits are also held up in the supreme reality, for in all stages of experience these distinguishing features have no reality but the ultimate reality, which holds them all in the oneness of pure consciousness. Since the distinguishing characteristics have no further reality beyond them than the unchangeable ground-consciousness, they ultimately have to be regarded as being homogeneous (*sama-rasa*) with ubiquitous reality.

The concept of *sama-rasa* is homogeneity. A thing which appears as different from another thing, but is in reality or essence the same, is said to be *sama-rasa* with the first one. It is also a way in which the *bhedābheda* theory of the reality and the appearance is explained. Thus a drop of water is in appearance different from the sheet of water in which it is held, but in fact it has no other reality and no other taste than that sheet of water. The ultimate reality, without losing its nature as such, shows itself in various forms, though in and through them all it alone remains as the ultimately real. It is for this reason that though the ultimate reality is endowed with all powers, it does not show itself except through its various manifesting forms. So the all-powerful Śiva, though it is the source of all power, behaves as if it were without any power. This power therefore remains in the body as the ever-awaking *kuṇḍalinī* or the serpentine force, and also as manifesting in different ways. The consideration of the body as indestructible is called *kāya-siddhi*.

We need not go into further detail in explaining the philosophical ideas of Gorakṣa as contained in *Siddha-siddhānta-paddhati*, for this would be to digress. But we find that there is a curious combination of Haṭha-yoga, the control of the nerve plexuses, the idea of the individual and the world as having the same reality, though they appear as different, as we find in the lecture attributed to Allama in *Prabhu-liṅga-līlā*. It also holds a type of *bhedābheda* theory and is distinctly opposed to the monistic interpretation of the Upaniṣads as introduced by Śaṅkara.

The idea of *ṣaṭ-sthala* must have been prevalent either as a separate doctrine or as a part of some form of Śaivism. We know that there were many schools of Śaivism, many of which have now become lost. The name *ṣaṭ-sthala* cannot be found in any of the sacred Sanskrit works. We have no account of Vīra-śaivism before *Siddhānta-śikhāmaṇi*. Descriptions of it are found in many works, some of the most important of which are *Prabhu-liṅga-līlā* and *Basava-purāṇa*. We also hear that Canna-basava, the nephew of Basava, was initiated into the doctrine of *ṣaṭ-sthala*. In *Prabhu-liṅga-līlā* we hear that Allama instructed the doctrine of *ṣaṭ-sthala* to Basava. We also find the interesting dialogue between Allama and Gorakṣa in the *Prabhu-liṅga-līlā*. We have also examined briefly some of the contents of *Siddha-siddhānta-paddhati* of Gorakṣa, and we find that the *ṣaṭ-sthala* doctrine preached by Allama was more or less similar to the *Yoga* doctrine found in the *Siddha-siddhānta-paddhati*. If we had more space, we could have brought out an interesting comparison between the doctrines of Allama and Gorakṣa. It is not impossible that there was a mutual exchange of views between Gorakṣa and Allama. Unfortunately the date of Gorakṣa cannot be definitely known, though it is known that his doctrines had spread very widely in various parts of India, extending over a long period in the Middle Ages.

The interpretation of *ṣaṭ-sthala* is rather different in different works dealing with it. This shows that, though the *ṣaṭ-sthala* doctrine was regarded as the most important feature of Vīra-śaivism after Basava, we are all confused as to what the *ṣaṭ-sthala* might have been. As a matter of fact we are not even certain about the number. Thus in *Vīra-śaiva-siddhānta* (MS.) we have a reference to 101 *sthalas*, and so also in *Siddhānta-śikhāmaṇi*. But elsewhere in Śrīpati's *bhāṣya*, *Anubhava-sūtra* of Māyi-deva, and in *Prabhu-liṅga-līlā* and *Basava-purāṇa* we find reference to six *sthalas* only.

In the same way the *sthalas* have not been the same in the various authoritative works. The concepts of these *sthalas* are also different, and they are sometimes used in different meanings. In some works *sthala* is used to denote the six nerve plexuses in the body or the six centres from which the power of God is manifested in different ways; sometimes they are used to denote the sixfold majestic powers of God and sometimes to denote the important natural elements, such as earth, fire, air, etc. The whole idea seems to be that the macrocosm and microcosm being the same identical entity, it is possible to control the dissipated forces of any centre and pass on to a more concentrated point of manifestation of the energy, and this process is regarded as the upward process of ascension from one stage to another.

Anubhava-sūtra of Māyi-deva[1].

Upamanyu, the first teacher, was born in Aaipura. The second teacher was Bhīma-nātha Prabhu. Then came Mahā-guru Kaleśvara. His son, well versed in *śrauta* and *smārta* literature and their customs and manners, was Śrī Boppa-nātha. Boppa-nātha's son was Śrī Nāka-rāja Prabhu, who was well versed in Vīra-śaiva rites and customs of religion. The disciple of Nāka-rāja was Saṅgameśvara. Saṅgameśvara's son was Māyi-deva. He is well versed in the knowledge of *Śivādvaita*, and he is a *ṣaṭ-sthala-Brahma-vādī*. The *Śaivāgamas* begin with *Kāmika* and end with *Vātula*. *Vātula-tantra* is the best. Its second part, called *Pradīpa*, contains the *Śiva-siddhānta-tantra*. *Ṣaṭ-sthala* doctrine is based on the principles of the *Gītā* together with the older views. It is supported by the instructions of teachers and self-realisation by *anubhūti* and by arguments. In the *Anubhava-sūtra* there are (1) the *guru-paramparā*; (2) the definition of *sthala*; (3) the *liṅga-sthala*; (4) the *aṅga-sthala*; (5) the *liṅga-saṃyoga-vidhi*; (6) the *liṅgārpaṇa-sadbhāva*; (7) the *sarvāṅga-liṅga-sāhitya*; and (8) the *kriyā-viśrānti*.

Sthala is defined as one Brahman identically the same with *sat*, *cit* and *ānanda*, which is called the ultimate category of Śiva—the ground of the manifestation of the world and dissolution. He is also the category from which the different categories of *mahat*, etc. have sprung forth. '*Stha*' means *Sthāna* and '*la*' means *laya*. It is the source of all energies and all beings have come from it and shall return into it. It is by the self-perturbation of the energy of this ultimate category that the various other *sthalas* are evolved. This one *sthala* may be divided into the *liṅga-sthala* and the *Aṅga-sthala*. As the empty space can be distinctively qualified as the space inside the room or inside the jar, so the dual bifurcation of *sthala* may appear as the object of worship and the worshipper.

Śiva remaining unchanged in Himself appears in these two forms. It is the same Śiva which appears as pure consciousness and also as the part of *liṅga*. The part of *liṅga*, *liṅgāṅga* is also called *jīva* or the individual souls.

[1] *Anubhava-sūtra* forms the second part of *Śiva-siddhānta-tantra*, which is complete in two parts. The first part is *Viśeṣārtha-prakāśaka*. *Anubhava-sūtra* is written by Māyi-deva; it is evident from the colophons of *Anubhava-sūtra*. It is also mentioned in the last colophon of *Śiva-siddhānta-tantra*.

As *sthala* is of two parts, Brahma and jīva, so His *śakti* is also twofold. It is indeterminate and is called Maheśvara. It assumes two forms by its own pure spontaneity. One part of it may be regarded as associated with *liṅga*, the Brahman, and the other with *aṅga*, the *jīva*. In reality *śakti* and *bhakti* are the same[1]. When the energy moves forward for creation it is called *śakti* as *pravṛtti*, and as cessation *nivṛtti* is called *bhakti*[2]. On account of the diverse nature of *bhakti* its indeterminateness disintegrates into various forms. The twofold functions of *śakti* as the upper and the lower show themselves in the fact that the upper one tends to manifest the world and the lower one, appearing as *bhakti*, tends to return to God. In these twofold forms the same *śakti* is called *māyā* and *bhakti*. The *śakti* in the *liṅga* appears as the *bhakti* in the *aṅga*, and the unity of *liṅga* and *aṅga* is the identity of Śiva and *jīva*.

The *liṅga-sthala* is threefold, as: (1) *bhāva-liṅga*; (2) *prāṇa-liṅga*; and (3) *iṣṭa-liṅga*. The *bhāva-liṅga* can only be grasped through inner intuition as pure Being, and this *bhāva-liṅga* is called *niṣkala*. *Prāṇa-liṅga* is the reality as grasped by thought and as such it is both indeterminate and determinate. The *iṣṭa-liṅga* is that which fulfils one's good as self-realisation or adoration, and it is beyond space and time.

The ultimate *śakti* as being pure cessation and beyond all, is *śāntyatīta*; the next one is *icchā-śakti*, called also *vidyā* as pure knowledge. The third one is called the *kriyā-śakti* which leads to cessation. The three *śaktis* of *icchā*, *jñāna* and *kriyā* become sixfold.

The six *sthalas* are again described as follows:

(1) That which is completely full in itself, subtle, having no beginning nor end, and is indefinable, but can be grasped only by the intuition of the heart as the manifestation of pure consciousness, is called the *mahātma-liṅga*.

(2) That in which we find the seed of development as consciousness beyond the senses, called also the *sādākhya-tattva*, is called *prasāda-ghana-liṅga*.

(3) The pure luminous *puruṣa*, which is without inward and outward, without any form, and known by the name Ātman, is called the *cara-liṅga*.

[1] *Śakti-bhaktyor na bhedo 'sti. Anubhava-sūtra*, p. 8.

[2] *śaktyā prapañca-sṛṣṭiḥ syāu,*
bhaktya tad-vilayo mataḥ. *Ibid.*

(4) When this by the *icchā-śakti* manifests itself as the ego, we have what is called *Śiva-liṅga.*

(5) When it by its own knowledge and power and omnipotence assumes the role of an instructor for taking all beings beyond the range of all pleasures, it is called *guru-liṅga.*

(6) The aspect in which by its action it upholds the universe and holds them all in the mind, is called the *ācāra-liṅga.*

There are further divisions and sub-divisions of these *sthalas*, *aṅga-sthala.*

'*Aṃ*' means Brahma and '*ga*' means that which goes. *Aṅga-sthala* is of three kinds as *yogāṅga*, *bhogāṅga* and *tyāgāṅga*. In the first, one attains the bliss of union with Śiva. In the second, *bhogāṅga*, one enjoys with Śiva, and in *tyāgāṅga* one leaves aside the illusion or the false notion of the cycle of births and rebirths. *Yogāṅga* is the original cause, the *bhogāṅga* is the subtle cause and *tyāgāṅga* is the gross one. *Yogāṅga* is the dreamless state, *bhogāṅga* is the ordinary state of sleep, and *tyāgāṅga* is the waking state. *Yogāṅga* is the state of *prajñā*, *bhogāṅga* is *taijas* and *tyāgāṅga* is *viśva*. *Yogāṅga* is called the unity with Śiva and *śaraṇa-sthala.* *Bhogāṅga* is twofold, *prāṇa-liṅgi* and *prasādi.* The gross is twofold, *bhakta-sthala* and *māheśvara sthala.* Again *prājña* is *aikya-sthala* and *śaraṇa-sthala.* The *taijas* is *prāṇa-liṅgi* and *prasādi.* *Viśva* again is twofold as *māheśvara* and *bhakta-sthala.* The unity, the *śaraṇa*, the *prāṇa-liṅgi*, the *prasādi*, the *māheśvara* and the *bhakta* may be regarded as the successive of the six *sthalas.*

Again omnipotence, contentment, and beginningless consciousness, independence, unobstructedness of power and infinite power —these are the parts of God, which being in *ṣaṭ-sthala* are regarded as six types of *bhakti* depending on various conditions. The *bhakti* manifests itself in diverse forms, just as water manifests in various tastes in various fruits. The *bhakti* is of the nature of Śiva. Then it is of the nature of *ānanda* or bliss. Then it is of the nature of *anubhava* or realisation. Then it is of the nature of adoration (*naiṣṭhikī*) and the sixth is of the nature of *bhakti* among good men. It is further said that all those classifications are meaningless. The truth is the identity of myself and everything, all else is false—this is *aikya-sthala.* By the self-illumination of knowledge, the body and senses appear as having no form, being united with God; when everything appears as pure, that is called the *śaraṇa-sthala.*

When one avoids all illusions or errors about body, etc., and conceives in the mind that one is at one with the *liṅga*, that is called the *prāṇa-liṅga*, or *cara-sthala*. When one surrenders all objects of gratification to God, it is called the *prasāda-sthala*, and when one fixes one's mind on God as being one with Him—it is called *māheśvara-sthala*. When the false appears as true and the mind is detached from it by the adorative action of *bhakti*, and the person becomes detached from the world—this is called *bhakti-sthala*. Thus we have another six kinds of *ṣaṭ-sthala*.

Again from another point of view we have another description of *ṣaṭ-sthala*, such as from Ātman comes *ākāśa*, from *ākāśa* comes *vāyu*, from *vāyu* comes *agni*, from *agni* comes water and from water—earth. Again the unity of Ātman with Brahman is called *vyomāṅga*. *Prāṇa-liṅga* is called *vāyvāṅga*, and *prasāda* is called *analāṅga*, and *maheśvara* is called *jalāṅga* and the *bhakta* is called *bhūmyaṅga*. Again from *bindu* comes *nāda*, and from *nāda* comes *kalā*, and reversely from *kalā* to *bindu*.

Unlike the Vaiṣṇavas, the *Anubhava-sūtra* describes *bhakti* not as attachment involving a sense-duality between the worshipper and the worshipped, but as revealing pure oneness or identity with God in the strongest terms. This implies, and in fact it has been specifically stated, that all ceremonial forms of worship involving duality are merely imaginary creations. In His sportive spirit the Lord may assume diverse forms, but the light of *bhakti* should show that they are all one with Him.

CHAPTER XXXVI

PHILOSOPHY OF ŚRĪKAṆṬHA

Philosophy of Śaivism as expounded by Śrīkaṇṭha in his Commentary on the *Brahma-sutra* and the Sub-commentary on it by Appaya Dīkṣita.

INTRODUCTORY

IT has often been stated in the previous volumes of the present work that the *Brahma-sūtra* attributed to Bādarāyaṇa was an attempt at a systematisation of the apparently different strands of the Upaniṣadic thought in the various early Upaniṣads, which form the background of most of the non-heretical systems of Indian philosophy. The *Brahma-sūtra* had been interpreted by the exponents of different schools of thought in various ways, for example, by Śaṅkara, Rāmānuja, Bhāskara, Mādhva, Vallabha, and others, and they have all been dealt with in the previous volumes of the present work. Vedānta primarily means the teachings of the Upaniṣads. Consequently the *Brahma-sūtra* is supposed to be a systematisation of Upaniṣadic wisdom; and its various interpretations in diverse ways by the different exponents of diverse philosophical views, all go by the name of the Vedānta, though the Vedānta philosophy of one school of thinkers may appear to be largely different from that of any other school. Thus while the exposition of the *Brahma-sūtra* by Śaṅkara is monistic, the interpretation of Mādhva is explicitly pluralistic. We have seen the acuteness of the controversy between the adherents of the two schools of thought, extending over centuries, in the fourth volume of the present work.

As Śrīkaṇṭha expounded his views as an interpretation of the *Brahma-sūtra* and accepted the allegiance and loyalty to the Upaniṣads, the work has to be regarded as an interpretation of the Vedānta. Like many other interpretations of the Vedānta (for example, by Rāmānuja, Mādhva, Vallabha, or Nimbārka), the philosophy of Śrīkaṇṭha is associated with the personal religion, where Śiva is regarded as the highest Deity, being equated with

Brahman. It can, therefore, be claimed as an authoritative exposition of Śaivism. Śaivism, or rather Śaiva philosophy, also had assumed various forms, both as expressed in Sanskritic works and in the vernacular Dravidian works. But in the present work, we are only interested in the exposition of Śaiva philosophy in Sanskrit works. The present writer has no access to the original Dravidian literature such as Tamil, Telegu and Canarese, etc., and it is not within the proposed scheme of the present work to collect philosophical materials from the diverse vernacular literature of India.

In introducing his commentary, Śrīkaṇṭha says that the object of his interpretation of the *Brahma-sūtra* is the clarification of its purport since it has been made turbid by previous teachers[1]. We do not know who were these previous teachers, but a comparison between the commentary of Śaṅkara and that of Śrīkaṇṭha shows that at least Śaṅkara was one of his targets. Śaṅkara's idea of Śaiva philosophy can briefly be gathered from his commentary on the *Brahma-sūtra* II. 2. 35–8, and his view of the Śaiva philosophy tallies more with some of the Purāṇic interpretations which were in all probability borrowed by Vijñāna Bhikṣu in his commentary on the *Brahma-sūtra* called *Vijñānāmṛta-bhāṣya*, and his commentary on the *Īśvara-gītā* of the *Kūrma-purāṇa*. Śaṅkara lived somewhere about the eighth century A.D., and his testimony shows that the sort of Śaiva philosophy that he expounded was pretty well known to Bādarāyaṇa, so that he included it as a rival system for refutation in the *Brahma-sūtra*. This shows the great antiquity of the Śaiva system of thought, and in a separate section we shall attend to this question.

Śaṅkara came from the Kerala country in the South, and he must have been acquainted with some documents of Śaiva philosophy or the *Śaivāgamas*. But neither Śaṅkara nor his commentators mention their names. But obviously Śrīkaṇṭha followed some *Śaivāgamas*, which were initiated in early times by one called Śveta, an incarnation of Śiva, who must have been followed by other teachers of the same school, and according to Śrīkaṇṭha's own testimony, twenty-eight of them had flourished before

[1] *Vyāsa-sūtram idaṃ netraṃ viduṣāṃ brahma-darśane.*
pūrvācāryaiḥ kaluṣitaṃ śrīkaṇṭhena prasādyate.
Śrīkaṇṭha's *bhāṣya*, introductory verse, 5.

Śrīkaṇṭha and had written *Śaivāgama* works. The original teacher Śveta has also been mentioned in the *Vāyavīya saṃhitā* of the *Śiva-mahāpurāṇa*[1].

In the initiatory adoration hymn Śrīkaṇṭha adores Śiva, the Lord, as being of the nature of ego-substance (*ahaṃ-padārtha*). The sub-commentator Appaya Dīkṣita (A.D. 1550), in following the characterisation of Śiva in the *Mahābhārata*, tries to give an etymological derivation in rather a fanciful way from the root *vaśa*, 'to will.' This means that the personality of Śiva, the Lord, is of the nature of pure egohood and that his will is always directed to the effectuation of good and happiness to all beings. This egohood is also described as 'pure being' (*sat*), 'pure consciousness' (*cit*) and 'pure bliss' (*ānanda*). Śrīkaṇṭha further says that his commentary will expound the essence of the teachings of the Upaniṣads or the Vedānta and will appeal to those who are devoted to Śiva[2]. Śrīkaṇṭha describes Śiva on the one hand as being the category of *aham* or egohood which forms the individual personality, and at the same time regards it as being of the nature of 'pure being,' 'pure consciousness,' and 'pure bliss.' He thinks that this individual personality can be regarded only in unlimited sense to be identified with the infinite nature of Śiva. Appaya Dīkṣita in commenting on this verse quotes the testimony of some of the Upaniṣads to emphasise the personal aspect of the God Śiva as a personal God. Ordinarily the word '*sac-cid-ānanda-rūpāya*' would be used in the writings of monistic Vedānta of the school of Śaṅkara, in the sense of a concrete unity of 'pure being,' 'pure consciousness,' and 'pure bliss.' But that kind of interpretation would not suit the purposes of a purely theistic philosophy. For this reason Appaya says that the words '*sac-cid-ānānda*' are the qualities of the supreme God Śiva and that this is indicated by the terminal word '*rūpāya*,' because Brahman as such is *arūpa* or formless. The expansion of the limited individual into the infinite nature of Śiva also implies that the individual enjoys with Him qualities of bliss and consciousness. In a Śaṅkarite interpretation the person who attains liberation becomes one with Brahman, that

[1] *Śiva-mahāpurāṇa*, *Vāyavīya saṃhitā* I. 5. 5 *et seq.* (Veṅkaṭeśvara Press, Bombay, 1925).

[2] *oṃ namo'haṃ-padārthāya lokānāṃ siddhi-hetave,*
saccidānanda-rūpāya śivāya paramātmane. I.
Preliminary adoration to Śiva by Śrīkaṇṭha.

is, with the unity of *sat*, *cit* and *ānanda*. He does not enjoy consciousness or bliss but is at once one with it. The Brahman in the system of Śaṅkara and his school is absolutely qualityless and differenceless (*nirviśeṣa*). Rāmānuja in his commentary on the *Brahma-sūtra* tries to refute the idea of Brahman as qualityless or differenceless and regards the Brahman as being the abode of an infinite number of auspicious and benevolent characters and qualities. This is called *saguṇa-brahman*, that is, the Brahman having qualities. The same idea is put forward in a somewhat different form by Śrīkaṇṭha. Except in the Purāṇas and some older Sanskrit literature, the idea of a Brahman with qualities does not seem to be available in the existent philosophical literature outside Rāmānuja. Rāmānuja is said to have followed the *Bodhāyana-vṛtti* which, however, is no longer available. It may, therefore, be suggested that Śrīkaṇṭha's *bhāṣya* was inspired by the *Bodhāyana-vṛtti*, or by Rāmānuja, or by any of the *Śaivāgamas* following a simple theistic idea.

On the one hand Lord Śiva is regarded as the supreme and transcendent Deity, and on the other he is regarded as the material cause of this material universe, just as milk is the material cause of curd. This naturally raises some difficulties, as the supreme God cannot at the same time be regarded as entirely transcendent and also undergoing changes for the creation of the material universe which is to be regarded as of the nature of God Himself. To avoid this difficulty Appaya summarises the view of Śrīkaṇṭha and tries to harmonise the texts of the Upaniṣads, pointing to monistic and dualistic interpretations. He thus says that God Himself is not transformed into the form of the material universe, but the energy of God which manifests itself as the material universe is a part and parcel of the entire personality of God. The material universe is not thus regarded either as illusion or as an attribute of God (in a Spinozistic sense), nor is the universe to be regarded as a part or a limb of God, so that all the activities of the universe are dependent on the will of God, as Rāmānuja holds in his theory of *Viśiṣṭādvaita*; nor does Śrīkaṇṭha regard the relation between the universe and God as being of the same nature as that between the waves or foam and the sea itself. The waves or foam are neither different from nor one with the sea; this is called the *bhedābheda-vāda* of Bhāskara. It may also be noted that this view of Śrīkaṇṭha is entirely different from the view of Vijñāna Bhikṣu as expressed in the *Vijñānāmṛta-bhāṣya*, a commentary on the *Brahma-sūtra* in which he tries to establish a view well known in the Purāṇas, that the *prakṛti* and the *puruṣa* are abiding entities outside God and are co-existent with Him; they are moved by God for the production of the universe, for the teleological purposes of enjoyment and experience of the *puruṣas*, and ultimately lead the *puruṣas* to liberation beyond bondage. It may not be out of place here to refer to the commentary of Śaṅkara on the *Brahma-sūtra* (II. 2. 37 *et seq.*) where he tried to refute a Śaiva doctrine which regards God as the instrumental cause that transforms the *prakṛti* to form the universe, a view somewhat similar to that found in the *Vijñānāmṛta-bhāṣya* of Vijñāna Bhikṣu. This Śaiva view seems to have been entirely different from the Śaiva view expressed by Śrīkaṇṭha, expressly based on the traditions of the twenty-eight yogācāryas beginning with Śveta. Lord Śiva, the supreme personal God, is regarded as fulfilling all our desires, or rather our beneficent wishes. This idea is brought out by Appaya in his somewhat fanciful etymology of the word '*śiva*,' a twofold derivation from the root *vaśa* and from the word '*śiva*' meaning good.

Śrīkaṇṭha adores the first teacher of the Śaiva thought and regards him (Śveta) as having made the various Āgamas. But we do not know what these Āgamas were. Appaya in his commentary is also uncertain about the meaning of the word '*nānāgama-vidhāyine*.' He gives two alternative interpretations. In one he suggests that the early teacher Śveta had resolved the various contradictions of the Upaniṣadic texts, and had originated a system of Śaiva thought which may be properly supported by the Upaniṣadic texts. In the second interpretation he suggests that the word '*nānāgama-vidhāyine*,' that is, he who has produced the various Āgamas, only means that the system of Śveta was based on the various *Śaivāgamas*. In such an interpretation we are not sure whether these Āgamas were based on the Upaniṣads or on other vernacular Dravidian texts, or on both.[1] In commenting upon the *bhāṣya* of Śaṅkara on the *Brahma-sūtra* (II. 2. 37), Vācaspati says in his *Bhāmatī* that the systems known as Śaiva,

[1] *asmin pakṣe 'nānāgama-vidhāyinā'ity*
asya nānāvidha-pāśupatādy-āgama-nirmātrā ity arthaḥ.
Appaya's commentary on Śrīkaṇṭha's *bhāṣya* (Bombay, 1908), Vol. I, p. 6.

Pāśupata, Kāruṇika-siddhāntin, and the Kāpālikas are known as the fourfold schools called the Māheśvaras[1]. They all believe in the Sāṃkhya doctrine of *prakṛti*, *mahat*, etc., and also in some kind of Yoga on the syllable *om*; their final aim was liberation and end of all sorrow. The individual souls are called *paśus* and the word '*pāśa*' means bondage. The Maheśvaras believe that God is the instrumental cause of the world as the potter is of jugs and earthen vessels.

Both Śaṅkara and Vācaspati regard this Maheśvara doctrine, based upon certain treatises (*Siddhānta*) written by Maheśvara, as being opposed to the Upaniṣadic texts. None of them mentions the name of the teacher Śveta, who is recorded in Śrīkaṇṭha's *bhāṣya* and the *Śiva-mahāpurāṇa*. It is clear therefore that, if Śaṅkara's testimony is to be believed, this word '*nānāgama-vidhāyine*' cannot mean the reconciliatory doctrine based on the Upaniṣads as composed by Śveta and the other twenty-seven Śaiva teachers[2]. We have already pointed out that the Śaiva doctrine, that we find in Śrīkaṇṭha, is largely different from the Maheśvara school of thought which Śaṅkara and Vācaspati wanted to refute. There Śaṅkara had compared the Maheśvara school of thought as being somewhat similar to the Nyāya philosophy.

What the Siddhānta treatises, supposed to have been written by Maheśvara, were, is still unknown to us. But it is certain that they were composed in the beginning of or before the Christian era, as that doctrine was referred to by Bādarāyaṇa in his *Brahma-sūtra*.

[1] Rāmānuja, however, in his commentary on the same *sūtra* mentions as the fourfold schools the Kāpālas, the Kālamukhas, the Pāśupatas, and the Śaivas.

[2] The *Vāyavīya-saṃhitā* section mentions the names of the twenty-eight yogācāryas beginning with Śveta. Their names are as follows:

Śvetaḥ sutāro madanaḥ suhotraḥ kaṅka eva ca,
laugākṣiś ca mahāmāyo jaigīṣavyas tathaiva ca. 2.
dadhivāhaś-ca ṛṣabho munir ugro 'trir eva ca,
supālako gautamaś ca tathā vedaśirā muniḥ. 3.
gokarṇaś-ca guhāvāsī śikhaḍī cāparaḥ smṛtaḥ,
jaṭāmālī cāṭṭahāso dāruko lāṅgulī tathā. 4.
mahākālaś ca śūlī ca daṇḍī muṇḍīśa eva ca,
saviṣṇus soma-śarmā ca lakulīśvara eva ca. 5.

Vāyavīya-saṃhitā II. 9, verses 2–5 (compare *Kūrma-purāṇa* I. 53, 4 *et seq.*). The names of their pupils are given from II. 9, verses 6–20 (compare *Kūrma-purāṇa* I. 53, 12 *et seq.*).

Each one of the yogācāryas had four disciples. The better known of them are as follows (*Vāyavīya-saṃhitā* II. 9, 10 *et seq.*): Kapila, Asuri, Pañcaśikha, Parāśara, Bṛhadaśva, Devala, Śālihotra, Akṣapāda, Kaṇāda, Ulūka, Vatsa.

Śrīkaṇṭha definitely says that the souls and the inanimate objects, of which the universe is composed, all form materials for the worship of the supreme Lord. The human souls worship Him directly, and the inanimate objects form the materials with which He is worshipped. So the whole universe may be regarded as existing for the sake of the supreme Lord. Śrīkaṇṭha further says that the energy or the power of the Lord forms the basis or the canvas, as it were, on which the whole world is painted in diverse colours. So the reality of the world lies in the nature of God Himself; the universe, as it appears to us, is only a picture-show based on the ultimate reality of God who is regarded as definitely described and testified in the Upaniṣads[1]. On the testimony of Śrīkaṇṭha, the philosophy of Śaivism as interpreted by him follows an interpretation of the Upaniṣads and is based on them. It is unfortunate that most of the scholars who have contributed articles to the study of Śaivism or written books on it, have so far mostly ignored the philosophy propounded by Śrīkaṇṭha, although his work had been published as early as 1908.

We have already seen that Śaṅkara in his *bhāṣya* on the *Brahma-sūtra* II. 2. 37, had attributed the instrumentality of God as being the doctrine of the Siddhānta literature supposed to have been written by Maheśvara. Appaya, in commenting upon the same topic dealt with by Śrīkaṇṭha, says that this is the view which may be found in the *Śaivāgamas* when they are imperfectly understood. But neither he nor Śrīkaṇṭha mentions the names of any of the *Śaivāgamas* which have come down to us, which describe the instrumentality of God. So Śrīkaṇṭha also undertakes to refute the view of Śaivism which holds that God is only the instrumental cause of the world. We may therefore infer that some of the *Śaivāgamas* were being interpreted on the line of regarding God as being the instrumental cause of the world.

Śrīkaṇṭha's *bhāṣya* on *Brahma-sūtra* II. 2. 37 and the commentary of Appaya on it bring out some other important points. We know from these that there were two types of Āgamaṣ, one meant for the three castes (*Varṇa*) who had access to the Vedic

1 *nija-śakti-bhitti-nirmita-nikhila-jagajjālā-citra-nikurumbaḥ,*
sa jayati śivaḥ parātmā nikhilāgama-sāra-sarvasvam. 2.
bhavatu sa bhavatām siddhyai paramātmā sarva-maṅgalo-petaḥ,
cidacinmayaḥ prapañcaḥ śeṣo' śeṣo' pi yasyaiṣaḥ. 3.
Introductory verses, Śrīkaṇṭha's *bhāṣya*.

literature, and the other for those that had no access to the Vedic literature. These latter Āgamas might have been written in the Dravidian vernaculars, or translated into the Dravidian vernaculars from Sanskrit manuals. Śrīkaṇṭha's own interpretation of the *Brahma-sūtra* is based mainly on the views propounded in the *Vāyavīya-saṃhitā* section of the *Śiva-mahāpurāna*. In the *Kūrma-purāṇa* and the *Varāha-purāṇa* also we hear of different types of *Śaivāgamas* and Śaiva schools of thought. Some of the Śaiva schools, such as Lakulīśa or Kāpālikas, are regarded in those Purāṇas (*Kūrma* and *Varāha*) as being outside the pale of Vedic thought, and the upholders of those views are regarded as following delusive Śāstras or scriptures (*mohā-śāstra*). In reply to this it is held that some of those schools follow some impure practices, and have on that account been regarded as *moha-śāstra*. But they are not fully opposed to the Vedic discipline, and they encourage some kinds of adoration and worship which are found in the Vedic practice. The Āgamas of this latter type, that is, which are for the Śūdras and other lower castes, are like the well-known Āgamas such as *Kāmika*, *Mṛgendra*, etc. It is urged, however, that these non-Vedic Āgamas and the Vedic Śaivism as found in the *Vāyavīya-saṃhitā* are essentially authoritative, and both of them owe their origin to Lord Śiva. Their essential doctrines are the same, as both of them regard Śiva as being both the material and the instrumental cause of the world. It is only that some superficial interpreters have tried to explain some of the Āgamas, emphasising the instrumentality of the supreme Lord, and the above topic of the *Brahma-sūtra* is intended to refute such a view of the supreme Lord as being only the efficient or instrumental cause.

It is curious to note that the two systems of Śaiva philosophy called *Lākulīśa-pāśupata* and the *Śaiva-darśana* as treated in the *Sarvadarśana-saṃgraha*, deal mainly with the aspect of God as the efficient cause of the universe; they lay stress on various forms of ritualism, and also encourage certain forms of moral discipline. It is also surprising to note that the *Sarva-darśana-saṃgraha* should not mention Śrīkaṇṭha's *bhāṣya*, though the former was written somewhere about the fourteenth century A.D. and Śrikaṇṭha's *bhāṣya* must have been written much before that time, though it is not possible for us as yet to locate his time exactly. Neither does the *Sarva-darśana-saṃgraha* refer to any Purāṇic materials as found in the *Śiva-mahāpurāṇa*, the *Kūrma-purāṇa* and the *Varāha-purāṇa*. But we shall treat of the systems later on in other sections and show their relation with the philosophy as propounded in Śrīkaṇṭha's *bhāṣya*, so far as manuscript material and other published texts are available.

In interpreting the first *sūtra* of the *Brahma-sūtra* '*athāto-brahma-jijñāsā*,' Śrīkaṇṭha first introduces a long discussion on the meaning of the word '*atha*.' The word '*atha*' generally means 'after,' or it introduces a subject to a proper incipient. Śrīkaṇṭha holds that the entire *Mīmāṃsā-sūtra* by Jaimini, beginning with "*athāto dharma-jijñāsā*" to the last *sūtra* of the *Brahma-sūtra* IV. 4. 22 "*anāvṛttiḥ śabdād anāvṛttiḥ śabdāt*," is one whole. Consequently the *brahma-jijñāsā* or the inquiry as to the nature of Brahman must follow the inquiry as to the nature of *dharma*, which forms the subject-matter of the *Pūrva-mīmāṃsā-sūtra* of Jaimini. We have seen in our other volumes that the subject-matter of the *Pūrva-mīmāṃsā* starts with the definition of the nature of *dharma*, which is regarded as being the beneficial results accruing from the dictates of the Vedic imperatives "*codanā-lakṣaṇoṛtho dharmaḥ*"). The sacrifices thus are regarded as *dharma*, and these sacrifices are done partly for the attainment of some desired benefits such as the birth of a son, attainment of prosperity, a shower of rain, or long residence in heaven after death; partly also as obligatory rites, and those which are obligatory on ceremonial occasions. Generally speaking these sacrificial duties have but little relation to an inquiry about the nature of Brahman. Śaṅkara, therefore, had taken great pains in his commentary on the *Brahma-sūtra* as well as in his commentary on the *Gītā*, to show that the sacrificial duties are to be assigned to persons of an entirely different character from those who are entitled to inquire about the nature of Brahman. The two parts of sacrifices (*karma*) and knowledge (*jñāna*) are entirely different and are intended for two different classes of persons. Again, while the result of *dharma* may lead to mundane prosperity or a residence in heaven for a time and will, after a time, bring the person in the cycle of transmigratory birth and death, the knowledge of Brahman once attained or intuited directly, would liberate the person from all bondage eternally. So, these two courses, that is the path of *karma* and the path of knowledge, cannot be regarded as complementary to each other. It is wrong to regard them as segments of the same circle. This is what is known as the refutation by Śaṅkara of the joint performance of *karma* and *jñāna*, technically called the *jñāna-karma-samuccaya-vāda*.

Śrīkaṇṭha here takes an entirely opposite view. He says that the Brāhmin who is properly initiated with the holy thread has a right to study the Vedas, has even an obligatory duty to study the Vedas under a proper teacher, and when he has mastered the Vedas he also acquaints himself with their meaning. So the study of the Vedas with a full comprehension of their meaning must be regarded as preceding any inquiry or discussion regarding the nature of Brahman. As *dharma* can be known from the Vedas, so the Brahman has also to be known by the study of the Vedas. Consequently, one who has not studied the Vedas is not entitled to enter into any discussion regarding the nature of Brahman. But then it cannot be said that merely after the study of the Vedas one is entitled to enter into a discussion regarding the nature of Brahman. For such a person must, after the study of the Vedas, discuss the nature of *dharma*, without which he cannot be introduced into a discussion regarding the nature of Brahman. So the discussion about the nature of Brahman can only begin after a discussion on the nature of *dharma*[1]. He further says that it may be that the principles and maxims used in the interpretation of Vedic injunctions as found in the *Pūrva-mīmāṃsā* were necessary for the understanding of the Upaniṣadic texts leading to a discussion on the nature of Brahman. It is for this reason that a discussion of the nature of *dharma* is indispensably necessary for the discussion of the nature of Brahman.

It cannot, however, be said that if sacrifices lead to an understanding of the nature of Brahman, what is the good of any discussion on its nature. One might rather indulge in a discussion of the nature of *dharma*, because when the Vedic duties are performed without desire for the fulfilment of any purpose, that itself might purify the mind of a man and make him fit for inquiring into the nature of Brahman, for, by such a purposeless performance of

[1] *tarhi kiṃ anantaram asyārambhaḥ. dharma-vicārānantaram.* Śrīkaṇṭha's *bhāṣya* I. I. I, Vol. I, p. 34.
na vayam dharma-brahma-vicāra-rūpayoś śāstrayor atyanta-b-hedavādinaḥ. kintu ekatva-vādinaḥ. Ibid.

Vedic sacrifices, one may be purified of one's sins, and this may lead to a proper illumination of the nature of Brahman[1]. He also makes references to Gautama and other *smṛtis* to establish the view that only those who are initiated in the Vedic ceremonial works are entitled to abide with Brahman, and get commingled with him. The most important point is that only those Vedic sacrifices which are done without any idea of the achievement of a purpose lead finally to the cessation of sins, and thereby making the Brahma-illumination possible. In the case of such a person the result of *karma* becomes the same as the result of knowledge. The *karmas* are to be performed until true knowledge dawns. Consequently one can say that the discussion on the nature of Brahman must be preceded by the discussion on the nature of *dharma* accruing from the prescribed Vedic duties. The inquiry after the nature of Brahman is not meant as the carrying out of any Vedic mandate, but people turn to it for its superior attraction as being the most valued possession that one may have, and one can perceive that only when one's mind is completely purified by performing the Vedic duties in a disinterested manner, can one attain the knowledge of Brahman. It is only in this way that we can regard the discussion on the nature of *dharma* as leading to the discussion of the nature of Brahman. If the mind is not purified by the performance of the Vedic duties in a disinterested manner, then the mere performance of the Vedic duties does not entitle anyone to inquire about the nature of Brahman.

Appaya Dīkṣita, in commenting on the above *bhāṣya* of Śrīkaṇṭha, says that the discussion on the nature of Brahman means a discussion on the texts of the Upaniṣads. Such discussions would naturally lead to the apprehension of the nature of Brahman. The word '*brahman*' is derived from the root '*bṛṃhati*' meaning 'great' which again is not limited by any qualification of time, space, or quality, that is, which is unlimitedly great. We have to accept this meaning because there is nothing to signify any limitation of any kind (*saṃkocakābhāvāt*). The Brahman is different from all that is animate (*cetana*) and inanimate (*acetana*). There are two kinds of energy: that which is the representative of the material power or energy (*jaḍa-śakti*), which transforms itself in the form of

[1] *tasya phalābhisandhi-rahitasya pāpāpanayana-rūpacitta-śuddhi-sampādana-dvārā bodha-hetutvāt.* Śrīkaṇṭha's *bhāṣya* I. I. I, Vol. I, p. 39.

the material universe under the direction or instrumentality of the Brahman; and there is also the energy as consciousness (*cicchakti*), and this consciousness energy, as we find it in animate beings, is also controlled by the Brahman[1]. The Brahman Himself is different from the phenomenal world consisting of inanimate things and conscious souls. But as the conscious souls and unconscious world are both manifestations of the energy of God called Brahman or Śiva or any other of His names, God Himself has no other instrument for the creation and maintenance of the world. So the greatness of Brahman is absolutely unlimited as there is nothing else beyond Him which can lend Him any support. The two energies of God representing the material cause and the spiritual force may be regarded somehow as the qualities of God.

Just as a tree has leaves and flowers, but still in spite of this variety is regarded as one tree, so God also, though He has these diversified energies as his qualities, is regarded as one. So, when considered from the aspect of material and spiritual energies, the two may be differentiated from the nature of Brahman, yet considered internally they should be regarded as being one with Brahman. These two energies have no existence separate from the nature of God. The word 'brahman' means not only unlimitedness, it also means that He serves all possible purposes. He creates the world at the time of creation and then leading the souls through many kinds of enjoyment and sorrow, ultimately expands them into His own nature when the liberation takes place.

Appaya Dīkṣita, after a long discussion, conclusively points out that not all persons who had passed through the discipline of sacrificial duties are entitled to inquire about the nature of Brahman. Only those who, by reason of their deeds in past lives, had had their minds properly purified could further purify their minds in this life by the performance of the Vedic duties without any desire for fruit, and can attain a discriminative knowledge of what is eternal and non-eternal, and have the necessary disinclination (*vairāgya*), inner control and external control of actions and desire for liberation, thereby qualifying themselves for making an

[1] *tasya cetanācetana-prapañca-vilakṣanatvā-bhyupagamena vastu-paricchinat-vād ity āśaṅkāṃ nirasitum ādya-viśeṣaṇam. sakala-cetanācetana-prapañcā-kāryayā tadrūpa-pariṇāminyā parama-śaktyā jaḍa-śakter māyāyā niyāmakatvena tata utkṛṣtayā cicchaktyā viśiṣṭasya. Śivārkamaṇi-dīpikā*, Appaya's commentary, Vol. I, p. 68.

inquiry about the nature of Brahman. Appaya Dīkṣita thus tries to bridge over the gulf between the standpoint of Śrīkaṇṭha and the standpoint of Śaṅkara. With Śaṅkara it is only those inner virtues and qualities, desire for liberation and the like that could entitle a person to inquire about the nature of Brahman. According to Śaṅkara the discussion on the nature of Vedic duties or their performance did not form an indispensable precedent to the inquiry about the nature of Brahman. But Appaya Dīkṣita tries to connect Śrīkaṇṭha's view with that of Śaṅkara by suggesting that only in those cases where, on account of good deeds in past lives, one's mind is sufficiently purified to be further chastened by the desireless performance of Vedic duties, that one can attain the mental virtues and equipments pointed out by Śaṅkara as an indispensable desideratum for inquiry into the nature of Brahman.

Appaya Dīkṣita tries to justify the possibility of a discussion regarding the nature of Brahman by pointing out that in the various texts of the Upaniṣads the Brahman is variously described as being the ego, the food, the bio-motor force (*prāṇa*), and the like. It is necessary, therefore, by textual criticism to find out the exact connotation of Brahman. If Brahman meant only the ego, or if it meant the pure differenceless consciousness, then there would be no scope for discussion. No one doubts his own limited ego and nothing is gained by knowing Brahman, which is pure differenceless consciousness. For this reason it is necessary to discuss the various texts of the Upaniṣads which give evidence of a personal God who can bestow on His devotee eternal bliss and eternal consciousness.

The Nature of Brahman.

Śrīkaṇṭha introduces a number of Upaniṣadic texts supposed to describe or define the nature of Brahman. These apparently are in conflict with one another, and the contradiction is not resolved either by taking those definitions alternately or collectively, and for this reason it is felt necessary to enter into a textual and critical interpretation of those texts as yielding a unified meaning. These texts describe Brahman as that from which everything has sprung into being and into which everything will ultimately return, and taht, it is of the nature of pure bliss, pure being and pure consciousness. Appaya Dīkṣita says that, such qualities being ascribed to various deities, it is for us to find out the really ultimate Deity, the Lord Śiva, who has all these qualities. He also introduces a long discussion as to whether the ascription of these diverse epithets would cause any reasonable doubt as to the entity or person who possesses them. He further enters into a long discussion as to the nature of doubt that may arise when an entity is described with many epithets, or when an entity is described with many contradictory epithets, or when several objects are described as having one common epithet. In the course of this discussion he introduces many problems of doubt with which we are already familiar in our treatment of Indian philosophy[1]. Ultimately Appaya tries to emphasise the fact that these qualities may be regarded as abiding in the person of Śiva and there can be no contradiction, as qualities do not mean contradictory entities. Many qualities of diverse character may remain in harmony in one entity or person.

Lord Śiva is supposed to be the cause of the creation of the world, its maintenance, and its ultimate dissolution, or the liberation of souls, through the cessation of bondage. All these qualities of the production of the world, its maintenance, etc., belong to the phenomenal world of appearance, and cannot therefore be attributed to the Lord Śiva as constituting His essential definition. It is true that a person may, by his good deeds and his disinclination to worldly enjoyments and devotion, attain liberation automatically. But even in such cases it has to be answered that, though the person may be regarded as an active agent with reference to his actions, yet the grace of God has to be admitted as determining him to act. So also, since all the epithets of creation, maintenance, etc., belong to the world of appearance, they cannot be regarded as in any way limiting the nature of Lord Śiva. They may at best be regarded as non-essential qualities by which we can only signify the nature of Brahman, but cannot get at His own true nature. The application of the concept of agency to individual persons or inanimate things is only one of emphasis; for, from certain points of view, one may say that a person attains liberation by his own action, while from another point of view the whole action of the individual may be

[1] See especially the third volume of the present work dealing with the problem of doubt in Venkaṭa.

regarded as being due to the grace of God. So, from one point of view the laws of the world of appearance may be regarded as natural laws, while from another all the natural laws may be regarded as being the manifestations of the grace of God.

It may be urged that if Lord Śiva is all-merciful why does He not remove the sorrows of all beings by liberating them? To this question it may be said that it is only when, by the deeds of the persons, the veil of ignorance and impurity is removed that the ever-flowing mercy of God manifests itself in liberating the person. Thus there is a twofold action, one by the person himself and the other by the extension of mercy on the part of God in consonance with his actions.

Again, the dissolution of the world of appearance is not a magical disappearance, but rather the return of the grosser nature of the *prakṛti* or primal matter into its subtle nature of the same *prakṛti*. The world as a whole is not illusion, but it had at one time manifested itself in a grosser form of apparent reality, and in the end it will again return into the subtle nature of the cosmic matter or *prakṛti*. This return into the nature of the subtle *prakṛti* is due to the conjoint actions of all animate beings as favoured by the grace of God.

The second *sūtra*, which describes or defines Brahman as that from which all things have come into being, into which all things will ultimately return, and wherein all things are maintained, regards these qualities of production, maintenance, and dissolution of all things, according to Śrīkaṇṭha as interpreted by Appaya, as being the final determinant causal aspect, both material and instrumental, by virtue of which the nature of Brahman as God or Īśvara can be inferred. So according to Śrīkaṇṭha and Appaya this *sūtra* '*janmādy-asya yataḥ*' should be regarded as a statement of infallible inference of the nature of Brahman. Śaṅkara in his commentary had definitely pointed out that those who regard Īśvara or God as the cause of all things and beings interpret this *sūtra* as an example of inference, by which the unlimited nature of Brahman could be directly argued; and that such a definition, in that it points out the reasons, is sufficient description, not too wide nor too narrow. Therefore, by this argument one can understand the Brahman as being the supreme and unlimited Lord of the whole of the material and spiritual universe. Śaṅkara definitely refuses to accept such an interpretation, and regards it as merely stating the general purport of the Upaniṣadic texts, which say that it is from Brahman that everything has come into being, and that it is in and through Brahman that everything lives, and that ultimately everything returns into Brahman. The main point at issue between Śaṅkara and Śrīkaṇṭha is that, while Śaṅkara refuses to accept this *sūtra* as establishing an argument in favour of the existence of Brahman, and while he regards the purpose of the *Brahma-sūtra* as being nothing more than to reconcile and relate in a harmonious manner the different texts of the Upaniṣads, Śrīkaṇṭha and the other Śaivas regard this *sūtra* as an inferential statement in favour of the existence of the unlimited Brahman or the supreme Lord Śiva[1].

Rāmānuja also does not interpret this *sūtra* as being an inferential statement for establishing the nature and existence of Brahman. He thinks that by reconciling the apparently contradictory statements of the Upaniṣadic texts, and by regarding Brahman as the cause of the production, maintenance, and dissolution of the world, it is possible to have an intuition or apprehension of the nature of Brahman through the Upaniṣadic texts[2].

Śrīkaṇṭha tries to interpret the various epithets of Brahman such as *ānanda* or bliss, *sat* or being, *jñāna* or consciousness, and the fact that in some texts Śiva is mentioned as the original cause of the world in the sense that Śiva is both the original and ultimate cause of the universe. He raises the difficulty of treating these epithets as applying to Brahman either alternately or collectively. He also further raises the difficulty that in some of the Upaniṣadic texts *prakṛti*, which is inanimate, is called the *māyā* and the cause of the inanimate world. If Brahman is of the nature of knowledge or consciousness then He could not have transformed Himself into the material world. The transformation of pure consciousness into the material universe would mean that Brahman is changeable and this would contradict the Upaniṣadic statement that the Brahman is absolutely without any action and in a state of pure passivity.

[1] *etad evānumānam saṃsāriv-vyatirikte-śvarāstitvādi-sādhanaṃ manyanta īśvara-kāraṇinaḥ. nanu ihāpi tad evopanyastam janmādi-sūtre, na; vedānta-vākya-kusuma-grathanārthatvāt sūtrāṇām.* Śaṅkara's *bhāṣya* on *Brahma-sūtra* I. I. 2.

[2] Rāmānuja's *bhāṣya* on *Brahma-sūtra* I. I. 2.

From this point of view the objector might say that all the epithets that are ascribed to Brahman in the Upaniṣads cannot be applied to it at the same time, and they may not be taken collectively as the defining characteristics of the nature of Brahman. Śrīkaṇṭha, therefore, thinks that the abstract terms as truth, consciousness, bliss, etc., that are applied to Brahman, are to be taken as personal qualities of the Supreme Lord. Thus, instead of regarding Brahman as pure consciousness, Śrīkaṇṭha considers the Supreme Lord as being endowed with omniscience, eternally self-satisfied, independent, that is, one who always contains his power or energy, and one who possesses omnipotence. He is eternally self-efficient (*nitya aparokṣa*) and never depends on any external thing for the execution of his energy or power (*anapekṣita-bāhya-karaṇa*). Lord Śiva, thus being omniscient, knows the deeds of all animate beings and the fruits of those deeds to which they are entitled, and He also knows the forms of bodies that these animate souls should have in accordance with their past deeds, and He has thus a direct knowledge of the collocation of materials with which these bodies are to be built up[1]. The fact that the Brahman is described as *ānanda* or bliss is interpreted as meaning that Lord Śiva is always full of bliss and self-contented[2].

In the Upaniṣads it is said that the Brahman has the *ākāśa* as his body (*ākāśa-śarīram brahma*). It is also said in some of the Upaniṣads that this *ākāśa* is bliss (*ānanda*). Śrīkaṇṭha says that this *ākāśa* is not the elemental *ākāśa* (*bhūtākāśa*); it merely means the plane of consciousness (*cidākāśa*), and in that way it means the ultimate material (*para-prakṛti*), which is the same as the ultimate energy. Appaya points out that there are people who think that the energy of consciousness is like an instrument for creating this universe, as an axe for cutting down a tree. But Appaya denies this view and holds that the ultimate energy is called the *ākāśa*[3]. It is this energy of consciousness

[1] *anena sakala-cetana-bahu-vidha-karma-phala-bhogānu-kūla-tat-tac-charīra-nirmāṇopāya-sāmagrī-viśeṣa jñam brahma nimittaṃ bhavati.* Śrīkaṇṭha's *bhāṣya* on *Brahma-sūtra* I. I. 2, p. 121.

[2] *parabrahma-dharmatvena ca sa eva ānando brahmeti pracuratvād brahmatvenopacaryate. tādṛśānanda-bhoga-rasikaṃ brahma nitya-tṛptam ity ucyate. Ibid.* p. 122.

[3] *yasya sā paramā devī śaktir ākāśa-saṃjñitā.* Appaya's commentary, Vol. I, p. 123.

(*cicchakti*) that is regarded as pervading through all things and it is this energy that undergoes the transformations for the creation of the universe. It is this *cicchakti* that is to be regarded as the original force of life that manifests itself in the activities of life. All kinds of life functions and all experiences of pleasure are based on the lower or on the higher level of this ultimate life force, called also the *cicchakti* or *ākāśa*.

Again, Brahman is described as being of the nature of being, consciousness and bliss (*ānanda*). In this case, it is held that Brahman enjoys His own bliss without the aid of any external instrumentality. And it is for this reason that the liberated souls may enjoy bliss of a superlative nature without the aid of any external instruments. The truth as consciousness is also the truth as pure bliss which are eternal in their existence not as mere abstract qualities, but as concrete qualities adhering to the person of Lord Śiva. Thus, though the Brahman or Lord Śiva may be absolutely unchangeable in Himself, yet His energy might undergo the transformations that have created this universe. Brahman has thus within Him both the energy of consciousness and the energy of materiality which form the matter of the universe (*cid-acit-prapañca-rūpa-śakti-viśiṣṭatvam svābhābikam eva brahmaṇaḥ*). As the energy of Brahman is limitless, he can in and through those energies form the material cause of the universe. As all external things are said to have 'being' as the common element that pervades them all, it represents the aspect of Brahman as 'being,' in which capacity it is the material cause of the world. The supreme Lord is called *Śarva*, because all things are finally absorbed in Him. He is called *Īśāna*, because He lords over all things, and He is hence also called *Paśupati*. By the epithet *paśupati* it is signified that He is not only the Lord of all souls (*paśu*), but also all that binds them (*pāśa*). The Brahman thus is the controller of all conscious entities and the material world[1].

It has been said that the *māya* is the primal matter, *prakṛti*, which is the material cause of the universe. But God or the Lord Śiva is said to be always associated with the *māyā*, that is, He has no separate existence entirely apart from the *māyā*. In such a view, if the *māyā* is to be regarded as the material cause of the universe,

[1] *anena cid-acin-niyāmakaṃ brahmeti vijñāyate.* Śrīkaṇṭha's *bhāṣya* on *Brahma-sūtra* I. I. 2, p. 127.

then the Lord Śiva, who is associated with the *māyā*, has also to be, in some distant sense, regarded as the material cause of the universe. So the final conclusion is that the Brahman as associated with subtle consciousness and subtle materiality is the cause, and the effect is the universe which is but gross consciousness as associated with gross matter[1]. It is true, indeed, that the facts of production, maintenance, and dissolution are epithets that can only apply to the phenomenal world, and therefore they cannot be regarded as essential characteristics determining the nature of Brahman as an inferential statement. Yet the production, maintenance, and dissolution of the world of phenomena may be regarded as a temporary phase (*taṭastha-lakṣaṇa*) of the nature of Brahman. It should also be noted that when *māyā* transforms itself into the world by the controlling agency of God, God Himself being eternally associated with *māyā*, may in some sense be regarded as being also the material cause of the world, though in His supreme transcendence He remains outside the *māyā*. The difference between this view and that of Rāmānuja is that, according to the latter, the Brahman is a concrete universal having the entire materiality and the groups of souls always associated with Him and controlled directly by Him, as the limbs of a person are controlled by the person himself. The conception is that of an entire organisation, in which the Brahman is the person and the world of souls and matter are entirely parts of Him and dominated by Him. The position of Śaṅkara is entirely different. He holds that the central meaning of the *sūtra* is just an interpretation of the texts of Upaniṣads which show that the world has come out of Brahman, is maintained in Him, and will ultimately return into Him. But it does not declare that this appearance of the world is ultimately real. Śaṅkara is not concerned with the actual nature of the appearance, but he has his mind fixed on the ultimate and

[1] *'māyāṃ tu prakṛtim vidyād' iti māyāyāḥ prakṛtitvam īśvarātmikāyā eva 'māyinaṃ tu maheśvaram' iti vākya-śeṣāt. sūkṣma-cid-acid-viśiṣṭam brahma kāraṇaṃ sthūla-cid-acid-viśiṣṭaṃ tat-kāryam bhavati.* Śrīkaṇṭha's *bhāṣya* on *Brahma-sūtra* I. I. 2, pp. 134 *et seq.*

satyaṃ māyopādānam iti brahmāpy upādānam eva. apṛthak-siddha-karyāvasthā śrayatva-rūpaṃ hi māyāyā upādānatvam samarthanīyaṃ. tat-samarthyamānam eva brahma-paryantam āyāti. nitya-yoge khalu māyinam iti māyā-śabdādi-nipratyayaḥ. tataś ca māyāyāḥ brahmā-pṛthak-śiddhyaiva tad-apṛthak-siddhāyāḥ kāryāvasthāyā api brahmāpṛthak-siddhis siddhyati.

Appaya Dīkṣita's commentary, Vol. I, p. 134.

unchangeable ground which always remains true and is not only relatively true as the world of appearance[1].

We have said above that Śrīkaṇṭha regarded the second *sūtra* as indicating an inference for the existence of God. But in the course of later discussions he seems to move to the other side, and regards the existence of Brahman as being proved by the testimony of the Vedas. The general argument from the unity of purpose throughout the universe cannot necessarily lead to the postulation of one creator, for a house or a temple which shows unity of purpose is really effected by a large number of architects and artisans. He also thinks that the Vedas were produced by God. That is also somehow regarded as additional testimony to His existence. The nature of Brahman also can be known by reconciling the different Upaniṣadic texts which all point to the supreme existence of Lord Śiva. In *Brahma-sūtra* II. I. 18, 19 Śrīkaṇṭha says that the Brahman as contracted within Himself is the cause while, when by His inner desire He expands Himself, He shows Himself and the universe which is His effect[2]. This view is more or less like the view of Vallabha, and may be regarded as largely different from the idea of Brahman as given by Śrīkaṇṭha in I. I. 2. Śrīkaṇṭha, in further illustrating his views, says that he admits Brahman to be the ultimate material cause of the universe only in the sense that the *prakṛti*, from which the world is evolved, is itself in Brahman. So as Brahman cannot remain without His *śakti* or energy, He can be regarded as the material cause of the world, though He in Himself remains transcendent, and it is only His *māyā* that works as an immanent cause of the production of the world. He thus says that there is a difference between the individual souls and the Brahman, and there is a difference between the *prakṛti* and the Brahman. He would not admit that the world of appearance is entirely different from Brahman; neither would he admit that they are entirely identical. His position is like that of the modified

[1] For the view of Śaṅkara and his school, see Vols. I and II. For the view of Rāmānuja and his school see Vol. III.

[2] "*cidātmaiva hi devo*" *ntaḥ-sthitam icchā-vaśād bahiḥ. yogīva nirupādānam arthajātaṃ prkāśayed' iti. nirupādānam iti anapekṣitopādānāntaraṃ svayam upādānaṃ bhūtvety arthaḥ. tataḥ parama-kāraṇāt parabrahmaṇaḥ śivād abhinnam eva jagat kāryam iti...yathā saṃkucitaḥ sūkṣma-rūpaḥ paṭaḥ prasārito mahāpaṭa-kuṭī-rūpeṇa kāryaṃ bhavati, tathā brahmāpi saṃkucita-rūpaṃ kāraṇaṃ prasārita-rūpam kāryaṃ bhavati.* Śrīkaṇṭha's *bhāṣya*, Vol. II, p. 29.

monists, like that of the *Viśiṣṭādvaita-vāda* of Rāmānuja. Brahman exists in quite a transcendent manner, apart from the individual souls and the inanimate world. But yet, since the individual souls and the material universe are emanations from His energy, the world of souls and matter may be regarded as parts of Him, though they are completely transcended by Himself[1].

Moral Responsibility and the Grace of God.

The question is, why did the supreme Lord create the whole universe? He is always self-realised and self-satisfied, and He has no attachment and no antipathy. He is absolutely neutral and impartial. How is it, then, that He should create a world which is so full of happiness to some (e.g. the gods) and so full of sorrow and misery to others? This will naturally lead us to the charge of partiality and cruelty. Moreover, since before the creation there must have been destruction, it will necessarily be argued that God Himself is so cruel as to indulge in universal destruction out of simple cruelty. So one may naturally argue that what purpose should God have in creating a world which is not a field for the attainment of our own desires and values. The reply given to this is that God indulges in the creation and destruction of the world in accordance with the diversity of human deeds and their results (*karma* and *karmaphala*).

It cannot be argued that before the creation there were no souls, for we know from the Upaniṣadic texts that the souls and God both exist eternally. As the souls have no beginning in time, so their deeds also are beginningless. This may lead to an infinite regress, but this infinite regress is not vicious. The series of births and deaths in the world in different bodies is within the stream of beginningless *karma*. Since God in His omniscience directly knows by intuition the various kinds of deeds that the individual

[1] *bhedābheda-kalpanaṃ viśiṣṭādvaitaṃ sādhayāmaḥ na vayaṃ brahma-prapañcayor atyantam eva bheda-vādinaḥ ghaṭa-paṭayor iva. tad-ananyatva-para-śruti-virodhāt. na vā'tyantā-bheda-vādinaḥ śukti-rajatayor iva. ekatara-mithyātvena tat-svābhāvika-guṇa-bheda paraśruti-virodhāt. na ca bhedābheda-vādinaḥ, vastu-virodhāt. kin tu śarīra-śarīriṇor iva guṇa-guṇinor iva ca viśiṣṭ-ādvaita-vādinaḥ. prapañca-brahm aṇor ananyatvam nāma mṛḍ-ghaṭayor iva guṇa-guṇinor iva ca kārya-kāraṇatvena viśeṣaṇa-viśeṣyatvena ca vinābhāva-rahitatvam.* Śrīkaṇṭha's *bhāṣya* on *Brahma-sūtra* II. I. 22, Vol. II, p. 31.

would perform, He arranges suitable bodies and circumstances for the enjoyment or suffering of such deeds already anticipated by Him. So the difference in creation is due to the diversity of one's deeds. The time of destruction comes when the souls become tired and fatigued by the process of birth and death, and require some rest in dreamless sleep. So the effectuation of dissolution does not prove the cruelty of God.

Now, since the pleasures and sorrows of all beings depend upon their deeds (*karma*), what is the necessity of admitting any God at all? The reply is that the law of *karma* depends upon the will of God and it does not operate in an autonomous manner, nor does it curb the freedom or independence of God. This, however, would lead us in a circular way to the same position, for while the pleasures and sorrows of men depend upon the deeds of men and the law of *karma*, and since the law of *karma* depends upon the will of God, it actually means that the pleasures and sorrows of beings are due indirectly to the partiality of God.

Again, since the *karma* and the law of *karma* are both unintelligent, they must be operated by the intelligence of God. But how could God before the creation, when beings were devoid of the miseries of death and birth, were not endowed with any bodies, and were therefore in a state of enjoyment, associate them with bodies, lead them to the cycle of birth and rebirth, and expose them to so much sorrow? The reply is that God extends His grace to all (*sarvānugrāhaka parameśvara*); and thus, since without the fruition of one's deeds (*karmapākam antareṇa*) there cannot be pure knowledge, and since without pure knowledge there cannot be the liberation of enjoying bliss in a superlative manner, and since also without the fruition of *karma* through enjoyment and suffering there cannot be the relevant bodies through which the souls could enjoy or suffer the fruits of *karma*, bodies have necessarily to be associated with all the souls which were lying idle at the time of the dissolution. So when in this manner the deeds of a person are exhausted through enjoyment or suffering, and the minds of beings become pure, it is only then that there may arise self-knowledge leading to the supreme bliss of liberation.

It may again be asked that, if God is absolutely merciful, why could not He arrange for the fruition of the deeds of all persons at one and the same time and allow them to enjoy the bliss of liberation? The reply is that, even if God would have extended His grace uniformly to all persons, then those whose impurities have been burnt up would be liberated and those whose impurities still remained could only attain salvation through the process of time. Thus, though God is always self-contented, He operates only for the benefit of all beings.

From the interpretation of Appaya it appears that the word grace (*annugraha*) is taken by him in the sense of justice. So God does not merely extend His mercy, but His mercy is an extension of justice in accordance with the deeds of persons, and therefore He cannot be regarded as partial or cruel[1]. Appaya anticipates the objection that in such a view there is no scope for the absolute lordship of God, for He only awards happiness and misery in accordance with the law of *karma*. It is therefore meaningless to say that it is He, the Lord, that makes one commit sins or perform good deeds merely as He wishes to lower a person or to elevate him. For God does not on His own will make one do bad or good deeds, but the persons themselves perform good or bad actions according to their own inclinations as acquired in past creations, and it is in accordance with those deeds that the new creation is made for the fulfilment of the law of *karma*[2]. Appaya further says that the good and bad deeds are but the qualities of the mind (*antaḥkaraṇa*) of the persons. At the time of dissolution these minds are also dissolved in the *māyā* and remain there as unconscious impressions or tendencies (*vāsanā*), and being there they are reproduced in the next creation as individual bodies and their actions in such a way that, though they were dissolved in the *māyā*, they do not commingle, and each one is associated with his own specific mind and deeds at the next birth[3]. In the Āgamas, where thirty-six categories

[1] *evaṃ ca yathā narapatiḥ prajānāṃ vyavahāra-darśane tadīya-yuktāyukta-vacanānusāreṇa anugraha-nigraha-viśeṣaṃ kurvan pakṣapātitva-lakṣaṇam vaiṣamyaṃ na pratipadyate evam īśvaro'pi tadīya-karma-viśeṣā-nusāreṇa viṣama-sṛṣṭiṃ kurvan na tatpratipadyate.* Appaya Dīkṣita's commentary, Vol. II, p. 47.

[2] *parameśvaro na svayam sādhvasādhūni karmāṇi kārayati, tais sukha-duḥkhādīni ca notpādayati, yenatasya vaiṣamyam āpatet. kin tu prāṇina eva tathābhūtāni karmāṇi yāni sva-sva-rucyanusāreṇa pūrva-sargeṣu kurvanti tāny eva punas-sargeṣu viṣama-sṛṣṭi-hetavo bhavanti. Ibid.* Vol. II, p. 48.

[3] *parmeśvarastu pūrva-sarga-kṛtānām tat-tad-antaḥkaraṇa-dharmarūpāṇāṃ sadhva-asādhu-karmaṇāṃ pralaye sarvāntaḥ-karaṇāṇām vilīnatayā māyāyām eva vāsanā-rūpatayā lagnānāṃ kevalam asaṅkareṇa phala-vyavasthāpakaḥ. anyathā māyāyām saṅkirṇeṣu karma-phalam anyo gṛhṇīyāt.* Appaya Dīkṣita's commentary, Vol. II, p. 48.

(*tattva*) are counted, the law of *karma* called *niyati* is also counted as one of the categories. Though the category of *niyati* is admitted, it cannot operate blindly, but only under the superintendence of God, so that the actions or fruits of action of one may not be usurped by another. Pure *niyati* or the law of *karma* could not have done it. The view supported here is that when, at the time of dissolution, all *karmas* are in a state of profound slumber, God awakens them and helps the formation of bodies in accordance with them, and associates the bodies with the respective souls, and makes them suffer or enjoy according to their own deeds.

The problem still remains unexplained as to how we are to reconcile the freedom of will of all persons with the determinism by God. If God is regarded as being responsible for making us act in the way of good or of evil, then deferring God's determination to beginningless lives does not help the solution of the difficulty. If God determines that we shall behave in a particular manner in this life, and if that manner is determined by the actions of our past lives *ad infinitum*, then when we seek for the original determination we are bound to confess that God is partial; for He must have determined us to act differently at some distant period and He is making us act and suffer and enjoy accordingly. So the ultimate responsibility lies with God. In reply to this it is held by Appaya, interpreting the commentary of Śrīkaṇṭha, that we were all born with impurities. Our bondage lies in the veil that covers our wisdom and action, and God, who possesses infinite and manifold powers, is always trying to make us act in such a manner that we may ultimately purify ourselves and make ourselves similar to Him. The dissolution of our impurities through natural transformation is like that of a boil or wound in the body which disappears only after giving some pain. The Vedic duties which are obligatory and occasional help to cure us of these impurities, just as medicine helps to cure a wound, and this may necessarily cause misery of birth and death. It is only when our deeds fructify that knowledge can spring from them. So also by the performance of obligatory and occasional deeds as prescribed in the Vedas, our *karmas* become mature and there arises in us a spirit of disinclination (*vairāgya*), devotion to Śiva and an inquiry after Him, which ultimately produces in us the wisdom that leads to liberation. The fruition of one's *karma* cannot take place without the environment of the world such as we have it. Thus, for the ultimate liberation we must perform certain actions. God makes us perform these actions, and according to the manifold character of our deeds He creates different kinds of bodies, making us do such actions as we may suffer from, and thereby gradually advance towards the ultimate goal of liberation. In accordance with the diversity of our original impurities and actions, we are made to perform different kinds of deeds, just as a medical adviser would prescribe different kinds of remedies for different diseases. All this is due to the supreme grace of God. Śrīkaṇṭha's usage of the word *karma* means that by which the cycle of birth and death is made possible through the agency of God[1]. In the dissolution, of course, there cannot be any process for the fulfilment or fruition of action, so that state is supposed to be brought about only for giving a rest to all beings.

In *Brahma-sūtra* II. 3. 41 Śrīkaṇṭha seems to make it definitely clear that the individual souls themselves do things which may be regarded as the cause of their acting in a particular way, or desisting from a particular way of action, in accordance with the nature of the fruition of their past deeds. It is further said that God only helps a person when he wishes to act in a particular way, or to desist from a particular action. So a man is ultimately responsible for his own volition, which he can follow by the will of God in the practical field of the world. The responsibility of man rests in the assertion of his will and the carrying of the will into action, and the will of God helps us to carry out our will in the external world around us. Man performs his actions in accordance with the way in which he can best satisfy his interests. He is therefore responsible for his actions, though in the actual carrying out of the will he is dependent on God. God thus cannot be charged with partiality or cruelty, for God only leads the individual souls to action in accordance with His own will and inner effort[2].

[1] *bhāṣye "karma-pākam antareṇe'tyādi-vākyeṣu karma-śabdaḥ kriyate" nena saṃsāra iti karaṇa-vyutpattyā vā parameśvareṇa pakvaḥ kriyata iti karma-vyutpattyā vā malāvaraṇaparo draṣṭavyaḥ.* Appaya Dīkṣita's commentary, Vol. II, p. 50.

[2] *ato jīva-kṛta-prayatnāpekṣatvāt karmasu jīvasya pravartaka īśvaro na vaiṣamyabhāk. tasyāpi svādhīna-pravṛtti-sadbhāvāt vidhi-niṣedhādi-vaiyarthaṃ ca na sambhavatīti siddham.* Śrīkaṇṭha's *bhāṣya* on *Brahma-sūtra* II. 3. 41, p. 157.

It is curious to note, however, that Appaya thinks that, even allowing for the inner human effort of will, the individual is wholly dominated by God. Appaya thus leaves no scope for the freedom of the will[1].

In *Brahma-sūtra* II. 2. 36–8 Śrīkaṇṭha makes a special effort to repudiate the view of Śaṅkara, that the Śaivas believed in a doctrine that God was the instrumental cause of the world, and could be known as such through inference. He also repudiates the view that the Brahman or Śiva had entered into the *prakṛti* or the primal matter, and thereby superintended the course of its evolution and transformation into the universe. For in that case He should be open to the enjoyment and suffering associated with the *prakṛti*. Śrīkaṇṭha therefore holds that according to the Śaiva view the Brahman is both the material and the efficient cause of the universe, and that He cannot be known merely by reason, but by the testimony of the Vedic scriptures. There is here apparently an oscillation of view on the subject as propounded by Śrīkaṇṭha. Here and in the earlier parts of his work, as has been pointed out, Śrīkaṇṭha asserts that, though God is the material cause of the universe, He is somehow unaffected by the changes of the world[2]. The ultimate Brahman or Śiva is associated with a subtle energy of consciousness and materiality which together are called *cicchakti*, and as associated with the *cicchakti*, God Śiva is one and beyond everything. When in the beginning of creation there comes out from this supreme *māyā* or *cicchakti* the creative *māyā* which has a serpentine motion, then that energy becomes the material cause of the entire world. It is from this that four categories evolve, namely as *śakti*, *Sadāśiva*, *Maheśvara*, and *Śuddha-vidyā*. After that comes the lower *māyā* of a mixed character, which is in reality the direct material cause of the world and the bodies. Then comes time (*kāla*), destiny (*niyati*), knowledge (*vidyā*), attachment (*rāga*), and the souls. In another line there comes from the impure *māyā* the entire universe and the bodies of living beings. From that comes intelligence (*buddhi*), egotism (*ahaṅkāra*), *manas*, the fivefold cognitive senses, the fivefold conative senses, the fivefold subtle

[1] *tathā ca parameśvara-kārita-pūrva-karma-mūla-svecchādhīne yatne, parameśvarādhīnatvan na hīyate.* Appaya's commentary, Vol. II, p. 156.

[2] *jagad-upādana-nimitta-bhūtasyāpi parameśvarasya "niṣkalam niṣkriyam" ityādi-śrutibhir nirvikāratvam apy upapadyate.* Śrīkaṇṭha's *bhāṣya* on *Brahma-sūtra* II. 2. 38, p. 109.

causes of gross matter called *tanmātra*, and also the fivefold elements of matter. Thus are the twenty-three categories. Counting the previous categories, we get thirty-six categories altogether. These are well known in the Śaiva texts and they have been established there both logically and by reference to the testimony of the scriptural texts. A distinction is made, as has been shown above, between the pure *māyā* and the impure *māyā*. The impure *māyā* includes within itself all the effects such as time and the impure souls. The word *vyakta* is used to denote the material cause or the purely material world, including the mental psychosis called *buddhi*.

The category of Śiva is also sometimes denoted by the term *śakti* or energy[1]. The word *śiva-tattva* has also been used as merely Śiva in the *Vāyavīya-saṃhitā*.

We have seen before that Śaṅkara explained this topic of the *Brahma-sūtra* as refuting the view of the different schools of Śaivas or Maheśvaras who regard God as being the instrumental cause of the universe. Śrīkaṇṭha has tried to show that God is both the material cause and the instrumental cause of the universe. In his support he addresses texts from the *Vāyavīya-saṃhitā* of the *Śiva-mahāpurāṇa* to show that, according to the Vedic authority, God is both the material and the instrumental cause of the universe. But Śrīkaṇṭha says that, though the Āgamas and the Vedic view of Śaivism are one and the same, since both of them were composed by Śiva, in some of the Āgamas, such as the *Kāmika*, the instrumental side is more emphasised; but that emphasis should not be interpreted as a refutation of the view that God is also the material cause of the universe. It is true that in some sects of Śaivism, such as the Kāpalikas or Kālamukhas, some of the religious practices are of an impure character and so far they may be regarded as non-Vedic; and it is possible that for that reason, in the *Mahābhārata* and elsewhere, some sects of Śaivism have been described as non-Vedic. Yet from the testimony of the *Varāha-purāṇa* and other Purāṇas, Śaivism or the *Pāśupata-yoga* has been regarded as Vedic. Śrīkaṇṭha and Appaya took great pains to bridge the gulf between the vernacular Śaivism and the

[1] *śiva-tattva-śabdena tu śiva evocyate. na tu atra śiva-tattva-śabdaḥ para-śaktiparaḥ. śakti-śabdas tat-kārya-dvitīya-tattva-rūpa-śaktiparaḥ.* Appaya Dīkṣita's commentary, Vol. II, p. 110.

Sanskritic, that is, those forms of Śaivism which were based on the authority of the Vedas and were open to the first three castes (*varṇa*), and those which are open to all castes. Both try to make out that the present topic was not directed against the views propounded in the *Śaivāgamas* as Śaṅkara explained, but against other views which do not form any part of the Śaiva philosophy.

In some texts of the *Kalpa-sūtras* we hear of objections against the valid authority of some of the texts, but these objections do not apply to the Āgamas composed by Śiva. It is said that Śiva cannot be the material cause of the universe, because the Upaniṣads hold that the Brahman is changeless, and in this way an attempt is made to refute the *pariṇāma* doctrine. *Pariṇāma* means "change from a former state to a latter state." It is further held that *śakti* or energy is in itself changeless. Even if that *śakti* be of the nature of consciousness, then such a change would also be inadmissible. Against this view it is held that there may be change in the spiritual power or energy (*cicchakti*) on the occasion of a desire for creation or a desire for destruction. The *cicchakti* which is within us goes out and comes into contact, in association with the senses, with the external objects, and this explains our perception of things. So, since we have to admit the theory of the functional expansion (*vṛtti*) of the *cicchakti*, it is easy to admit that the original *śakti* has also its functional expansion or contraction[1].

According to the Śaiva school as propounded by Śrīkaṇṭha, the individual souls have not emanated from God, but they are co-existent with Him. The apparent scriptural texts that affirm that souls came out of Brahman like sparks from a fire are interpreted as meaning only the later association of souls with *buddhi* and *manas*, and also with the different bodies. It must also be said that the souls are the conscious knowers, both by way of senses and by the *manas*. The *manas* is explained as a special property or quality of knowledge which the soul possesses and by virtue of which it is a knower. This *manas* must be differentiated from a lower type of *manas* which is a product of *prakṛti*, and which becomes associated with the soul in the process of birth and rebirth through association

[1] *teṣvapi sisṛkṣā-saṃjihīrṣādi-vyavahāreṇa śiva-cicchakteḥ "cicchaktir artha-saṃyogo-'dhyakṣam indriya-mārgata" iti cicchakti-vṛtti-nirgama-vyavahāreṇa jīva-cicchakteś ca pariṇāmitvam āviṣkṛtam eveti bhāvaḥ.* Appaya Dīkṣita's commentary, Vol. II, p. 112.

with the power of *māyā*. This power gives it a special character as a knower, by which it can enjoy or suffer pleasure and pain, and which is limited to the body and the egoism. It is by virtue of this *manas* that the soul is called a *jīva*. When through Brahma-knowledge its threefold association with impurities is removed, then it becomes like Brahman, and its self-knowledge in a liberated state manifests itself. This knowledge is almost like Brahma-knowledge. In this state the individual soul may enjoy its own natural joy without the association of any of the internal organs, merely by the *manas*. The *manas* there is the only internal organ for the enjoyment of bliss and there is no necessity of any external organs. The difference between the individual soul and God is that the latter is omniscient and the former knows things only particularly during the process of birth and rebirth. But in the actual state of liberation the souls also become omniscient[1]. Śrīkaṇṭha also holds that the souls are all atomic in size, and that they are not of the nature of pure consciousness, but they all possess knowledge as their permanent quality. In all these points Śrīkaṇṭha differs from Śaṅkara and is in partial agreement with Rāmānuja. Knowledge as consciousness is not an acquired quality of the soul as with the Naiyāyikas or the Vaiśeṣikas, but it is always invariably co-existent in the nature of the selves. The individual souls are also regarded as the real agents of their actions, and not merely illusory agents, as some philosophical theories hold. Thus Sāṃkhya maintains that the *prakṛti* is the real agent and also the real enjoyer of joys and sorrows, which are falsely attributed to the individual souls. According to Śrīkaṇṭha, however, the souls are both real agents and real enjoyers of their deeds. It is by the individual will that a soul performs an action, and there is no misattribution of the sense of agency as is supposed by Sāṃkhya or other schools of thought. The souls are ultimately regarded as parts of Brahman, and Śrīkaṇṭha tries to repudiate the monistic view that God falsely appears as an individual soul through the limitations of causes and conditions (*upādhi*)[2].

[1] *tat-sadṛśa-guṇatvāt apagata-saṃsārasya jīvasya svarūpānandānubhava-sādhanaṃ manorūpam antaḥ-karaṇam anapekṣita-bāhya-karaṇam asti iti gamyate. jñājñau iti jīvasya ajñatvam kiṃcij jñatvam eva. asaṃsāriṇaḥ parameśvarasya tu sarvajñatvam ucyate. ataḥ saṃsāre kiṃcij jñatvaṃ muktau sarvajñatvam iti jñātā eva ātmā.* Śrīkaṇṭha's *bhāṣya* on *Brahma-sūtra*, II. 3. 19, pp. 142–3.

[2] Śrīkaṇṭha's *bhāṣya* on *Brahma-sūtra*, II, 3. 42–52.

Regarding the view that *karmas* or deeds produce their own effects directly, or through the intermediary of certain effects called *apūrva*, Śrīkaṇṭha holds that the *karmas* being without any intelligence (*acetana*) cannot be expected to produce the manifold effects running through various births and various bodies. It has therefore to be admitted that, as the *karmas* can be performed only by the will of God operating in consonance with the original free will of man, or as determined in later stages by his own *karma*, so the prints of all the *karmas* are also distributed in the proper order by the grace of God. In this way God is ultimately responsible on the one hand for our actions, and on the other for the enjoyment and suffering in accordance with our *karmas*, without any prejudice to our moral responsibility as expressed in our original free inclination or as determined later by our own deeds.[1]

In the state of liberation the liberated soul does not become one with the Brahman in its state of being without any qualities. The Upaniṣadic texts that affirm that the Brahman is without any qualities do so only with the view to affirm that Brahman has none of the undesirable qualities, and that He is endowed with all excellent qualities which are consistent with our notion of God. When in the state of liberation the liberated souls become one with the Brahman, it only means that they share with God all His excellent qualities, but they never become divested of all qualities, as the monistic interpretation of Śaṅkara likes to explain. It has been pointed out before that God may have many attributes at one and the same time, and that such a conception is not self-contradictory if it is not affirmed that he has many qualities of a contradictory character at one and the same time. Thus, we can speak of a lotus as being white, fragrant and big, but we cannot speak of it as being both blue and white at the same time.[2]

Śrīkaṇṭha holds that only those *karmas* which are ripe for producing fruits (*prārabdha-karma*) will continue to give fruits, and will do so until the present body falls away. No amount of knowledge or intuition can save us from enjoying or suffering the fruits of *karma* that we have earned, but if we attain true knowledge by continuing our meditation on the nature of Śiva as being one with ourselves, we shall not have to suffer birth and rebirth of the

[1] Śrīkaṇṭha's *bhāṣya* on *Brahma-sūtra*, III. 2. 37–40.
[2] Śrīkaṇṭha's *bhāṣya* on *Brahma-sūtra*, III. 3. 40.

accumulated *karmas* which had not yet ripened to the stage of giving their fruits of enjoyment or suffering[1].

When all the impurities (*mala*) are removed and a person is liberated, he can in that state of liberation enjoy all blissful experiences and all kinds of powers, except the power of creating the universe. He can remain without a body and enjoy all happiness through his mind alone, or he can at one and the same time animate or recreate many spiritual bodies which transcend the laws of *prakṛti*, and through them enjoy any happiness that he wishes to have. In no case, however, is he at that stage brought under the law of *karma* to suffer the cycles of birth and rebirth, but remains absolutely free in himself in tune with the Lord Śiva, with whom he may participate in all kinds of pleasurable experiences. He thus retains his personality and power of enjoying pleasures. He does this only through his mind or through his immaterial body and senses. His experiences would no longer be of the type of the experiences of normal persons, who utilise experiences for attaining particular ends. His experience of the world would be a vision of it as being of the nature of Brahman[2].

[1] Śrīkaṇṭha's *bhāṣya* on *Brahma-sūtra*, IV. I. 19.
[2] Śrīkaṇṭha's *bhāṣya* on *Brahma-sūtra*, IV. 4. 17–22.

CHAPTER XXXVII

THE ŚAIVA PHILOSOPHY IN THE PURĀṆAS

The Śaiva Philosophy in the *Śiva-mahāpurāṇa*.

WE shall discuss the antiquity of the Śaiva religion and philosophy in a separate section. It is a pity that it is extremely difficult, nay, almost impossible, to trace the history of the continuous development of Śaiva thought from earliest times. We can do no more than make separate studies of different aspects of Śaiva thought appearing in different contexts, and then try to piece them together into an unsatisfactory whole. This is largely due to various factors. First, the Śaiva thought was expressed both in Sanskrit and also in Dravidian languages. We do not yet know definitely if the Dravidian texts were but translations from Sanskrit sources, or were only inspired by Sanskrit writings. Later writers, even in the Purāṇas, hold that Śiva was the author of all Śaiva scriptures either in Sanskrit or in Dravidian. This, of course, refers to the earliest writings, the Āgamas.

We do not know the exact date of the earliest Āgamas. The word '*āgama*' needs a little explanation. It means "texts that have come down to us", and which are attributed either to God or to some mythical personage. We have a list of twenty-eight Śivācaryas in the *Vāyavīya-saṃhitā* of the *Śiva-mahāpurāṇa*, and these have been referred to as late as the tenth century A.D. But there is nothing to prove the historical existence of these Śaiva teachers, nor do we know what Āgamas we owe to each of them. We have no direct knowledge of any Dravidian philosophical culture before the Aryan culture had penetrated into the South. It is, therefore, difficult to imagine how there could be Dravidian works of philosophy which ran parallel to the Sanskrit works.

The other difficulty is that most of these supposed Āgamas of the past are not now available. Most of the Āgamas that we get now are written in Sanskrit in various Dravidian scripts. The records of the schools of Śaiva philosophy mentioned by Śaṅkara in his *bhāṣya* on the *Brahma-sūtra* must have been written in Sanskrit, but the present writer is quite unable to identify all the schools referred to in the seventh or eighth centuries with the existing records of Śaiva thought. There was a great upheaval of Śaiva thought from the twelfth century, contemporaneously with the revival of Vaiṣṇava thought in Rāmānuja, but Rāmānuja himself does not refer to all the schools of Śaivism referred to by Śaṅkara and Vācaspati Miśra in his *Bhāmatī* commentary. Rāmānuja only mentions the Kālamukhas and the Kāpālikas, and no literature about their philosophical views is now available. The Kāpālika sect probably still exists here and there, and one may note some of their practices, but so far we have not been able to discover any literature on the practices of the Kālamukhas. But we shall revert again to the problem when we discuss the antiquity of Śaiva thought and its various schools. The three schools of Southern Śaivism that are now generally known are the Vīraśaivas, the Śivajñāna-siddhi school and the school of Śaivism as represented by Śrīkaṇṭha. We have dealt with the Śaivism of Śrīkaṇṭha in two sections. The school of Pāśupata-Śaivism is mentioned in the fourteenth century in Mādhava's *Sarva-darśana-saṃgraha* and the Pāśupata school is referred to in the *Mahābhārata* and many other Purāṇas. In the *Śiva-mahāpurāṇa*, particularly in the last section called the *Vāyavīya-saṃhitā*, we have a description of the Pāśupata philosophy. I shall, therefore, now try to collect the description of the Pāśupata system of thought as found in the *Vāyavīya-saṃhitā* of the *Śiva-mahāpurāṇa*.

The *Śiva-mahāpurāṇa*, according to the testimony of the Purāṇa itself, is supposed to have been a massive work of one hundred thousand verses divided into seven sections, written by Śiva Himself. This big work has been condensed into twenty-four thousand verses by Vyāsa in the Kaliyuga. We know nothing about the historicity of this Vyāsa. He is supposed to have written most of the Purāṇas. The present *Śiva-mahāpurāṇa*, however, contains seven sections, of which the last section called the *Vāyavīya-saṃhitā* is divided into two parts and is supposed to elucidate the view of the different schools of Śaivism. According to our interpretation it shows only one school of Śaivism, namely the Pāśupata-Śaivism in two variant forms. None of the works that we have been able to discover so far have been attributed to Śiva or Maheśvara, though Śaṅkara in his *bhāṣya* on the *Brahma-sūtra* II. 2, 37 refers to Siddhānta works written by Maheśvara. We have traced some of the Āgamas, but these Āgamas are not called Siddhānta, nor are they supposed to owe their authorship to Maheśvara. On the evidence of the *Śiva-mahāpurāṇa*, we have quite a number of Śaiva teachers who are regarded as incarnations of Śiva and also many of their disciples, but we know nothing about these mythical teachers. One teacher called Upamanyu is often referred to in the *Vāyavīya-saṃhitā* section as instructing the principles of Śaivism. The account of Śaivism given by Śaṅkara in his *bhāṣya* referred to above, is very meagre, but it seems to indicate that the Śaivas regarded *prakṛti* as the material cause and Śiva as the instrumental or efficient cause; and it is this latter view that Śaṅkara mainly criticises as the school of Īśvara-kāraṇins, implying thereby the view that the Upaniṣads cannot tolerate the idea of a separate efficient cause as Īśvara. Vācaspati also points out that the *prakṛti* being the material cause could not be identified with the efficient cause, the Īśvara. In Śaivism we are faced with the problem of solving the issue between Śaṅkara and the Śaivas. Our treatment of Śrīkaṇṭha's *bhāsya* has shown the direction in which the Śaivas want to solve the difficulty, but Śrīkaṇṭha's *bhāsya* is probably a work not earlier than the eleventh century, and many other works of Śaivism can be traced only as far back as the twelfth century A.D. On the testimony of the *Śiva-mahāpurāṇa*, which must have been written before the time of Śaṅkara, we know that Śaiva works by great Śaiva teachers were written both for those who adhered to the *Varṇāśrama dharma* and for those who did not care for the *Varṇāśrama dharma* and were not privileged to study the Vedas. The latter class of works must therefore have been the Dravidian works of the South, many of which are now lost, and of which only some traditions are available in the Sanskrit Āgamas. We have already dealt with these in another section. We shall have occasion to show that the Kāśmīr form of Śaivism was more or less contemporaneous with Śaṅkara.

In the second section of the *Śiva-mahāpurāṇa* called the *Rudra-saṃhitā*, we are told that at the time of the great dissolution, when all things were destroyed, there was only darkness, no sun, no planets, no stars, no moon, and no day and night; there is only pure vacuity devoid of all energy. There was no sensibility of any kind; it was a state when there was neither being nor non-being; it was beyond all mind and speech, beyond all name and form. But yet in that neutral state there existed only the pure being, the pure consciousness, infinite and pure bliss, which was immeasurable and a state in itself; it had no form and was devoid of all qualities[1]. This was purely of the nature of pure consciousness, without beginning and end and without any development. Gradually there arose a second desire or will by which the formless was changed into some form by its own playful activities. This may be regarded as the all-creating pure energy, of which there is no parallel. The form created by this energy is called *sadāśiva*. People also call Him Īśvara, or God. The lone energy, spontaneously moving, created from itself its own eternal body, which is called *pradhāna*, *prakṛti*, or *māyā*, and which generates the category of *buddhi*. This *māyā* or *prakṛti* is the creator of all beings and is regarded as coming into contact with the supreme *puruṣa*, the Śiva, called *Śambhu*, who is different from God. This *śakti* or energy is also regarded as *kāla* or time.

From *prakṛti* came the *mahat* or *buddhi* and from *buddhi* came the three *guṇas*, *sattva*, *rajas* and *tamas*, and from them the three-fold *ahaṅkāra*. From *ahaṅkāra* came the *tanmātras*, the five *bhūtas*, the five conative senses, and the five cognitive senses, and *manas*.

In the *Kailāsa-saṃhitā* of the *Śiva-mahāpurāṇa* the view of Śaivism is described as being the Śivādvaita system or the monistic theory of Śaivism[2]. It is said here that since all living beings are constituted of a male and a female part, the original cause must also be represented by a male and a female principle united. As a matter of fact, the Sāṃkhyas had taken that idea from this statement, and had regarded the original cause as being *prakṛti* and *puruṣa*. But they tried to establish it merely on rational grounds; they were not disposed to establish it in a theistic sense. For that reason, though some of the Sāṃkhya categories may be accepted, yet the Sāṃkhya philosophy as a whole, being a purely rationalistic system, ought to be abandoned. The Brahman is regarded in the Vedas as being the unity of *sat*, *cit* and *ānanda*, and it is in the neuter gender. The

[1] *satyaṃ jñānam anantaṃ ca parānandaṃ paraṃ-mahaḥ.*
aprameyam anādhāram avikāram anākṛti,
nirguṇaṃ yogigamyañ ca sarva-vyāpyeka-kārakam.
Śiva-mahāpurāṇa, II. 1. 6, 11*c*, *d*–12.

[2] *utpāṭya ajñāna-sambhūtaṃ saṃśayākhyaṃ viṣa-drumam,*
śivādvaita-mahā-kalpa-vṛkṣa-bhūmir yathā bhavet.
Ibid. VI. 16. 11.

being represented in Brahman means that all negation of being is excluded. The neuter character of the being represents the fact that it is the *puruṣa*, and this *puruṣa* also is of an illuminating nature. The pure consciousness in the unity of *sat-cid-ānanda* represents the female part. So the two parts that are regarded as male and female are the illuminating part (*prakāśa*) and the pure consciousness, and these two together are the generating causes of the world. So in the unity of *sac-cid-ānanda* we have the unity of Śiva and Śakti. This illumination is also sometimes impeded, as the flame of a wick is impeded by smoke and other impurities. These are the *malas* which do not belong to Śiva, but are seen in the fire of pure consciousness. It is on this account that the *cicchakti* or the energy of pure consciousness is seen in an impure state in human souls. It is for the expulsion of this *mala* that the pervasiveness of *śakti* or energy is to be assumed as existing in all time. *Śakti* thus is the symbol of *bala* or strength. In the *paramātman* there is both the Śiva-aspect and the *śakti*-aspect. It is by the connection of Śiva and Śakti that there is *ānanda* or bliss. The Ātman is pure consciousness and this consciousness holds within it all knowledge and all energy; it is independent and free, and that is its nature. In the *Śiva-sūtra*, *jñāna* or knowledge has been described as a bondage, but the word *jñāna* there means only finite, limited or turbid knowledge which all human beings have, and in this way alone can knowledge be regarded as bondage.

The Śakti or energy is also called *spanda* or vibration. Knowledge, movement and will are like the three sides of Śiva, and human beings get their inspiration from between these. As we have said above, the Śiva and Śakti combined gives the supreme *śakti* called *parāśakti*, and from this *parāśakti* there evolves the *cicchakti* or power of consciousness. From this comes the *śakti* or bliss or *ānanda-śakti*, from this the will-power or *icchā-śakti*, and from this come *jñāna-śakti*, or power of knowledge, and the power of motivation, or *kriyā-śakti*. The first category of vibration in the category of Śiva is called *śiva-tattva*. The world and the souls are entirely identical with Śiva, and such a knowledge leads to liberation.

The supreme Lord contracts Himself and manifests Himself as the individual *puruṣas* or souls who enjoy the qualities of the *prakṛti*. This enjoyment takes place through the function of fivefold *kalā*, such as that which leads the individual to action; that which leads him to discover the true reality of twofold *vidyā*; that which attaches him to the objects of sense (*rāga*); *kāla* or time which makes things happen in succession; *niyati*, which is used in a peculiar sense, not of destiny but of conscience, that is, it is the factor by which one decides what one should do or not do[1].

The *puruṣa* or the individual souls possess in a cumulative way the qualities of knowledge, will, etc. The so-called *citta* or the psychic plane is constituted of the various qualities existent in the *prakṛti*. From *buddhi* come the various senses and subtle matter.

The system of thought referred to above, the Śivādvaita system, is arranged in rather a clumsy manner. The points that emerge from the above statements can be briefly summarised. First, it regards the Brahman as being an undifferentiated Being or Non-being, when there is nothing but void in the universe. From this Being-and-Non-being, the Brahman, there sprang forth an entity which represents within it the two principles of male and female energy which pervades all living beings. It is out of this principle, the Śiva, that we have, on the one hand the individual selves which are but contractions of the nature of the supreme Lord, and on the other we have the world evolving out of the female energy side, the *prakṛti*, more or less in the Sāṃkhya fashion. The *puruṣa* is supposed to have within him fivefold categories, through which he can experience joys and sufferings of his intercourse with the world as such. These individuals, on account of the contraction that they suffered, show themselves as impure as a flame in a wick appears smoky. Thus the whole system tends towards a sort of monism without being purely idealistic. The closeness or its affinity with Śrīkaṇṭha's philosophy will be immediately apparent, though there are differences in the mode of expression. There are certain passages which remind us of some form of Kāśmīr Śaivism, which though a monism, is largely different from the monism as expressed herein. We also find here a reference to the *spanda* theory of Kāśmīr Śaivism. But in spite of this we need not think that the monistic Śaivism was first enunciated in this Purāṇa or in this chapter. We shall have occasion to show that some form of distinctly monistic Śaivism with relative

[1] *idaṃ tu mama kartavyam idaṃ neti niyāmikā,*
niyatis syāt.... *Śiva-mahāpurāṇa*, vi. 16. 83.

bias could be traced to the beginnings of the Christian era. The Kāśmīr Śaivism flourished probably from the seventh to the eleventh century A.D. It may, therefore, be thought that the chapter under reference of the *Śiva-mahāpurāṇa* was probably written somewhere about the ninth or the tenth century A.D., which may also be regarded as the time of Śrīkaṇṭha, though we are not sure if he flourished somewhere at the eleventh century A.D. after Rāmānuja. We discuss these matters further in the appropriate sections.

In the second chapter of the *Rudra-saṃhitā* of the *Śiva-mahāpurāṇa*[1], Śiva is supposed to say that the highest reality, the knowledge of which brings liberation, is pure consciousness, and in that consciousness there is no differentiation between the self and the Brahman[2]. But strangely enough Śiva seems to identify *bhakti* or devotion with knowledge. There can be no knowledge without *bhakti*[3]. When there is *bhakti* or devotion, there is no distinction of caste in the way of attaining the grace of God. Śiva then classifies the different types of *bhakti*. The nature of devotion, as described in this chapter under consideration, shows that *bhakti* was not regarded as an emotional outburst, as we find in the Caitanya school of *bhakti*. Here *bhakti* is regarded as listening to the name of Śiva, chanting it, and meditating on Him as well as worshipping Him and regarding oneself as the servitor to Śiva, and also to develop the spirit of friendship through which one can surrender oneself to God Śiva. The chanting of the name of Śiva is to be associated with the legendary biography of Śiva as given in the Purāṇas. The meditation on Śiva is regarded as amounting to the development of the idea that Śiva is all-pervasive and is omnipresent. And this makes the devotee fearless. It is through *bhakti* that true knowledge and the disinclination to worldly things can occur.

In IV. 41 four types of liberation are described as *sārūpya*, *sālokya*, *sānnidhya*, and *sāyujya*. We have already discussed in the fourth volume the nature of those types of liberation which are also

[1] *Śiva-mahāpurāṇa* II. 2. 23.

[2] *paratattvaṃ vijānīhi vijñānaṃ parameśvari*
dvitīyaṃ smaraṇaṃ yatra nāhaṃ brahmeti śuddhadhiḥ.
Śiva-mahāpurāṇa II. 2. 23. 13.

bhaktau jñāne na bhedo hi...
vijñānaṃ na bhavaty eva sati bhakti-virodhinaḥ.
Ibid. II. 2. 23. 16.

admitted by the followers of the Mādhva school of Vaiṣṇavas. And this liberation is only granted by Śiva who is beyond all the *guṇas* of *prakṛti*.

The ultimate nature of Śiva is described here (iv. 41) as being changeless (*nirvikārin*) and beyond *prakṛti*. He is of the nature of pure knowledge, unchangeable, all-perceiving. The fifth kind of liberation called the *kaivalya* can be attained only by the knowledge of Śiva and His ultimate nature. The whole world springs out of Him and returns to Him and is always pervaded by Him. He is also designated as being the unity of being, consciousness, and bliss (*sac-cid-ānanda*); He is without any qualities or conditions, pure, and cannot be in any way made impure. He has no colour, no form and no measure. Words cannot describe Him and thoughts cannot reach Him. It is the Brahman which is also called Śiva. Just as space (*ākāśa*) pervades all things, so He pervades all things. He is beyond the range of *māyā* and beyond conflict (*dvandvātīta*). He can be attained either through knowledge or through devotion, but the way of devotion is easier to follow than the way of knowledge. In the next chapter (iv. 42) it is said that it is from Śiva, the ultimate Brahman, that *prakṛti* as associated with *puruṣa* (individual souls) is produced[1]. This evolution of *prakṛti* as associated with *puruṣa* is called the category of *Rudra*, which is only a transformation of Śiva, the highest Brahman, just as golden ornaments may be regarded as transformations of gold. The formless Śiva is considered as having a form only for the advantage of meditation.

All that one can know or see in the universe, in the highest or the lowest, is only Śiva, and the character of things in their plurality is formed from Him. Śiva alone remains the same unchangeable reality before the creation, and at the dissolution of the creation. The pure Śiva is regarded as qualified only when one considers Him as being the possessor of *śakti* or energy with which in reality He is identical. It is through the will of Śiva that all operations in the world can go on. He knows them all, but no one knows Him. Having created the world He remains away from it and is not involved with it. But it is in His form as pure consciousness that He is seen in and through the world, as the sun is seen in

[1] *tasmāt prakṛtir utpannā puruṣeṇa samanvitā.* *Ibid.* iv. 42. 3.

his reflections. In actuality Śiva does not enter into this world of change. In reality Śiva is the whole of the world, though the world appearances seem to occur in a time series of discontinuity. *Ajñāna* or nescience only means misunderstanding, it is not a substance that stands by Brahman and could be regarded as a dual entity[1].

According to the Vedāntins the reality is one, and the individual soul (*jīva*), which gets deluded by *avidyā* or nescience and thinks itself to be different from the Brahman, is only a part of it. But when released from the grasp of nescience it becomes one with Śiva, and Śiva, as we have already said, pervades all things without being actually in them. One can attain liberation by following the path indicated by the Vedānta. As fire, which exists in the wood, can be manifested by the constant rubbing of the wood, so by the various processes of devotion one can attain Śiva, but one must be convinced of the fact that whatever exists is Śiva, and it is only through illusion that various names and forms appear before us[2]. Just as the ocean, or a piece of gold, or a piece of mud may appear in various shapes, though actually they remain the same, so it is only by various conditions through which we look at things that they appear so different, though they are actually nothing but Śiva. There is actually no difference between the cause and the effect[3], yet through illusion one thinks of something as cause and something else as effect. From the seed comes the shoot, appearing as different from the seed, but ultimately the shoot grows into a tree and fructifies and thereby reduces itself into fruit and seed. The seed stays on and produces other shoots and the original tree is destroyed. The true seer is like the seed from which there are many transformations, and when these have ceased we have again the true seer. With the removal of nescience (*avidyā*) a person is dissociated from egoism and becomes pure, and then through the grace of God Śiva he becomes what he really is, that is, Śiva. Just

1 *ajñānaṃ ca mater bhedo nāsty anyacca dvayaṃ punaḥ.*
9: *darśaneṣu ca sarveṣu mati-bhedaḥ pradarśyate.*
Śiva-mahāpurāṇa IV. 43. 8*c*, *d*.

2 *bhrāntyā nānā-svarūpo hi bhāsate śaṅkaras sadā.*
Ibid. IV. 43. 15*c*, *d*.

3 *kārya-kāraṇayor bhedo vastuto na pravartate,*
kevalaṃ bhrānti-buddhyaiva tad-abhāve sa naśyati.
Ibid. IV. 43. 17.

as in a mirror one can see one's body reflected, so one can see oneself reflected in one's pure mind, that is Śiva, which is one's real character.

We thus see that in this school of Śaivism as described in the *Śiva-mahāpurāṇa* IV. 43, we have a monistic system of Śaivism which is very much like the monistic system of Śaṅkara. It believes that the plurality of appearance is false, and that the only reality is Brahman or Śiva. It also believes that this false appearance is due to the interference of nescience. It does not admit any difference between cause and effect, but yet it seems to adhere to the monotheistic faith that God Śiva can bestow liberation on those who are devoted to Him, though it does not deny that the Brahman can be attained by the way indicated in the Upaniṣads. It says that *jñāna* comes from *bhakti* or devotion, from *bhakti* comes love (*prema*), and from *prema* one gets into the habit of listening to episodes about the greatness of Śiva, and from that one comes into contact with saintly people, and from that one can attain one's preceptor. When in this way true knowledge is attained, one becomes liberated. The practice of the worship of the preceptor is also introduced here. It is said that if one gets a good and saintly preceptor, one should worship him as if he were Śiva Himself, and in this way the impurities of the body will be removed, and it will be possible for such a devotee to attain knowledge.

We thus see that in this chapter, though Śaivism is interpreted purely on Vedāntic lines, the doctrine of theism and the doctrine of preceptor worship are somehow grafted into it, though such doctrines cannot fit in with the monism of the Upaniṣads as interpreted by Śaṅkara. This system, therefore, seems to present a specimen of Śaivism different from what we had in the second book of the *Śiva-mahāpurāṇa*, and different also from the philosophy of Śaivism as presented by Śrīkaṇṭha and Appaya Dīkṣita.

Śaiva Philosophy in the *Vāyavīya-saṃhitā* of the *Śiva-mahāpurāṇa*.

§ 1

The *Śiva-mahāpurāṇa* seems to be a collection of seven treatises, called Saṃhitās, dealing with different aspects of the worship of Śiva, myths of Śiva, and philosophy of Śaivism. Though there is a general agreement on the fundamental patterns of Śaiva thought in the various systems of Śaivism, yet these patterns often present marked differences, which ought to be noted for the sake of a detailed study of Śaivism. This is particularly so, as no other system of thought which had spread so far and wide all over India from the days of the hoary past has suffered so much mutilation and destruction of its literature as did Śaivism. We have some older records in the Vedas and the Upaniṣads, and also in the Indus Valley Civilization period, but the systematic Śaiva thought has lost most of its traces from pre-Christian times, until we come to the ninth or tenth centuries A.D. Most of the Āgama works written in Sanskrit and in Dravidian are not now available, and it is even difficult to identify the systems of Śaiva thought as referred to by Śaṅkara in the eighth century A.D. Our treatment of Śaivism can therefore be only gleanings from here and there, and it will not have any proper historical perspective. Even writers in the eleventh or the fourteenth and fifteenth centuries are unable to indicate the proper texts and their mutual relations, at least so far as Sanskrit works are concerned. Much of what is written about the Dravidian texts and their authors is either mythological or largely unhistorical. Even the *Śiva-mahāpurāṇa* seems to be a composite work written at different times. It consists of collections of thought more or less different from each other, and points to different levels of attitude of Śaiva thought. It is not therefore possible to give a consistent account of the whole work of the *Śiva-mahāpurāṇa*; I have accordingly attempted to give an estimate of Śaivism as delineated in Chapters II, IV, VI and VII. But as the philosophical level of the seventh Saṃhitā, the *Vāyavīya-saṃhitā*, seems to be somewhat different from that of the *Śiva-mahāpurāṇa*, I shall try briefly to review the contents of the

Vāyavīya-saṃhitā, which may be regarded as a school of Pāśupata Śaivism. I shall try later on to give estimates of other forms of Śaivism so far as they have been available to me.

In vii. i. 2. 19 of the *Vāyavīya-saṃhitā*, the ultimate God is regarded as being the original cause, the cause of maintenance, as the ground, and also as the cause of destruction of all things. He is called the ultimate *puruṣa*, the Brahman, or the *paramātman*. The *pradhāna* or the *prakṛti* is regarded as His body, and He is also regarded as the agent who disturbs the equilibrium of *prakṛti*[1]. He manifests Himself in twenty-three different categories and yet remains absolutely undisturbed and unchanged. Though the world has been created and maintained by the supreme Lord, yet people do not know him under the delusion of *māyā* or nescience.

In vii. i. 3 it is said that the ultimate cause is that which is unspeakable and unthinkable, and it is that from which the gods Brahmā, Viṣṇu and Rudra have sprung forth, together with all gross matter and sense faculties. He is the cause of all causes and is not produced from any other cause. He is omnipotent and the Lord of all. The supreme Lord stands silent and rooted in one place like a tree and yet He pervades the whole universe. Everything else in the universe is moving excepting their final cause, the Brahman. He alone is the inner controller of all beings, but yet He Himself cannot be recognised as such, though He knows all. Eternal power, knowledge, and action belong naturally to Him. All that we know as destructible (*kṣara*) and indestructible (*akṣara*) have sprung from the supreme Lord, by whose ideation they have come into being. In the end of the *māyā*, the universe will vanish with the disappearance of the individual souls[2]. The supreme Lord, like an omnipotent artist, has painted the canvas of world appearance, and this appearance will ultimately return to Him. Every being is under His control and He can only be realised through supreme devotion (*bhakti*). Only the true devotees can have any real communication with Him. The creation is gross and subtle, the former is visible to all, and the latter only to the yogins, but beyond that there is a supreme Lord of eternal knowledge and

[1] *namaḥ pradhāna-dehāya pradhāna-kṣobha-kāriṇe,*
trayo-viṃśati-bhedena vikṛtāy-āvikāriṇe.
Vāyavīya-saṃhitā vii. i. 2. 19.

[2] *bhūyo yasya paśor ante viśva-māyā nivartate.*
Ibid. vii. i. 3. 13.

bliss, and unchangeable. Devotion to God is also due to the extension of grace by God. As a matter of fact, the grace is produced out of devotion and the devotion is produced out of grace, just as the tree grows out of a seedling and a seedling grows out of a tree.

When one tries to think oneself as being of the nature of the supreme Lord, then His grace is extended to such a person and this increases his merit and his sins are attenuated. By a long process of attenuation of sins through many births, there arises devotion to God, as the supreme Lord with the proper consciousness of it. As a result of that there is a further extension of grace, and in consequence of that one can leave off all desires for the fruits of one's action, though one may be working all the same.

By the renunciation of the fruits of *karma*, one becomes associated with the faith in Śiva. This can be either through a preceptor or without a preceptor. The former is much preferable to the latter. Through knowledge of Śiva one begins to discover the sorrows of the cycles of birth and rebirth. In consequence of that there is a disinclination to all sense-objects (*vairāgya*). From this comes emotion (*bhāva*) for the supreme Lord, and through this emotion one is inclined to meditation, and one is then naturally led to renounce actions. When one thus concentrates and meditates on the nature of Śiva one attains the state of *yoga*. It is through this *yoga* again that there is a further increase of devotion, and through that a further extension of the grace of God. At the end of this long process the individual is liberated, and he then becomes equal to Śiva (*śiva-sama*), but he can never become Śiva. The process of the attainment of liberation may be different in accordance with the fitness of the person concerned.

In VII. I. 5 Vāyu is supposed to say that the knowledge of *paśu*, the individual souls, *pāśa* or the bondage, and *pati*, the supreme Lord, is the ultimate object to all knowledge and faith, and this only can lead to supreme happiness. All sorrows proceed from ignorance, and they are removed through knowledge. Knowledge means limitation by objectivity. This objectivisation through knowledge may be with reference to material objects and non-material things (*jaḍa* and *ajaḍa*). The supreme Lord controls them both. The individual souls are indestructible and are therefore called *akṣara*; the bondage (*pāśa*) is destructible and therefore called *kṣara*; and that, which is beyond these two, is the supreme Lord.

Vāyu, in further explaining the subject, says that *prakṛti* can be regarded as *kṣara*, and *puruṣa* as the *akṣara*, and the supreme Lord moves them both to action. Again *prakṛti* is identified with *māyā* and *puruṣa* is supposed to be encircled by *māyā*. The contact between *māyā* and the *puruṣa* is through one's previous deeds by the instrumentality of God. The *māyā* is described as the power of God. The impurity or *mala* consists in its power to veil the nature of consciousness of the souls. When divested of this *mala* the *puruṣa* returns to its original natural purity. The association of the veil of *māyā* with the soul is due, as we have said before, to previous deeds and this gives the opportunity for enjoying the fruits of our actions. In connection with this, one should also note the category of *kalā* which means knowledge, attachment, time, and *niyati* or destiny. The individual person enjoys all this through his state of bondage. He also enjoys and suffers the fruits of his good and bad deeds. The association with the impurities (*mala*) is without a beginning, but it may be destroyed with the attainment of liberation. All our experiences are intended for experiencing the fruits of our *karma* through the gates of our external and internal senses and our body.

Vidyā or knowledge is here defined as that which manifests space and action (*dik-kriyā-vyañjakā vidyā*). Time or *kāla* is that which limits or experiences (*kālo'vacchedakaḥ*), and *niyati* is that which determines the order of things, and *rāga* or attachment impels one to do actions. The *avyakta* is the cause consisting of the three *guṇas*; from it come all objects and to it everything returns. This *prakṛti*, called also *pradhāna* or *avyakta*, manifests itself in the form of pleasure, pain, and numbness. The method of the manifestation of the *prakṛti* is called *kalā*. The three *guṇas*, *sattva*, *rajas* and *tamas* come out of *prakṛti*. This is distinctively a new view, different from the classical Sāṃkhya theory. In the classical Sāṃkhya theory, *prakṛti* is merely the state of equilibrium of the three *guṇas*, and there *prakṛti* is nothing but that which is constituted of the equilibrium between the three *guṇas*. These *guṇas* permeate through the *prakṛti* in a subtle state as oil permeates through the seeds of sesamum. It is out of the modification of the *avyakta* or *pradhāna* that the five *tanmātras* and five gross matter-elements, as well as five cognitive and five conative senses and the *manas*, come into being. It is the causal state as such that is called the unmanifested or the *avyakta*. The effects as transformations are called the *vyakta* or the manifested; just as a lump of clay may be regarded as the unmanifested and the earthen vessels made out of it are regarded as the manifested. The manifold world of effects find their unity in the unmanifested *prakṛti*, and all bodies, senses, etc. are regarded as being enjoyed through *puruṣa*.

Vāyu, in further explaining the subject, says that, though it is difficult to find out any proper reason for admitting a universal soul, yet one is forced to admit a universal entity which experiences the enjoyments and sufferings, and which is different from intellect, the senses, and the body. This entity is the permanent enjoyer of all human experiences, even when the body perishes (*ayāvad-deha-vedanāt*). It is this universal entity to which all objects of experience appeal, it is called the inner controller in the Vedas and the Upaniṣads. It pervades all things, yet it manifests itself here and there under certain circumstances and is itself unperceivable. It cannot be seen by the eye nor by any of the senses. It is only by the right wisdom of the mind that this great soul or Ātman can be realised. It is unchangeable in all changes and it is the perceiver of all things, though it cannot be perceived itself. Such a great soul is different from the body and the senses, and those who consider it as being identical with the body cannot perceive it. It is by being associated with the body that it undergoes all impurities and suffering, and is drawn to the cycles of births and rebirths by its own deeds. As a field that is flooded with water soon generates new shoots, so in the field of ignorance the *karma* begins to shoot up and produce bodies which are the source of all miseries. Through the cycle of birth and rebirth one has to experience the fruits of one's *karma* and so the process goes on. This universal entity appears as many and manifests various intellectual shades in different persons[1]. All our human relations are accidental and contingent, like two pieces of floating wood drawn together by the waves and then separated again. All beings, from the plants to Brahma, are the *paśus* or manifestations of this

1 *chāditaś ca viyuktaś ca śarīrair eṣu lakṣyate,*
candra-bimba-vad ākāśe taralair abhra-sañcayaiḥ,
aneka-deha-bhedena bhinnā vṛttir ihātmanaḥ.
Śiva-mahāpurāṇa VII. I. 5. 56 *et seq.*

puruṣa. It is the *puruṣa* that is bound by the ties of pleasure and pain, and is like the plaything of the great Lord. It is ignorant and impotent, and cannot provide for its pleasure or arrange for the dispelling of sorrow.

We have already seen the nature of the *paśu* and the *pāśa*. The *pāśa* is the energy or *śakti* of Śiva manifesting itself as *prakṛti*; it evolves the material world, the subjective world, as well as pleasures and pains, which fetter the universal soul, the *paśu*, appearing as many under different conditions and circumstances. We cannot fail to note that the *puruṣa* or *Ātman* here is not many as the *puruṣas* of the Sāṃkhya or the *Ātmans* of the Nyāya, or of some other systems of Śaiva thought. The idea of the Vedāntic monism is eclectically introduced here, and we are faced with the conception of one *puruṣa* which appears as many in different bodies under different conditions. This one *puruṣa* is all-pervading, and it is on account of its being reflected through various conditions that it appears in various divergent forms of things, ranging from Brahma to a blade of grass.

But the supreme Lord who possesses an infinite number of excellent and attractive qualities is the creator of both the *paśu* and the *pāśa*. Without Him there could not be any creation of the universe, for both the *paśu* and the *pāśa* are inanimate and without knowledge. We must remember that according to Sāṃkhya the *puruṣas* are nothing but pure consciousness, but here they are regarded as the reflection of one conscious entity appearing as many through its being reflected in various conditions or environments. Beginning from the *prakṛti* down to the atoms, we have only the inanimate things entering into various modifications. This could not have been if they were not created and moulded by an intelligent creator. This world consisting of parts is an effect, and must therefore have an agent to fashion it. The agency as the supreme Lord, the Creator, belongs to Śiva and not to the soul or to the bondage. The soul itself is moved into activity by the motivity of God. When an individual thinks of himself as the agent of his action, it is only a wrong impression of the nature of causality (*ayathā-karaṇa-jñāna*). It is only when one knows oneself to be different from the true motivating agent that one may ultimately attain immortality. The *kṣara* and *akṣara*, that is, the *pāśa* and the *paśu*, are all associated with each other and they are both maintained by the supreme Lord in their manifested and unmanifested forms. The so-called plurality itself is pervaded by the supreme Lord. God alone is the Lord of all and the refuge of all. Though one, He can uphold the universe by His manifold energies.

This sixth chapter of the first part of the *Vāyavīya-saṃhitā* deals mostly with the contents derived from the Śvetāśvatara Upaniṣad and may be regarded as an expansion of the philosophy of the Śvetāśvatara Upaniṣad. The Lord Himself pervades all things and there is no tinge of impurity in Him. Various other texts of the Upaniṣad are also collated with it for the same purpose, and the Brahman is identified with Śiva. In the previous volumes of the present work, attempts have been made to show that the Upaniṣads were interpreted in the *Brahma-sūtras*, in the *Gītā*, and also in the commentaries of the various schools of interpreters of the *Brahma-sūtras* in accordance with the specific views of the relevant authors. In the *Śiva-mahāpurāṇa* we find also the same attempt to adapt the Upaniṣadic texts for the promulgation of the Śaiva view of philosophy. It is again and again emphasised that there is only one Lord and there is no one second to Him, yet the idea of *māyā* or *prakṛti* is introduced to explain the transformation of the world of appearance. We have seen before that *māyā* is regarded as the energy or *śakti* of Brahman. But we do not find much discussion about the relationship of this energy with God. It is said also in accordance with the Upaniṣads that God is naturally endowed with knowledge and power. But we have not the philosophical satisfaction to know what is exactly the nature of knowledge and power, and how this power is exerted, and what knowledge can mean in relation to the supreme Lord, who has no senses and no *manas*.

In VII. I. 6. 67 the Lord is described as one who produces time and is the Lord of all the *guṇas* and the liberator of all bondage. A question is raised as regards the nature of *kāla* or time. In reply to such a question Vāyu says that *kāla* appears before us in the form of successive moments and durations. The real essence of *kāla* is the energy of Śiva. *Kāla* therefore cannot be outstripped by any being whatsoever. It is, as it were, the ordering power of God[1]. The *kāla* thus is an energy of God that emanates from Him

1 *niyogarūpam īśasya balaṃ viśva-niyāmakam.*
Śiva-mahāpurāṇa VII. I. 7. 7.

and pervades all things. For this reason everything is under the domination of time. But Śiva is not fettered by time; He is the master of all time. The unrestricted power of God is manifested through time, and for this reason no one can transcend the limits of time. No amount of wisdom can take us beyond time, and whatever deeds are done in time cannot be outstripped. It is time which decides the fates and destinies of persons in accordance with their deeds, yet no one can say what is the nature of the essence of time.

We have so far seen that the *prakṛti* as superintended by *puruṣa* evolves as the world before us by the inexorable will and order of God. The order of the evolution of the *prakṛti* or the *avyakta* into different categories is more like what we have in the classical Sāṃkhya. The creation is a process of emanation or emergence from the state of *avyakta* in the well-known classical line of Sāṃkhya, and the dissolution takes place by a process of retrogression, in which the same process is reversed until the whole world of appearance returns to *avyakta* or *prakṛti*.

Turning again to the nature and function of Śiva, the supreme Lord, it is said that there is nothing but the tendency for helping others that may be regarded as the essential nature of Śiva. He has nothing to do but help all beings to attain their best through their actions. He is otherwise without any specific character, except to be of service to the world consisting of the *paśu* and the *pāśa*. This extension of the grace of the Lord is often described as His ordering will. It is for the fulfilment of the function of the Lord's will that one has to admit the existence of something for the good of which the will of the Lord goes forward. For this reason God may not be said to be dependent on others for the exercise of His will. It is in and through the function of His will that things come into being and move forward in an orderly process in accordance with *karma*. The independence of God means that He is not dependent on anything else; dependence means the condition in which one thing depends on another[1].

The whole world is supposed to be dependent on *ajñāna* or nescience, there is nothing of reality in the visible appearance of the world. All the characters of Śiva as described in the scriptures

[1] *ataḥ svātantrya-śabdārthān anapekṣatva-lakṣaṇaḥ.*
Ibid. VII. 1. 31. 7.

are only conditional assumptions; in reality there is no form that one can ascribe to Śiva[1].

All that has been said so far about the evolution of the world is based upon logical assumptions, while the transcendental reality of God is beyond all logic. It is by imagining God to be something of the nature of our *Ātman* that we attribute the supreme lordship to Him. Just as fire is different from the wood but cannot be seen without it, so we ascribe the lordship to Śiva, in and through the persons in whom He is manifested. It is by a similar extension of thought that the image of Śiva is also regarded as Śiva and is worshipped.

Śiva always helps all beings and never does harm to anyone. When it may seem apparent that he has punished somebody, it is only for the good of others. In many cases the punishment awarded by Śiva is for purging the impurities of the beings concerned. The basis of all good and evil deeds is to be found in the ordinance of God, that one must behave in this way and not in the other way. Goodness means abidance in accordance with His will. He who is engaged always in doing good to others is following the commandment of God, and he cannot be made impure. God only punishes those who could not be brought to the right path by any other course, but his punishment is never due to any spirit of anger or resentment. He is like the father who chastises the son to teach him the proper course. He who tyrannises over others deserves to be chastened. God does not injure others to cause them pain, but only to chasten them and make them fitter for the right path. He is like a doctor who gives bitter medicine for curing a malady. If God remained indifferent to the vices and sins of beings, then that would also be improper for Him, for that would be a way of encouraging people to follow the wrong path; and that also would be denying the proper protection to persons who ought to be protected and whom God is able to protect. The Lord Śiva is like fire; on contact with Him all impurities are resolved. When a piece of iron is put into fire, it is the fire that burns and not the iron; so all the inanimate objects of the world are pervaded by Śiva, the supreme Lord, and He alone shines through all the appearances.

1 *ajnānādhiṣṭhitaṃ śambhor na kiñcid iha vidyate,*
yenopalabhyate 'smābhis sakalenāpi niṣkalaḥ.
Śiva-mahāpurāṇa VII. I. 31. 9 *et seq.*

The grace of Śiva is not like the ordinary good qualities of friendship, charity, etc., but it cannot be regarded as a good or a bad quality. It means only the will of God leading to the benefit of all beings. Obedience to His commandments may be regarded as identical with the highest good, and the highest good is the same as obedience to His commandments. God, therefore, may be regarded as doing good to all and not merely to one individual. In this manner the individual good is associated with the good of humanity at large, and this can only be effected when all beings follow the commandments of God. The things in the world would behave in their own manners according to their specific nature. It is the function of God to make them grow in consonance with one another as far as their nature should permit. The natural character of things is an important limitation to the scope of this development. One can only melt gold by fire, but not charcoal, so God can only liberate those whose impurities have been purged, but not those who are still in an impure condition. Things which naturally can evolve into some other thing can be made to do so by the will of God. So God's will is only effective when it acts in co-operation with the natural tendency and the effective limits of the things. The individual souls are naturally full of impurities, and it is for that reason that they pass through the cycle of birth and rebirth. The association of the souls with *karma* and illusion is really what is called *saṃsāra*, the passage through the cycle of birth and rebirth. Since Śiva is not associated with any such *karma* and is absolutely pure, He can be the real agent for the motivation for the development of the animate and inanimate world. The impurity of the soul is natural to the soul and not accidental.

In the theory of the classical Sāṃkhya as represented in the *kārikā* of Īśvarakriṣṇa or the *Sāṃkhya-sūtra*, the teleology is made to abide in the *prakṛti*, which out of its own necessity impels the *prakṛti* to evolve in the twofold scheme of the psychical and the physical world for serving the *puruṣas* in twofold ways of the experience of pleasure and pain, and the attainment of liberation through knowledge. In this sense *prakṛti* is supposed to move for the fulfilment of the purpose of the *puruṣas*. In the Pātañjala school of Sāṃkhya, called also the *Yoga-sūtra* as explained by Vyāsa and Vācaspati, the *guṇas* forming the *prakṛti* have a natural obstruction which limits their scope of development. It is admitted that there is the permanent will of God, that things would evolve in particular directions in accordance with the *karma* of the individuals. The energy of the *prakṛti* or the *guṇas* flows naturally in the direction from which the obstruction has been removed. God does not of Himself push the *prakṛti* to move in a particular direction. The function lies in the removal of obstructions in the way of the development in particular channels. Had there been no such obstruction or if all obstructions were removed, then every thing could have become every other thing. There would be no definite order of evolution and no limitation to various conditions and by time and place. In the system that we are now dealing with the natural obstructions of individuals are frankly admitted as being due to the existence of impurities, and it is held that by the all-pervading nature of God the souls can be emancipated only when the natural obstructions are washed off. For this purpose the individual persons have to exert themselves and through the near proximity of God, the process of pacification is held; this is called the grace of God, not grace in the ordinary sense of the term, but a cosmic operation which helps all things and persons to develop in accordance with their respective deserts. The commandment of God is not like the commandment of a Mosaic god, but it simply means the carrying on of the cosmic process for the good of all. In the carrying out of this process some people must suffer for their own good and some people may attain rewards according to their merits. God Himself transcends all the appearances of the world; He does not actually exert His will to effect anything, but the very fact that all things are pervaded by Him produces the removal of such impurities as are consistent with the development of the cosmos as a whole.

Though the soul is the same, yet some of the souls are in bondage, as also, there are others who are in a state of liberation. Those who are in bondage may also be in different conditions of progress and may have accordingly different kinds of knowledge and power. The impurities associated with the soul may be regarded as green (*āma*) and ripe (*pakva*), and in these two forms they are responsible for the commission of all actions leading to birth and rebirth. But even though all souls are associated with *mala* or impurities, they are pervaded in and through by Śiva; and as the *malas* are purged, the proximity of Śiva becomes more manifest, and the individual becomes more and more pure, until he becomes like Śiva. The differences of the souls are only due to the conditioning factor of the *mala*. It is in accordance with the nature and condition of the *mala* that one soul appears to be different from the other. The root cause for all the suffering in the world is the impurities, and it is the function of the divine doctor, Śiva, to lead us through knowledge far away from the impurities. Knowledge alone is a means by which all sins may be removed. It may be objected that, since God is all-powerful He could liberate human beings without making them undergo suffering. To this question it is suggested in reply that misery and suffering constitute the nature of the *saṃsāra* of birth and rebirth. It has already been stated before that God's omnipotence is somehow limited by the natural conditions of the materials on which the will of God operates. The nature of the *malas* or the impurities being of the nature of sorrow and pain, it is not possible to make them painless, and for this reason, in the period in which one passes through the process of the expurgation of *malas* through *saṃsāra*, one must necessarily suffer pain. The individual souls are by nature impure and sorrowful, and it is by the administration of the order which acts as medicine, that these individuals are liberated. The cause of all impurities that generate the *saṃsāra* is the *māyā* and the material world, and these would not be set in motion in any way without the proximity of Śiva. Just as iron filings are set in motion by the presence of a magnet without the magnet's doing anything by itself, so it is by the immediate proximity of God that the world process is set in motion for its benefit. Even though God is transcendent and does not know the world, the fact of His proximity cannot be ruled out. So He remains the superintending cause of the world. All movement in the world is due to Śiva. The power by which He controls the world is His ordering will which is the same as His proximity. We are reminded of the analogical example introduced by Vācaspati in his commentary on the *Yogasūtra-bhāṣya*, where it is said that though the *puruṣa* does not do anything, yet its proximity produces the special fitness (*yogyatā*) on account of which the *prakṛti* moves for the fulfilment of the purposes of the *puruṣa*. The example of the magnet and the iron filings is also given in that connection. As the whole world is but a manifestation of Śiva's own power, we may quite imagine that when there was nothing in the world, He alone existed with His majestic order of will and there in the functioning of that will He was not in any way polluted by the worldly impurities.

In this connection Vāyu is supposed to say that knowledge is of two kinds, mediate (*parokṣa*) and immediate (*aparokṣa*). That which is known by reason or by instruction is called mediate knowledge. Immediate knowledge, however, can only dawn through practice of a high order, and without such immediate knowledge there cannot be any liberation.

§2

In the present section of the *Vāyavīya-saṃhitā* VII. 2, we find a modification of the philosophical view as expressed in the previous section, and this deserves some special attention. In the previous section it was stated that the impurities of the individual souls were natural to themselves, and God's will had to refashion them or remould them or purge the impurities through the cycles of birth and rebirth, in accordance with the natural limitations of the individual souls, so that though God's will operates uniformly through all, the development is not uniform. The sufferings of human beings are due to the obstacles and resistance offered by the inherent impurities of different souls. For this reason it is not possible for God to liberate all souls without making them undergo the cycles of birth and rebirth and sorrow.

The view that the souls are by nature impure is found also among the Jainas and among the followers of the Pañcarātra school[1]. In the Vedānta view, as explained in the school of Śaṅkara, the individual souls are no doubt regarded as the same as Brahman, but yet it is believed that the individual souls are associated with the beginningless nescience or *Avidyā* which can be destroyed later on by the realisation of the true nature of the Self. Thus in a way, the individual souls remain within a covering of impurity from beginningless time. But in the second section of the *Vāyavīya-saṃhitā* that we are now dealing with, it is said that God Himself binds all beings through the impurities, the *māyā* and the like,

[1] See the relevant portion of Jainism in Vol. I (pp. 169 *et seq.*) and the philosophy of Pañcarātra, especially of the *Ahirbudhnya-saṃhitā* in Vol. III (pp. 21 *et seq.* and 34 *et seq.*).

and He alone can liberate them when He is pleased to do so in accordance with the devotion of the beings concerned[1]. All the twenty-four categories of Sāṃkhya are to be regarded as being due to the action of *māyā*[2], and they are called the *viṣayas* or objects which are the bonds or ties by which the individuals are bound. By binding all beings, from the blade of a grass up to Brahman, the highest god, the great Lord makes them perform their own duties. It is by the order of the Lord that the *prakṛti* produces the *buddhi* for the service of the *puruṣas*, and from *buddhi* there arise the ego, the senses, the subtle matters (*tanmātras*), and the gross matter. It is by the same order that the different beings are associated with different bodies suitable to them. The world order is maintained in its uniform process by the will of God. This will or order of God cannot be transcended by anybody. It is in accordance with the same commandment of God as controlling all processes that one attains riches and knowledge through the performance of meritorious deeds, or that the sinners are punished. The parable of the Kena Upaniṣad is quoted to show that the powers of all deities and natural forces are derived from God. The whole world thus may be regarded as manifestations of Lord Śiva.

In different forms and functions and superintendence Lord Śiva is called by different names. Thus, when He enjoys the *prakṛti* and the *puruṣa* He is called *īśāna*. This *īśāna* appears in its eightfold form, technically called *aṣṭamūrti*; these are: earth, water, fire, air, the *ākāśa*, the soul, the sun and the moon. So these are the forms of Śiva as performing different functions and called by different names such as *śārvī*, *bhāvī*, *raudrī*, etc. *Raudrī* is the form in which the whole world is vibrating. The soul itself, as we have seen above, is a form of Śiva.

The proper worship of Śiva consists in giving protection from fear to all people, to do good to everybody, and to be of service to

[1] *mala-māyā-dibhiḥ pāśaiḥ sa badhnāti paśūn patiḥ,*
sa eva mocakas teṣāṃ bhaktyā samyag-upāsitaḥ.
Śiva-mahāpurāṇa. VII. 2. 2. 12 *et seq.*

[2] *Māyā* is twofold: the *prakṛti* and the *śuddhamāyā*. From the latter spring up the deities Brahmā, Viṣṇu and Rudra. The former is the *prakṛti* of the Sāṃkhya into which all beings return, and for that reason *prakṛti* is called *liṅga*, whereas the classical Sāṃkhya restricts the term to the *mahat* and calls *prakṛti* the *aliṅga*. There *mahat* is called *liṅga*, as it points to some original cause behind it and *prakṛti* being the ultimate cause does not point to any other original cause behind it. See *ibid.* VII. 2. 34. 7 *et seq.*

everybody. It is by satisfying all people that God becomes satisfied. Any injury done to any living being is an injury done to one of the forms of God itself.

We have seen above that the whole world is a personification of God. This pantheistic doctrine should be distinguished from the monism of the Vedānta as explained by Śaṅkara and his followers. In the Vedānta the reality is Brahman as *sac-cid-ānanda*, and everything else that we perceive is but an imposition on the reality of Brahman. They are ultimately false and their falsehood is discovered when the person attains liberation. So the world appears, but there may be a time when it may absolutely disappear before a liberated person. Here, however, the material world as such in all its various forms of the living and non-living is regarded as but different real forms of God, which are controlled by God, and are set in motion by God for the benefit of the souls, which latter again are but forms of God.

In this connection the question is raised as to the way in which God pervades the world as the male and the female powers. In reply to such a question Upamanyu is supposed to have replied that the energy or *śakti* called the great female Deity (*mahādevī*) belongs to *mahādeva*, the Great Lord, and the whole world is a manifestation of them both. Some things are of the nature of consciousness and some things are of the nature of the unconscious. Both of them can be pure or impure. When consciousness is associated with the unconscious elements, it passes through the cycles of birth and rebirth and is called impure. That which is beyond such associations is pure. Śiva and His *śakti* go together, and the whole world is under their domination. As it is not possible to distinguish the moon from the moonlight, so it is not possible to distinguish the *śakti* from Śiva. So the *śakti* or the power of the *śaktimān*, the possessor of the power, the supreme Lord, are mutually dependent. There cannot be *śakti* without Śiva, and there cannot be Śiva without *śakti*. It is out of this *śakti* that the whole world is created through the process of *prakṛti* or *māyā* and the three *guṇas*. Everywhere the operation of the *śakti* is limited by the will of Śiva and ultimately this goes back into Śiva. From the original *śakti* as inherent in Śiva, there emanates the 'active energy' (*kriyākhyā śakti*). By the disturbance of the original equilibrium there arises *nāda*, and from that arises *bindu*, and from *bindu* arises *sadāśiva*, and from *sadāśiva* arises Maheśvara, and from him arises true knowledge (*śuddha-vidyā*), and this is called the logos or the power of speech. This also manifests itself in the form of the alphabetical sounds. From this manifestation of *māyā* comes *kāla* or time, *niyati*, *kalā* and *vidyā*. From this *māyā* again come out the three *guṇas* constituting the unmanifested (*avyakta*). From the *avyakta* there evolve the categories as described in the Sāṃkhya. In brief it may be said that as the body is permeated by the inner controller, so the whole world is permeated by Śiva in His form as *śakti*. For this reason all the living and the non-living are but manifestations of the *śakti*. It is the supreme Lord that is associated with knowledge, activity and will, and through them all the supreme Lord controls and pervades the world. The order of the world and the world process is also determined by His will.

That which is imaginatively perceived by the supreme Lord is put into a fact by His will; so, just as the three *guṇas* arise in Him as the three manifested energies, so the whole world, which is identified with Śiva, is also the form of His energy, because it has come into being through His energy[1]. This *śakti* of Śiva is the *māyā*.

The *Śiva-mahāpurāṇa* refers to the *Śaivāgamas* as being instructions given by Śiva to Śivā. It seems, therefore, that the *Śaivāgamas* were written long before the *Śiva-mahāpurāṇa*, and it is the substance of the *Śaivāgamas* that is collected in the *Śiva-mahāpurāṇa* in the elucidation of the Pāśupata view. The instructions of the *Śaivāgamas* are supposed to have been given as the means for the attainment of the highest good through the mercy of Śiva, for the benefit of the devotees of Śiva[2].

Turning to the practical side of the attainment of direct or intuitive knowledge, we find that Śiva says that He is only properly approached through sincere faith in Him (*śraddhā*) and not by

[1] *evaṃ śakti-samāyogāc chaktimān ucyate śivaḥ,*
śakti-śaktimaduttham tu śāktaṃ śaivam idaṃ jagat.
Śiva-mahāpurāṇa VII. 2. 4. 36.

[2] *śrīkaṇṭhena śivenoktaṃ śivāyai ca śivāgamaḥ,*
śivāśritānāṃ kāruṇyāc chreyasām ekasādhanam.
Ibid. VII. 2. 7. 38 *et seq.*

It is difficult to say whether this is a reference to the Mahākāruṇika school of Śaiva thought, as referred to by Śaṅkara in the *bhāṣya* in the penultimate topic of the criticism of Śaivism. *Brahma-sūtra* II. 2.

tapas, chanting, or various postures of the body (*āsanas*), or even by instructional knowledge. Faith is the basis on which one should stand and this faith can be attained by following the natural duties of the four *varṇas* or castes and the *āśramas* or the stages of life. Faith is thus regarded not as a spontaneous emotion but as the consequence of a long traditional practice of the duties assigned to each caste and to each stage of life.

The *Śaiva dharma* consists of knowledge, action, rigid conduct, and *yoga*. The knowledge is the knowledge of the nature of souls, the objects, and the supreme Lord. Action is the purification in accordance with the instruction of the preceptor. *Caryā* or the right conduct means the proper worship of Śiva in accordance with the caste rights as instructed by Śiva. *Yoga* means the arresting of all mental states, excluding the constant thinking of God. Knowledge arises from *vairāgya* or disinclination towards worldly things, and from knowledge comes *yoga*; sense-control, called *yama*, and *niyama* remove the sins and when a man is disinclined to worldly objects he gradually turns to the path of *yoga*. In this connection, universal charity, non-injury, truthfulness, abstention from stealing, and supreme faith, teaching, performing sacrifices and meditation on one's identity with God are regarded as natural accessories. For this reason those who wish to attain liberation should keep themselves away from virtue and vice, merit and demerit. Those who have attained the state in which the stone and gold are of equal value, or have no value, need not worship God, because they are liberated beings.

Purity of mind is a hundredfold better than purity of body, because without the purity of the mind nobody can be pure. God accepts only the internal states of man (*bhāva*); that which is performed without any sincere emotion is merely an imitation. Devotion to God ought to be spontaneous, not practised for any advantage. Even when a man is attached to God for the attainment of some advantage, it may please God according to the depth of the emotion which is displayed by him. We find that the external expression of emotion as manifested in bodily movements, interest in listening to the adoration of Śiva, the choking of the voice, the shedding of tears, and the constant meditation and dependence on God, are regarded as the significant signs of a true devotee, whatever may be his caste and status in society.

We have already seen that the practical way towards liberation should be through the attainment of knowledge of the nature of souls, the objects that bind them and the supreme Lord. This knowledge should be supplemented by action in accordance with the direction of the Teacher, who in Śaiva cult is to be regarded as the incarnation of Śiva. This action called *kriyā* is to be supplemented by the prescriptive duties allotted to the different castes and stages of life in the scriptures, and the duty which consists of the worship of God goes by the name of *caryā*. This has further to be supplemented by a process of devotional meditation, with Śiva as the centre of attention, when all other mental states have been inhibited. The scriptures dealing with these subjects are twofold, one of Vedic origin, the other of independent origin. These latter are of twenty-eight kinds (like the Āgamas), called *Kāmika*, etc., which also go by the name of *Siddhānta*[1].

In VII. 1. 32 certain esoteric and obscure physiological processes are described by which one can bring oneself in contact with immortality as inherent in Śiva, the Mahādeva[2].

In VII. 2. 37 the *yoga* is described as being of five kinds: *mantrayoga*, *sparśayoga*, *bhāvayoga*, *abhāvayoga* and *mahāyoga*. The *mantrayoga* is that in which by constant repetition of certain *mantras* the mental states becomes steady. When this is associated with breath control it is called *sparśayoga*. When this state is further on the progressive scale and becomes dissociated from the necessity of chanting the *mantras*, it is called the *bhāvayoga*. By further advancement of this *yoga* process, the world appearance in its various forms entirely disappears, and this is called the *abhāvayoga*. At this stage the yogin is not concerned with the world. He

[1] H. W. Schomerus in his *Śaiva-siddhānta*, p. 3, says that there are six and sixteen schools of Śaivism, according to a commentary on *Śiva-jñāna-bodha* which we shall refer to later on. These schools as referred to by Schomerus are:

I. Pāśupata, Māvratavāda (?), Kāpālika, Vāma, Bhairava and Aikyavāda.

II. Ūrdhvaśaiva, Anādiśaiva, Ādiśaiva, Mahāśaiva, Bhedaśaiva, Abhedaśaiva, Antaraśaiva, Guṇaśaiva, Nirguṇaśaiva, Adhvanśaiva, Yogaśaiva, Jñānaśaiva, Anuśaiva, Kriyāśaiva, Nālupādaśaiva (?) and Śuddhaśaiva.

We do not know what were the contents of these different schools of Śaivism and we cannot also identify any particular texts giving the views of any of these schools of Śaivism. In our treatment we have noted different types of Śaivism, and many of them go by the name of Pāśupata-Śaivism, but whether this Pāśupata-Śaivism was also divided into different schools having different names, it is impossible for us to judge for want of definite materials, either published or unpublished.

[2] See verses 45–56 (VII. 1. 32).

thinks of himself as being of the nature of Śiva, and of being one with Him, and he is dissociated from all conditions. This is called the state of *mahāyoga*. At this stage one becomes disinclined to all worldly objects of attachment, whether as experiences by the senses or as prescribed by the scriptures. Of course, this practice of *yoga* includes the practices of *yama* and *niyama* as prescribed in the *Yoga-sūtras*, and also the practice of the different postures, the breath-control (*prāṇāyāma*), the holding back of the mind from other objects (*pratyāhāra*), the practice of concentration on particular objects (*dhāraṇā*), and also meditation (*dhyāna*), and becoming one with the object (*samādhi*). The processes of the different kinds of *yoga* and their accessories are described in the Śaiva scriptures, and also in the *Kāmika* and the other Āgamas. So far as the *Śiva-mahāpurāṇa* is concerned we do not find much difference between the practices of the different accessories such as *yama*, and *niyama*, *āsana*, etc., and those that are described in the *Yogaśāstra* of Patañjali. The only important difference is that, while in Patañjali's *yoga* the mind has to be concentrated first on the gross objects, then on the subtle entities or *tanmātras*, then on the *ahaṅkāra* or egohood, and then on *buddhi*, here in the Śaiva *yoga*, the yogin has to meditate on the divine nature of Śiva. In the *Yogaśāstra* also it is prescribed that one may meditate upon Īśvara, and it is through devotion to him that liberation may be granted to any yogin. The treatment of a yogin in *Yogośāstra* may take a twofold course: one meditation on Īśvara, the other the ascending scale of meditation on subtler and subtler categories, as a result of which the mind becomes absolutely shorn of all primitive tendencies and impressions, and becomes ultimately lost in the *prakṛti* itself, never to return again. The *Yoga* of Patañjali, therefore, seems to be a double synthesis of associating the Sāṃkhya doctrine and Sāṃkhya metaphysics with the pre-existent system of *yoga*-practice which we find in Buddhism, and the association of the theistic cult of Īśvara, who hangs rather loosely with the *yoga* system.

The *Śiva-mahāpurāṇa* goes on with the description of *prāṇāyāma*, consisting of: *pūraka*, the filling of the body with air through the nose; *recaka*, the expelling of the air out of the body; and *kumbhaka*, the process of keeping the body still after inflating it. By the processes of *prāṇāyāma* one may leave the body at will.

The advancement of *prāṇāyāma* is made gradually by lengthening the respiratory and inhibitory time. In this way there are four different classes of *prāṇāyāma* called *kanyaka*, *madhyama*, *uttama*, and *para*. That which is associated with the emotional expression of sweating, shivering, etc., is due to the expression of the sentiment of bliss on account of which tears flow spontaneously and there is sometimes incoherent speech, swooning. It should be noted that such states do not occur nor are recommended in the *yoga* of Patañjali. In this connection the discussion about *prāṇāyāma* is introduced and we hear of the five vāyus or bio-motor forces called *prāṇa*, *apāna*, *samāna*, *udāna*, and *vyāna*. The *prāṇavāyu* consists of five other types of *vāyu*, namely *nāga*, *kūrma*, *kṛkara*, *devadatta*, and *dhanañjaya* which performs the different functions of the *prāṇavāyu*. The *apānavāyu* is the bio-motor force by which all that is taken in by way of food and drink is assimilated and drawn down to the lower cavities. The *vyāna* is the bio-motor force that pervades the whole body and develops it. The *udāna* is that which affects the vital glands and the body. The *samāna* is that which provides the circulation through the body. When the functions and the forces of these *vāyus* are properly co-ordinated in accordance with the will of the yogin, he is able to burn up all the defects and maladies of the body and preserve his health in the proper manner, his power of assimilation becomes greater and his exertions become less. He becomes light in body, can move about quickly, and has energy and excellence of voice. He suffers from no diseases and has sufficient strength and vigour. He has power of retention, memory, usefulness, steadiness, and contentedness. He can perform asceticism and destroy his sins and perform sacrifice and make gifts as people should.

Pratyāhāra is effort of mind, by which the mind controls itself in relation to the objects to which the senses may be attracted. One who desires happiness should practise the virtue of disinclination and also try to attain true knowledge. It is by controlling one's senses that one can raise oneself up. When in this way the mind can be steadily attached to some object we have the state of *dhāraṇā*. This object to which the mind should be steadily attached is nothing but Śiva. In the proper state of *dhāranā* the mind should not be dissociated even for a moment from its object, Śiva. It is from the steadiness of the mind that *dhāraṇā* can proceed. So by continuous practice of *dhāraṇā* the mind should be made constant and steady. The word '*dhyāna*' is derived from the root *dhyai* denoting the thinking of Śiva with an undisturbed mind. Therefore this state is called *dhyāna*. When a person is in the state of *dhyāna*, the object of his meditation is constantly repeated in the same form without the association of any other idea. This constant flow of the same sort of image or idea is called *dhyāna*[1]. It is remembered that one should perform *tapa* or chanting the name or the *mantras* and pass into *dhyāna*, and when *dhyāna* is broken one should go on with *tapa* and from that again to *dhyāna*, and so on until the *yoga* is firmly attained. *Samādhi* is regarded as the last state of *yoga* in which the mind is illuminated with intuitive wisdom (*prajñāloka*). It is a state which itself seems to be nothing in essence and where the object alone shines like a limitless, waveless ocean[2]. After fixing the mind on the object of meditation, the saint looks like a fire which is being extinguished, he does not hear nor smell nor see nor touch anything, nor does his mind think. He does not understand anything, he is like a piece of wood. So when one's soul becomes lost in Śiva one is said to be in the state of *samādhi*. It is like a lamp that burns in a steady flame. From this state of *samādhi* the saint never breaks off.

It must, however, be noted that in the course of the practice of this *yoga* many obstacles come in, and they have to be conquered. Some of these are indolence, troublesome diseases, carelessness, doubt as to the proper object of meditation, inconstancy of mind, absence of faith, illusory notions, pain, melancholia, attachment to objects. Indolence refers both to bodily and mental laziness. The diseases, of course, come through the disturbances of the three *dhātus*—*vāyu*, *pitta*, and *kapha*. Carelessness (*pramāda*) comes through the non-utilisation of the means of performing the *yoga*. A doubtful inquiry as to what may be the true object of meditation is called *sthāna-samasyā*. Absence of faith means the

1 *dhyeyāvasthita-cittasya sadṛśaḥ pratyayaś ca yaḥ,*
pratyayāntara-nirmuktaḥ pravāho dhyānam ucyate,
sarvam anyat parityajya śiva eva śivaṅkaraḥ.
Siva-mahāpurāṇa VII. 2. 37. 52–3.

2 *samādhinā ca sarvatra prajñālokaḥ pravartate,*
yad-artha-mātra-nirbhāsaṃ stimitodadhi-vat-sthitaṃ,
svarūpa-śūnyavad bhānaṃ samādhir abhidhīyate.
Ibid. VII. 2. 37. 61–2.

continuance of the *yoga* process without the proper emotion. All sorrow comes through false knowledge. These sorrows are divided into three classes, in accordance with the classical Sāṃkhya classification, as *ādhyātmika*, *ādhibhautika*, and *ādhidaivika*. Disappointment is the frustration of one's desires, and causes mental troubles which are called *daurmanasya*. When the mind is drawn to various objects of desire it is said to be in a state of flirtation. When these obstacles are overcome then come other obstacles in the way of the appearance of miraculous powers.

The word '*yoga*' in the *Pāśupata-yoga* is used as a derivative from the root '*yujir yoge*,' and not from '*yuj samādhau*,' as we find the word used in Patañjali's *Yoga*. The true *yoga* can only arise by the proper integrative knowledge of the meditation, the object of meditation, and the purpose of meditation. In meditating on Śiva one should also meditate upon the energy of Śiva, as the whole world is pervaded by them both.

Among the miraculous powers which are regarded as obstacles in the progressive path of *yoga* one counts *pratibhā*, which means the power of knowing subtle things, things that are passed, and things that are obscure from our eyes, and things that are to come in future. In the *Nyāya-mañjarī* Jayanta mentions the word *pratibhā* in an entirely different sense. He means by *pratibhā* there an inexplicable intuition as to what may occur in the future, for example, "tomorrow my brother will come." It also includes the power of understanding all kinds of sound without effort, all that may be communicated by any animal in the world, and also the power of having heavenly visions. So by these miraculous powers one may taste heavenly delights and exquisite pleasures of touch and smell of a higher order. So one may attain all kinds of miraculous powers, and one has a full command of all things that one may wish to have. It is unnecessary for us to dilate further on the various types of miraculous powers which the yogin may attain, and which may detract him from his onward path toward attaining the *mahāyoga* or the highest *yoga*, that is, the union with Śiva.

But it is interesting to notice that the same chapter on the *Pāśupata-yoga* introduces certain methods which are not to be found in Patañjali's *Yoga*. Thus in VII. 2. 38, in a description of a particular posture of *yoga*, one is advised to fix one's attention on the tip of the nose and not to look at one side or the other. One sits down unmoved, like a piece of stone, and tries to think of Śiva and Śakti within oneself, as if they were installed in the seat of the heart, and meditates on them. One may also concentrate on one's navel, throat, palatal cavity and the spot between the eyebrows. One should think of a lotus having two, six, ten, twelve or sixteen petals, or a sort of quadrangle wherein one may place the Śiva. The lotus in the spot between the eyebrows consists of two petals which are as bright as lightning. So in the case of other lotuses having a number of petals the vowels are associated with each of the petals from the bottom upwards. The consonants beginning with *ka* and ending in *ṭa* may also be regarded as being associated with the lotus, and should be meditated upon. In rather an obscure manner the different consonants are supposed to be associated with the different petals of the imaginary lotuses, and one should steadily meditate upon Śiva and *Śakti* as associated with the letters of the petals.

In order to proceed on the path of *yoga* it may be necessary to meditate upon some of the recognised images of Śiva, such as the different gross images of Śiva mentioned in the Śaiva scriptures.

Meditation should at first commence with an object, and later on it becomes objectless. But the learned people always discard the state of meditation in which there is no object, and it is said that *dhyāna* consists in the stretching out of an intellectual state[1]. For this reason, in the state of *dhyāna* it is the mere *buddhi*, or the intellectual state that flows on, which may often be regarded as having no object. So what is called an objectless (*nirviṣaya*) *dhyāna* is only meditation on subtle entities. It is also often said that when meditation is upon some particular form of Śiva it is called *saviṣaya*, and when this is in a formless state as an extension of the knowledge of self, it is called *nirviṣaya*, This *saviṣaya dhyāna* is also called *sabīja*, and the *nirviṣaya dhyāna* is called *nirbīja*. As a result of *prāṇāyāma* and meditation, the mind becomes transparent, and then thoughts of Śiva continually recur. As we have said above, *dhyāna* means nothing more than the constant flow of an intellectual state (*buddhi*) of the form of Śiva. It is this continuous flow of

1 *tatra nirviṣayaṃ dhyānaṃ nāstīty eva satāṃ matam,*
buddher hi santatiḥ kācid dhyānam ity abhidhīyate.
Śiva-mahāpurāṇa VII. 2. 39. 5.

an intellectual state that is regarded as an object of *dhyāna*[1]. Both happiness and liberation come from *dhyāna*; for this reason, one should always try to practise *dhyāna*. There is nothing greater than *dhyāna*[2]. Those who perform *dhyāna* are dear to Śiva, not those who only perform the rituals.

[1] *buddhi-pravāha-rūpasya dhyānasyāsyāvalambanam,*
dhyeyam ity ucyate sadbhis tacca sāmbaḥ svayaṃ śivaḥ.
Śiva-mahāpurāṇa VII. 2. 39. 19.

[2] *nāsti dhyāna-samaṃ tīrthaṃ nāsti dhyānasamaṃ tapaḥ,*
nāsti dhyānasamo yajñas tasmād dhyānaṃ samācaret.
Ibid. VII. 2. 39. 28.

CHAPTER XXXVIII

ŚAIVA PHILOSOPHY IN SOME OF THE IMPORTANT TEXTS

The Doctrine of the *Pāśupata-sūtras*.

SOME of the philosophical doctrines of the Pāśupata system of Śaivism are discussed in the relevant sections. But the formal and ritualistic sides of the system, which have often been referred to elsewhere, as for example in the treatment of Śaivism in the *Sarva-darśana-saṃgraha*, need an authoritative explanation. This is found in the *Pāśupata-sūtras* with the *bhāṣya* of Kauṇḍinya, published in 1940 by the Oriental Manuscripts Library of the University of Travancore, Trivandrum. It is said that Śiva incarnated Himself as Nakulīśa and so was the author of the *Pāśupata-sūtras*. The *bhāṣya* by Kauṇḍinya is also an ancient one, as may be judged from the style of the writing. The editor of the *Pāśupata-sūtras*, A. Śāstri, thinks that Kauṇḍinya may have lived between the fourth and sixth centuries. The *Pāśupata-sūtras* together with the *bhāṣya* of Kauṇḍinya do not give us any philosophy of Śaivism. They deal almost wholly with the rituals, or rather modes of life. It may be quite possible that such ascetic forms of life existed from early times, and that later the philosophy of Śaivism was added. Though these ascetic forms of life had but little connection with the Śaiva philosophy as propounded later, they have a general anthropological and religious interest, as these forms of asceticism remain connected with the life of those who believe in the Śaiva philosophy. In the *Sarva-darśana-saṃgraha* of Mādhava the Pāśupata system is not identified with any form of philosophy, but with different kinds of ascetic practices. When Śaṅkara refutes the Śaiva system, he does not specifically mention any philosophical doctrines of an elaborate nature. He only brands the Śaivas as those who believe in God as the creator of the world (*īśvara-kāraṇin*). Of course, the Naiyāyika is also an *īśvara-kāraṇin* and he is also a Śaiva by faith. The other doctrines of the Naiyāyika are largely taken from the Vaiśeṣika, and Śaṅkara in his joint criticism of Nyāya and Vaiśeṣika had referred to them. The Naiyāyika thus shares his theistic conviction with the Śaivas. But while the Śaivas of the Pāśupata school lay emphasis on ascetic rituals, the Naiyāyika laid stress on logical arguments. It will therefore not be out of place if we treat the general outline of the Pāśupata sect on its ascetic side, though it may not be regarded as a contribution of philosophical value.

Kauṇḍinya, the commentator, in the beginning of his *bhāṣya*, offers adoration to Pāśupati who had created the whole world, beginning from the Brahman for the good of all. He says that the five subjects of discussion in the Pāśupata system are effect (*kārya*), cause (*kāraṇa*), meditation (*yoga*), behaviour (*vidhi*), and dissolution of sorrow (*duḥkhānta*)[1].

The teaching of the Pāśupata system is for the total annihilation of all kinds of sorrow and this teaching can only be communicated to proper disciples. When the disciple follows the ascetic practices recommended by the Lord, he attains liberation through His grace. It has been noticed before that the Śaiva is called Mahākāruṇika. In our exposition of the Śaiva thought we have examined carefully the doctrine of grace or *karuṇā*, and have also seen how this doctrine of grace is associated with the doctrine of *karma* and the theory of rebirth, in accordance with the justice implied in the theory of *karma*. But here in the *Pāśupata-sūtra* we are told that liberation comes directly from the grace of Śiva. The word *paśu* means all conscious beings, excluding the saints and the all powerful ones. Their animality or *paśutva* consists in the fact that they are impotent and their impotence is their bondage. This bondage, which means their complete dependence on the causal power, is beginningless. The word *paśu* is connected with the word *pāśa*, which means "cause and effect", and is technically also called *kalā*. All animals are thus bound by cause and effect, the sense images and their objects, and become attached to them. The word *paśu* is also derived from *paśyati*. Though the animals are all-pervasive and are of the nature of pure consciousness, they can only perceive

[1] The editor of the *Pāśupata-sūtras* gives the following list of the succession of teachers from Nakulīśa: Nakulīśa, Kauśika, Gārgya, Maitreya, Kauruṣa, Īśāna, Paragārgya, Kapilāṇḍa, Manuṣyaka, Kuśika, Atri, Piṅgala, Puṣpaka, Bṛhadārya, Agasti, Santāna, Rāśīkara (Kauṇḍinya), and Vidyāguru. The seventeenth *guru* called Rāśīkara has been identified with Kauṇḍinya by the editor. This has been done on the supposition that Kauṇḍinya occurs as the *gotra* name in the Bṛhadāraṇyaka Upaniṣad VI. 2 and 4.

their bodies; they do not understand the nature of cause and effect and they cannot go beyond them. The Pāśupati is so called because He protects all beings. Kauṇḍinya definitely says that the liberation from sorrow cannot be attained by knowledge (*jñāna*), disinclination (*vairāgya*), virtue (*dharma*) and giving up of one's miraculous powers (*aiśvarya-tyāga*), but by grace (*prasāda*) alone[1].

The person who is regarded as fit for receiving the Śaiva discipline must be a Brahmin with keen senses. The instruction of the teacher, leading to devotional practices and exciting desire for becoming Śiva, is given out of a spirit of charity to those who wish to annihilate all sorrow.

The word '*yoga*' is used to denote the contact of the self with *īśvara* or God (*ātmeśvara-saṃyogo yogaḥ*). The contact thus means that the person who was otherwise engaged leads himself to the supreme object of *īśvara*; or it may also mean that the contact is due to the dual approach of both God and the person, until they meet. The *yoga* must have disinclination to worldly things as the first condition.

Yoga cannot be attained by mere knowledge but one has to take to a certain course of action called *yoga-vidhi*. *Vidhi* means action. Thus we have the effect (*kārya*) which is the dissolution of pleasure and pain, the cause, the *yoga* and the *vidhi*, and these are the five categories which form the subject-matter of discussion of the *Pāśupata-śāstra*.

Describing the two kinds of perceptual knowledge Kauṇḍinya distinguishes between sense perception and self-perception. By the senses one can perceive various kinds of sense objects, such as sound, touch, colour, taste, smell and the objects to which they belong. In reality, most perceptions occur through sense-object contact, and are manifested in their totality in diverse aspects through such a contact, and are regarded as valid (*pramāṇa*). Self-perception means the totality of the relation that is produced by *citta* and *antaḥkaraṇa*, the mind and the thought. Inference (*anumāna*) is naturally based upon perception. The relationship between the thought, the mind, and the self expresses itself in diverse forms and produces diverse impressions and memories.

[1] *tasmāt prasādāt sa duḥkhāntaḥ prāpyate. na tu jñāna-vairāgya-dharma-iśvarya-tyāga-mātrād ity arthaḥ. Pāśupata-sūtras* (commentary, p. 6).

And these lead to other kinds of awareness, or those which can be inferred from them.

Inference is of two kinds, *dṛṣṭa* (perceived) and *sāmānyato dṛṣṭa* (perceived through universals). The first again is of two kinds, called *pūrvavat* and *śeṣavat*. *Pūrvavat* is that which is affiliated with a previous experience. It has been seen to have six fingers, and now we find it of six fingers; therefore it is the same as the previous one. When an animal is recognised as a cow on the evidence of its horns and the hanging neck, this is said to be an inference of the type of *śeṣavat*. The *śeṣavat* inference is intended to distinguish a class of things from others. As an example of *sāmānyato dṛṣṭa* (perceived through universals), it is said that as the location at different places of the same object cannot take place, one can infer that the moon and the stars which change places are travelling in the sky. Āgama or testimony is the scriptural testimony that is handed down to us from Maheśvara through His disciples. The *Pāśupata-śāstra* only admits perception, inference, and testimony; all other kinds of *pramāṇas* are regarded as falling within them.

It is the individual perceiver to whom things are proved by means of the *pramāṇas*. The object of the *pramāṇas* are the fivefold categories, namely *kārya*, *kāraṇa*, *yoga*, *vidhi*, and the dissolution of sorrow. Awareness or thought product is called *saṃvid*, *saṃcintana*, or *sambodha*. It is through these that knowledge is revealed. The process of knowledge continues from the first moment of inception to the completion of the knowledge.

Turning to the practices, it is said that one should collect ashes and bake them, and then smear the body in the morning, midday, and afternoon with these ashes. The real bathing is of course through the attainment of virtue by which the soul is purified. One should also lie down on the ashes and remain awake, for the person who is afraid of the cycles of birth and rebirth cannot have time to sleep. The ashes are to be used for bathing instead of water, both for purification and for bearing the signs of a Śaiva. The ashes (*bhasman*) are therefore called *liṅga*, or sign of a Pāśupata ascetic. We must note here that the word *liṅga*, which is often used in connection with the Śaiva doctrine for a phallic sign, is here regarded as a mere indicatory sign of a person's being a Pāśupata ascetic. The ashes which besmear the body are indicators of the person being a Pāśupata ascetic. The *bhasman* therefore is regarded as *liṅga*. These ashes distinguish the Pāśupata ascetic from the adherents of other sects.

The Pāśupata ascetic may live in the village, in the forest, or in any place of pilgrimage, and there he may employ himself in muttering the syllable *oṃ*, laughing, singing, dancing, and making peculiar sounds through his mouth and lips.

In introducing moral virtues, great emphasis is laid on the *yamas* consisting of non-injury, celibacy, truthfulness, and non-stealing. Next to these are the *niyamas* consisting of non-irritability (*akrodha*), attendance on the teachers, purity, lightness of diet, and carefulness (*apramāda*). Of these two *yama* and *niyama*, *yama* is regarded as being most important. Non-injury in the fashion of the Jainas is highly emphasised, and is regarded as the best of all virtues. We have translated *brahma-carya* by celibacy, but in reality it means all kinds of sense control, particularly the palate and the sex organs; association with women is strongly deprecated. Though verbal truth implying agreement of statements to facts is appreciated, it is held that the final standard of truth is the amount of good that is rendered to people by one's words. Even a misstatement or a false statement, if beneficial to all beings, should be regarded as preferable to a rigorous truthful statement. It is interesting to note that the Pāśupata system forbids all kinds of commercial dealings and trades, as they may cause pain to persons involved in mutual intercourse. Absence of anger (*akrodha*) has been enumerated above as a virtue. This includes both mental apathy consisting of jealousy, enmity, vanity and desire for the evil of others in one's own mind, as well as any action that may be committed in accordance with them. The Pāśupata ascetic has to earn his living by mendicancy alone.

It has been said above that the Pāśupata ascetic should be a Brahmin. It is prohibited for him to address women or Śūdras, except under special circumstances. Under such exceptional circumstances one should purify oneself by bathing in ashes and also *prāṇāyāma*, and the muttering of the *raudrī gāyatrī*. This prescription of practising *prāṇāyāma*, etc., in case one has to meet a woman or a Śūdra and to talk to them, is suggested for purifying the mind of the ascetic, for otherwise on being forced to meet them the ascetic may get angry in his mind, and that may cause injury to his own mind.

When the mind is purified, and one proceeds on the line of *yoga* with the Maheśvara, the supreme Lord, one attains various miraculous powers[1].

The Maheśvara, regarded also as Brahman, is beginningless and indestructible; He is unborn and without any kind of attachment. When one knows the nature of the Lord, one should take refuge in Him and follow the practices described by Him in His scriptures.

The supreme Lord is regarded as producing and destroying all things out of His nature as a playful being. The Lord is supreme as he controls the movements and tendencies of all beings. His eternity consists in his continual knowledge and action, by which he pervades all. He is called Rudra because he is associated with fear on the part of all[2].

The supreme Lord, being in Himself, creates, maintains and destroys the universe, that is, in Him the universe appears and dissolves like the stars in the sky. God creates the world at His will, as the world of effects exists in His own power and energy, and remains also by virtue of His power.

In explaining the position further, it is said in the *bhāṣya* (II. 5) that the category of Maheśvara is the all-pervasive one, and that the twenty-five categories like *puruṣa*, *pradhāna*, etc., are permeated by the supreme category. So also the category of the *puruṣa*, being the category of the self, is the all-pervading one, and the twenty-four categories of *pradhāna*, etc., are permeated by *puruṣa*. So also in the field of the categories, the *buddhi* is all-pervasive and the twenty-two other categories, beginning with *ahaṅkāra*, are permeated by *buddhi*. So also the *ahaṅkāra* is all-pervasive and the eleven senses are permeated by it; so again the eleven senses are the all-pervasive ones and the subtle five *tanmātras* are permeated by them. So also in the case of gross matter, where the same processes may be assigned to *ākāśa*, *vāyu*, *tejas*, etc.

The question is raised as regards the starting-point of difference between the cause and the effect. The writer of the *bhāṣya* (II. 5) says that it has to be understood on the analogy of a mixture of

[1] See *Pāśupata-sūtras* I. 21–37.

[2] *rutasya bhayasya drāvaṇāt saṃyojanād rudraḥ.*
Pāśupata-sūtras II. 4 (commentary).

turmeric and water; in turmeric water you have on the one hand the qualities of water, and on the other the qualities of turmeric. So when the supreme Lord is considered as being associated with the pleasures and pains that He gives to all beings, and the bodies with which He associates them, we may have a conception of a whole. So God can be associated with pleasures and pains that belong to the *prakṛti*, though He himself is absolutely unchangeable. The same analogy may explain the other categories of *pradhāna* and *prakṛti*. Being all-pervasive, the supreme Lord naturally pervades both the causal and the efficient states. The effect as identified in the cause is eternal; the cause, the Lord, is eternal, and all creation takes place in and through Him. Arguing in this way the world becomes eternal, for if the protector is eternal, the things to be protected must also be eternal. The world being eternal, the supreme Lord only connects the relevant parts of it in a relevant order. The grace of God consists in bringing about the proper association of the relevant parts.

God's will being all powerful and unlimited, He can create changes in the world and in the destinies of men according to His own pleasure. He does not necessarily depend upon the person or his *karma* or action[1]. God's will may operate either as the evolutionary process or as an interference with the state of things by inducing bondage or liberation. There is, however, a limit to the exercise of God's will in that the liberated souls are not associated with sorrow again. The limit of the effect world is that it is produced, helped and dissolved or changed by the causal category, the supreme Lord. This, therefore, is the sphere of cause and effect. Those who want the cessation of all sorrows should devote themselves to the worship of the Lord Śiva and to no one else.

It is advised that the Pāśupata ascetic should not be too much delighted on the attainment of miraculous powers. He should go on behaving like a Pāśupata ascetic, smearing his body with ashes and smiling and so on, both in places of pilgrimage and temples, and also among people in general. These are called *caryā*. In this *caryā* the joy of the ascetic should be manifested in its pure form

[1] *karma-kāminaś ca maheśvaram apekṣante, na tu bhagavān īśvaraḥ karma puruṣaṃ vā'pekṣate. ato na karmāpekṣa īśvaraḥ. Pāśupata-sūtras* II. 6 (commentary).

and not associated with any form of vanity which goes with the attainment of miraculous powers.

The process of spiritual worship can only be done through the surrendering of oneself in one's mind to the supreme Lord, and to continue to do it until the goal is reached. When one gives oneself up entirely to Śiva alone, he does not return from the state of liberation. This is the secret of self-surrender[1].

The supreme Lord, called Vāmadeva, *jyeṣṭha*, Rudra, is also called Kāla. It is within the scope of His function to associate the different beings in different kinds of bodies and in different states of existence, with different kinds of experiences, pleasurable and painful, through the process of time. The individual beings are called *kālya* as they happen to be in God or Kāla. The term *kalā* is given to the effects (*kālya*) and their instruments (*kāraṇa*). Thus, the five elements, earth, water, etc., are called *kalā* as *kārya* or effect. So also are their properties. The eleven senses together with *ahaṅkāra* and *buddhi* are called *kāraṇa*. God Himself is *vikaraṇa* or without any senses, so there is nothing to obstruct His powers of perception and action. It is God who associates all things and beings with the different *kalās* as *kālya* and *kāraṇa*. The supreme Lord is regarded as *sakala* and *niṣkala*, immanent and transcendent, but even in His transcendental aspect He has in Him all the powers by which He can extend His grace to all beings.

In the third chapter it is said that the real Śaiva ascetic may dispense with all the external practices, so that no one will recognise him as a Śaiva ascetic, and will not give him a high place in society. When the Śaiva ascetic is thus ignored by the people among whom he lives, this very degradation of him serves to remove his sins. When the ascetic bears the insults showered upon him by ignorant persons, he naturally attains fortitude. People may often abuse him as a lunatic, an ignorant man, or a dullard, etc., and in such circumstances he should get away from the public attention and fix his mind on God. With such behaviour he is not only purified but is spiritually ennobled. When a person thus moves about like a poor lunatic, besmeared with ashes and dirt, with

[1] *aikāntikātyantika-rudra-samīpa-prapter ekāntenaiva anāvṛtti-phalatvād asā-dhāraṇa-phalatvāc cātma-pradānam atidānam. Ibid.* II. 15 (commentary).

beard and nails and hair uncut, and when he does not follow habits of cleanliness, he is naturally regarded as an outcast. This leads him further on the path towards disinclination, and the insults he bears meekly make him advanced spiritually.

When a person is firm in *yama* and *niyama* practices, and meekly suffers the indignities and abuses showered on him by other people, he is well established in the path of asceticism.

Throughout the whole of the fourth chapter of the *Pāśupata-sūtras* the *pāśupata-vrata* is described as a course of conduct in which the ascetic behaves or should behave as a lunatic, ignorant, epileptic, dull, a man of bad character, and the like, so that abuses may be heaped on him by the unknowing public. This will enliven his disinclination to all worldly fame, honours, and the like, and the fact the people had unknowingly abused him would raise him in the path of virtue. When by such a course of action and by *yoga* one attains the proximity of the great Lord, one never returns again. India is supposed to have performed the *pāśupata-vrata* in the earliest time.

In the fifth chapter the process of *pāśupata-yoga* is more elaborately discussed. The supreme Lord is referred to by many names, but they all refer to the same being, the supreme Lord, and *yoga* means a steady union of the soul with Him. For this purpose the person should be completely detached from all objects, present, past and future, and be emotionally attached to Maheśvara[1]. The union of the self with Śiva must be so intimate that no physical sounds and disturbances should lead the person away. In the first stages the attachment with Śiva takes place by the withdrawal of the mind from other objects, and making it settle on the Lord; then the association becomes continuous.

The soul or the Ātman is defined as the being that is responsible for all sense cognitions, all actions, and all attachments to objects. The constant or continuous contact of the self with the supreme Lord constitute its eternity. We can infer the existence of the self from the experiences of pleasure, pain, desire, antipathy, and consciousness. The self is regarded as unborn in the sense that it is not born anew along with the chain of sensations and other activities of the mind, or in other words it remains the same

[1] *evaṃ maheśvare bhāvasthis tadasaṅgitvam ity arthaḥ. Pāśupata-sūtras* V. I (commentary).

through all its experiences. It is called *maitra* in the sense that it can remain in a state of equanimity and in attachment with the supreme Lord, when all its desires, antipathies, and efforts have disappeared.

The detachment referred to above can only be attained by the control of all the cognitive and conative senses, *manas* and *buddhi* and *ahaṅkāra*. The control of the senses really means that their activities should be directed towards good acts, and they should not be allowed to stray away into the commission of evil deeds[1].

Kauṇḍinya says that the definition of the goal as described by Sāṃkhya and Yoga is not true. That is not the way to liberation. The teachings of Sāṃkhya and Yoga are impure. To be liberated means to be connected with Lord Śiva, and not to be dissociated from all things[2].

The ascetic should live in some vacant room; he should devote himself to study and meditation, and make himself steady. He should be in continuous meditation for at least six months; and as he advances on the path of *yoga*, he begins to attain many miraculous powers through the grace of the supreme Lord.

The Pāśupata ascetic should live on mendicancy and should bear all hardships like animals. The yogin who has realised his goal, is not affected by any actions or sins. He is also unaffected by any mental troubles or physical diseases.

To sum up the whole position, one may say that when one becomes absolutely detached from all one's actions and sins, one should continue to meditate by drawing one's mind from all other objects and concentrating the mind on Śiva or on some symbolic name. We have already seen that *yoga* has been defined as the continuous connection of the self with the Lord, and this is also called *sāyujya*, that is, being with God. The supreme Lord has the infinite power of knowledge and action by which He controls everything, and this Lord should be meditated upon in His aspect as formless (*niṣkala*). God should not be approached with the association of any of the qualities attributed to Him. This is expressed by the *sūtra* v. 27, in which it is said that God is

[1] *tasmād akuśalebhyo vyāvartayitvā kāmataḥ kuśale yojitāni* (*yadā*), *tadā jitāni bhavanti. Pāśupata-sūtras* v. 7 (commentary).

[2] *ayaṃ tu yukta eva. na mukta iti viśuddham etad darśanam draṣṭavyam. Ibid.* v. 8 (commentary).

unassociated with anything that can be expressed by speech. The supreme Lord is therefore called *vāg-viśuddha*. The ascetic should often better stay in the cremation grounds where, not having any association, he will have greater time to devote to meditation, and attain merit or *dharma* which is identified with the greatness that is achieved by *yama* and *niyama*. In this way the ascetic cuts asunder all impurities. This cutting asunder of impurities means nothing more than taking away the mind from all sense objects and concentrating the mind on the Lord (*yantraṇa-dhāranātmakaś chedo draṣṭvyaḥ*). This *cheda* or dissociation means the separating of the self from all other objects. By this means all the network of causes that produce the defects are cut asunder. The defects are the various sensations of sound, touch, etc., for from these we get in our minds desire, anger, greed, fear, sleep, attachment, antipathy, and delusion. Then again these defects manifest themselves in our efforts to earn things, to preserve them, to be attached to them, and to indulge in injuring others. As a result of this, one afflicts oneself and also others. When one is afflicted oneself, one suffers, and if one afflicts others, then also on account of this vice one suffers. All such suffering thus is associated with the self. The sense objects are like the fruits of a poisoned tree which at the time of taking may appear sweet, but in the end will produce much suffering. The suffering of a man commences from the time of his being born, and continues throughout life till the time of death, so one should see that one may not have to be born again. The pleasures of enjoying sense objects have to be maintained with difficulty, and they produce attachment; when they disappear they produce further sorrow. Moreover, it is hardly possible to enjoy a sense object without injuring other persons. Even in wearing ordinary apparel one has to kill many insects. So one should refrain from enjoyment of all sense objects and be satisfied with whatever one gets, vegetable or meat, by begging.

The dissociation recommended above is to be done through *buddhi*, the internal organ (*antaḥkaraṇa*) which is conceived as being put in motion through merit, meditation, commandments and knowledge. The *buddhi* is also called *citta*. *Citta* means to know and to give experience of pleasure and pain, to collect merit and demerit and other impressions. So, as *buddhi* is called *citta*, it is also called *manas* and the internal organ, *antaḥkaraṇa*. The mind has thus to be dissociated from all sense objects by the self, and attached to Rudra or Śiva. When this is done then all intention of merit and demerit disappears; it slides away from the self like the old coil of a snake, or falls down like a ripe fruit. The self which is thus fixed in Śiva becomes static (*niṣkriya*) and is also called *niṣkala*. The mind in this state is devoid of all good and bad thoughts. When this *yoga* ideal is reached, the person becomes omniscient, and he cannot any further be drawn to any kind of illusory notions. So the liberated person, according to this *śaiva-yoga*, does not become a *kevalin* like the yogin following the Pātañjala discipline, but he becomes omniscient and has no sorrows, and this happens by the grace of God. He becomes absolutely liberated in the sense that he can arrest any future aggression of evil or time, and he is not dependent on anybody. In this way he attains or he shares the supreme power of the Lord. Neither does he become subject to all the sufferings of being in the mother's womb, or being born, and the like. He is free from the sorrows due to ignorance, from which is produced egotism, which leads one to forget that one is bound. So the liberated person becomes free from all sorrows of birth and rebirth and all bodily and mental sorrows as well.

The supreme Lord is also called Śiva, because He is eternally dissociated from all sorrows.

We thus see that there are five categories in this system. First, there is the *pati* or the Lord which is the cause, which is called by various names, Vāma, Deva, Jyeṣṭha, Rudra, Kāmin, Śaṅkara, Kāla, Kala-vikaraṇa, Bala-vikaraṇa, Aghora, Ghoratara, Sarva, Śarva, Tatpuruṣa, Mahādeva, Oṃkāra, Ṛṣi, Vipra, Mahānīśa, Īśāna, Īśvara, Adhipati, Brahmā, and Śiva[1]. The Sāṃkhya system admits *pradhāna* as the cause, but in the Pāśupata system God, as distinguished from the *pradhāna*, is the cause.

The category of effect is the *paśu*, and *paśu* is described as knowledge, the means of knowledge, and the living beings. They are produced changed, or dissolved. By knowledge we understand the scriptures, wisdom, merit, attainable objects, values, desires, etc., leading up to the dissolution of all sorrows. The second constituent of *paśu* called *kalā* is of two kinds: as effect, such as

[1] *Pāśupata-sūtras* v. 47 (commentary).

earth, water, air, etc., and as the instrument of knowledge, such as *buddhi*, egoism, *manas*, and internal organs, etc. The living beings, the *paśus*, are of three types, the gods, men and animals. The category of *pradhāna*, which is regarded as cause in Sāṃkhya, is regarded as effect in the *Pāśupata-śāstra*. Whatever is known or visible (*paśyana*) is called *pāśa*, and is regarded as effect. So *puruṣa*, which is regarded as cause elsewhere, is regarded as an effect, a *paśu*, here. We have already discussed the categories of *yoga* and *vidhi* leading to the dissolution of all sorrows.

A survey of the *Pāśupata-sūtras* with Kauṇḍinya's *bhāṣya* leads us to believe that it is in all probability the same type of Lakulīśa-Pāśupata system as referred to by Mādhava in his *Sarva-darśana-saṃgraha* in the fourteenth century. It may also be the same system of Pāśupatas as referred to by Śaṅkara in his *bhāṣya* on the second book of the second chapter of the *Brahma-sūtra*. There is no reference here to the doctrine of *māyā*, nor to the doctrine of monism as propounded by Śaṅkara. Even at the time of emancipation the liberated souls do not become one with Śiva, the supreme Lord, but the emancipation only means that by mental steadiness the devotee is in perpetual contact with Śiva, and this is what is meant by the word *sāyujya*. We also hear that, though God is omnipotent, He has no power over the liberated souls. Apparently the world and the beings were created by God, but this Pāśupata system does not make any special effort to explain how this world came into being. It is only in acknowledging Śiva as the instrumental cause of the world in this sense, that this Pāśupata system is very different from the Śaiva system of Śrīkaṇṭha and of the *Vāyavīya-saṃhitā*, where the monistic bias is very predominant. Here we have monotheism, but not monism or pantheism or panentheism. It may also be pointed out that the Pāśupata system as represented in this work is a Brahmanical system. For it is only Brahmins who could be initiated to the Pāśupata doctrines, but at the same time it seems to break off from Brahmanism in a variety of ways. It does not recommend any of the Brahmanical rites, but it initiates some new rites and new ways of living which are not so common in the Brahmanical circle. It keeps some slender contact with Brahmanism by introducing the meditation on the syllable *oṃ*. But as regards many of its other rituals it seems to be entirely non-Vedic. It does not refer to any of the Dravidian works as its source book, and yet it cannot be identified with the Pāśupata system of Śrīkaṇṭha or the *Vāyavīya-saṃhitā*.

It is also important to know that the Pāśupata system of the *Pāśupata-sūtras* has but little connection with the idea of *prakṛti* as energy or otherwise, as we find in the Purāṇic Pāśupata system. None of the categories of Sāṃkhya appear to be of any relevance regarding the creation of the world. About Yoga also one must always distinguish this *Pāśupata-yoga* and the *Pāśupata-yogas* referred to in the Purāṇas or in the *Yoga-sūtra* of Patañjali. The word *yoga* is used in the sense of continuous contact and not the suppression of all mental states (*citta-vṛtti-nirodha*), as we find in the *Pātañjala-yoga*. The emphasis here is on *pratyāhāra*, that is, withdrawing the mind from other objects and settling it down to God. There is therefore here no scope for *nirodha-samādhi*, which precedes *kaivalya* in *Pātañjala-yoga*. It may not be impossible that the Śaiva influence had somehow impressed upon the *Yoga-sūtra* of Patañjali, which apparently drew much of its material from Buddhism, and this becomes abundantly clear if we compare the *Vyāsa-bhāṣya* on the *Yoga-sūtra* with the *Abhidharmakosa* of Vasubandhu. The *Sāṃkhya-sūtra* that we now possess was probably later than the *Yoga-sūtra*, and it therefore presumed that the metaphysical speculations of Sāṃkhya could be explained without the assumption of any God for which there is no proof. The *Yoga-sūtra* did not try to establish Īśvara or God which is also the name for Śiva, but only accepted it as one of its necessary postulates. As a matter of fact, none of the systems of Indian philosophy tried to establish God by any logical means except the Naiyayikas, and according to tradition the Naiyāyikas are regarded as Śaivas.

In this connection, without any reference to some Āgama works to which we may have to refer later on, we can trace the development of the Pāśupata system in the tenth, eleventh, and up to the fourteenth centuries. It has been said before that the Īśvara-kāraṇins, referred to by Śaṅkara, may refer to the Naiyāyikas, and now I shall be referring to *Gaṇakārikā*, a Pāśupata work attributed to Haradattacarya, on which Bhāsarvajña wrote a commentary, called the *Ratnaṭīkā*. Bhāsarvajña is well known as the author of the *Nyāya-sāra*, on which he wrote a commentary called *Nyāya-bhūṣana*. In this he tried to refute the views of Diṅnāga, Dharma-kīrti, Prajñā-karagupta, the author of *Pramāṇa-vārttikālaṃkāra*, who lived about the middle of the tenth century and is quoted by Ratnākaraśānti of about A.D. 980. Bhāsarvajña, therefore, seems to have lived in the second half of the tenth century. The *Gaṇakārikā* consists of eight verses, and its purport is the same as that of the *Pāśupata-sūtras*. The *Pāśupata-sūtra* that we have dealt with is the same as that which is referred to as *Pāśupata-śāstra*, as the *Sarva-darśana-saṃgraha* quotes the first *sūtra* of the *Pāśupata-śāstra*[1].

Guṇaratna in his commentary on Haribhadra's *Ṣaḍdarśana-samuccaya* says that the Naiyāyikas are also called Yaugas and they walk about with long staffs and scanty loin-cloths, covering themselves up with blankets. They have matted locks of hair, smear their bodies with ashes, possess the holy thread, carry utensils for water, and generally live in the forests or under trees. They live largely on roots and fruits, and are always hospitable. Sometimes they have wives, sometimes not. The latter are better than the former. They perform the sacrificial duties of fire. In the higher state they go about naked; they purify their teeth and food with water, smear their bodies with ashes three times, and meditate upon Śiva. Their chief *mantra* is *oṃ namaḥ śivāya*. With this they address their *guru* and their *guru* also replies in the same manner. In their meetings they say that those men or women who follow the practices of Śaiva initiation for twelve years attain ultimately salvation or *Nirvāṇa*. Śiva the omniscient being, the creator and destroyer of the world, is regarded as a god. Śiva has eighteen incarnations (*avatāra*), namely Nakulīśa, Kauśika, Gārgya, Maitreya, Kauruṣa, Īśāna, Para-gārgya, Kapilāṇḍa, Manuṣyaka, Kuśika, Atri, Piṅgala, Puṣpaka Bṛhadārya, Agasti, Santāna, Rāśīkara, and Vidyāguru. They adore the aforesaid saints.

They further say that the ultimate being that they worship is not associated with any of the Purāṇic characteristics of Śiva, such as having matted locks, or the lunar digit in the hair, etc. Such a supreme being is devoid of all such characteristics and passions. Those who desire mundane happiness worship Śiva with such associated qualities, and as possessing attachment or passion. But those who are really absolutely unattached, they worship Śiva as unattached. People attain just those kinds of fruits that they wish to have, and the manner in which they wish to worship the deity.

[1] *Sarva-darśana-saṃgraha, Nakulīśa-pāśupata-darśana: Tatredam ādi-sūtram, "athātaḥ paśupateḥ pāśupata-yoga-vidhiṃ vyākhyāsyāmaḥ" iti.*

Guṇaratna says that the Vaiśeṣikas also follow the same kind of external insignia and dress, because the Vaiśeṣikas and the Naiyāyikas are very much similar in their philosophical attitudes. Guṇaratna further says that there are four types of Śaivas—Śaivas, Pāśupatas, Mahāvratadharas, and Kālamukhas, as well as other subsidiary divisions. Thus there are some who are called Bharaṭa who do not admit the caste rules. He who has devotion to Śiva can be called a Bharaṭa. In the Nyāya literature the Naiyāyikas are called Śaivas, because they worship Śiva, and the Vaiśeṣikas are called Pāśupatas. So the Naiyāyika philosophy goes by the name of Śaiva and Vaiśeṣika by the name of Pāśupata. Guṇaratna says that he gives this description just as he has seen it and had heard of it. Their main dialectical works are *Nyāya-sūtra*, *Vātsyāyana-bhāṣya*, Udyotkara's *Vārttika*, Vācaspati Miśra's *Tātparya-ṭīkā*, and Udayana's *Tātparya-pariśuddhi*. Bhāsarvajña's *Nyāya-sāra* and its commentary *Nyāya-bhūṣaṇa* and Jayanta's *Nyāya-kalikā* and Udayana's *Nyāya-kusumāñjali* are also mentioned as important works.

The statement of Guṇaratna about the Śaivas is further corroborated by Rājaśekhara's description of the Śaiva view in his *Ṣaḍdarśana-samuccaya*. Rājaśekhara further says that Akṣapāda, to whom the *Nyāya-sūtras* are attributed, was the primary teacher of the Nyāya sect of Pāśupatas. They admit four *pramāṇas*, perception, inference, analogy, and testimony, and they admit sixteen categories of discussion, namely, *pramāṇa*, *prameya*, *saṃśaya*, *prayojana*, *dṛṣṭānta*, *siddhānta*, *avayava*, *tarka*, *nirṇaya*, *vāda*, *jalpa*, *vitaṇḍā*, *hetvābhāsa*, *chala*, *jāti* and *nigrahasthāna*. These are just the subjects that are introduced in the first *sūtra* of Akṣapāda's *Nyāya-sūtra*. The ultimate object is the dissolution of all sorrow preparatory to liberation. Their main logical work is that by Jayanta and also by Udayana and Bhāsarvajña.

Kauṇḍinya's commentary on the *Pāśupata-sūtras* seems to belong to quite an early period, and it may not be inadmissible to say that it was a writing of the early period of the Christian era. But whether Kauṇḍinya can be identified with Rāśīkara, is more than we can say. Rāśīkara is mentioned in *Sarva-darśana-saṃgraha*, and there is of course nothing to suggest that Kauṇḍinya could not have been the *gotra* name of Rāśīkara.

Apart from the *Ratnaṭīkā* on the *Gaṇakārikā*, it seems that there was also a *bhāṣya*, but this *bhāṣya* was not on *Gaṇakārikā*, but it was the *bhāṣya* of Kauṇḍinya on the *Pāśupata-sūtras* which we have already examined. In the *Gaṇakārikā*, a reference is made to eight categories of a fivefold nature and also one category of a tripartite nature. Thus in speaking of strength or power (*bala*), which must be a source of the attainment of the other categories, we hear of faith in the teacher, contentment (*mateḥ prasāda*), fortitude (that is, power of bearing all kinds of sorrow), merit or *dharma*, and also conscious carefulness (*apramāda*).

The question of *bala* or strength may naturally come when one has to conquer one's enemies. One may, therefore, ask the significance of the attainment of *bala* or strength in following a course for the attainment of liberation. The answer to such an inquiry is that strength is certainly required for destroying ignorance, demerit, and the like. These are counted as destruction of ignorance in all its dormant seats, destruction of demerit, dissolution of all that leads to attachment, preservation from any possible failure, and also the complete cessation of the qualities that lead to animal existence as *paśu* through the meditation of God.

This strength may be exercised under different conditions and circumstances. First, when one shows oneself as a member of the Pāśupata sect, smearing the body with ashes and lying on the ashes, and so on; secondly, in the hidden stage, when one hides from other people the fact of one's being a member of the Pāśupata sect, and when one behaves like an ordinary Brāhmin. The third stage is a stage when one conquers all one's sense propensities. Next is the stage when all attractions cease. These include the other behaviours of a Pāśupata ascetic, such as dancing and acting like a madman. The final stage is the stage of *siddhi*, the final emancipation.

The fifth *kārikā* refers to the process of initiation (*dīkṣā*), which consists of the necessary ceremonial articles, the proper time, the proper action, the phallic insignia of Śiva, and the teachers.

The *kārikās* then go on to enumerate the different kinds of attainment (*lābha*). Of these the foremost is knowledge. This knowledge is to be attained methodically by the enumeration of the categories of knowledge, and thereafter by a sufficient description of them as we find in the *Nyāya-sūtras*. This will also include the various kinds of *pramāṇas* or proof, the differentiation between substance and attitude, the definition of action leading up to the final action of dissociation of all sorrows. In other philosophies the dissociation of sorrows is merely a negative quality, but in this system the dissolution of sorrow involves within it the possession of miraculous powers. This attainment of miraculous powers is called also *jñāna-śakti* and *kriyā-śakti*. *Jñāna-śakti* means *jñāna* as power. This *kriyā-śakti* consists of various kinds of powers of movement. As this system does not hold the idea of evolution or self-manifestation, the attainment of these powers is by association with superior powers. This is quite in accordance with the Nyāya theory regarding the origination of qualities. All the categories of knowledge, merit, etc., are included as being within the range of attainment. This also includes the inanimates and the animate characters such as the elements, the five cognitive senses, the five conative senses, and the *manas*.

God is called the Lord or *pati*, because He is always associated with the highest powers; these powers do not come to Him as a result of any action, but they abide in Him permanently. For this reason He can by His will produce any action or effect which stands before us as creation and it is for this reason that the creation of the world is regarded as a sort of play by Him. This is what distinguishes Him from all other animate beings, and this is His greatness.

The whole course of *vidhi* or proper religious behaviour consists of those kinds of action which would ultimately purify the individual and bring him close to God. In this connection *tapas* is recommended for the destruction of sins and for the generation of merit. *Dharma*, also consisting of various kinds of ritualistic behaviour, is recommended for the attainment of knowledge. The continuous meditation on God with emotion (*nityatā*) and the complete dissociation of the mind from all defects (*sthiti*) are also advised. These ultimately lead to the final liberation when the individuals become associated with great miraculous powers liked Śiva Himself. In other systems the liberated souls have no miraculous powers; they have only all their sorrows dissolved.

The above attainments should be made by residence with the teacher, or where people live who follow the caste and the *Aśrama* rules, or in any vacant place which is cleaned up and which has a covering on it, or in the cremation ground; or finally the aspirant with the cessation of his body may live in fixed association with the supreme Lord.

We must now turn to the means by which the aspirant may attain his desired end. The first is technically called *vāsa.* It means many things; it means the capacity to understand the proper meanings of words of texts, to remember them, to be able to collate and complete that knowledge in association with knowledge gained in other places, the ability to criticise the teachings of opposite schools in favour of one's own school, to be able to grasp the correct meaning of texts which have been differently interpreted, to be able to carry one's own conviction to other people, the ability to speak without contradiction and repetition and without any kind of delusion, and thereby to satisfy the teacher. To these must be added the proper courtesy and behaviour towards the teacher. This latter is called *caryā*, *paricaryā*, or *kriyā*. The term *caryā* is also used to denote various kinds of action, such as smearing the body with ashes, and so on. According to the Pāśupata system the bathing of the body with ashes is equivalent to proper sacrifice, that is, *yajña*. Other kinds of sacrifice are regarded as bad sacrifices.

Bhāsarvajña follows Kauṇḍinya's *bhāṣya* in describing *caryā* as being twofold or threefold. Thus the bathing of the body with ashes, lying down, muttering *mantras*, etc., are called *vrata*, which produces merit and removes demerit. All the other recommendations found in Kauṇḍinya's *bhāṣya* as regards shivering, laughing, making noises, etc., are also repeated here. In fact, the *Gaṇakārikā* and the *Ratnaṭīkā* closely follow the teachings of Kauṇḍinya in his *bhāṣya*, which is regarded as the most prominent work of the Pāśupata school.

One important point in this system deserves to be noticed. God Himself is absolutely independent. The introduction of the idea of *karma* and its fruit is not so indispensable, for the simple reason that no *karmas* can produce any fruit without the will of God. All *karmas* can be frustrated by God's will. So the introduction of the *karma* theory, which is held in so high an esteem in other systems of philosophy, is here regarded as superfluous. That this was the idea of the Nakulīśa-Pāśupata philosophy from the time of the *Pāśupata-sūtras* and Kauṇḍinya's *bhāṣya* to the fourteenth century when the *Sarva-darśana-saṃgraha* was written, is thoroughly borne out by texts. The action of all living beings depends upon the will of God. God Himself having no purpose to fulfil, does not want *karma* as an intermediary between His will and His effect.

After considerable difficulty we obtained a copy of *Mṛgendrāgama* from the Government Manuscript Library of Madras. It appears that this Āgama was one of the important texts of the Pāśupata sect. But the portions that we have recovered deal mainly with various kinds of rituals and they have no philosophical interest.

The Śaiva Ideas of Māṇikka-vāchakar in the *Tiru-vāchaka*.

In the present work the writer has refrained from utilising material from a Dravidian language such as Tamil, Telegu, and Kanarese. This is due to more than one reason. The first is that the writer has no knowledge of the Dravidian languages, and it is too late for him to acquire it, as it might take a whole life time to do so. The second is that this history in all its past volumes has only taken note of material available in Sanskrit. Thirdly, so far as the present author can judge, there is hardly anything of value from the philosophical point of view in Dravidian literature which is unobtainable through Sanskrit. A Tamil work could, however, be taken in hand, if there were any trustworthy translation of it, and if the work were of any great reputation. It is fortunate that Māṇikka-vāchakar's *Tiru-vāchaka*, which is held in very high esteem, has a trustworthy translation by the Rev. G. U. Pope, who devoted his life to the study of Tamil, and may be regarded as a very competent scholar in that language. It appears that Tamil was particularly rich in poetry, and we have many devotional songs both in Tamil and in Kanarese, but I do not know of any systematic philosophical work either in Tamil or in Kanarese which is not presented in Sanskrit. The Tamil literature also abounds in mythical and legendary accounts of many of the saints, which go by the name of Purāṇas, such as *Periya-purāṇa* and *Tiru-vātavurār-purāṇa*, *Nampiyāṇdār-nampi-purāṇa* and *Sekkilar-purāṇa*.

Tiru-vāchaka is a book of poems by Māṇikka-vāchakar. It is full of devotional sentiments and philosophical ideas, but it is not a system of philosophy in the modern sense of the term. Pope wishes to place Māṇikka-vāchakar in about the seventh or eight century, apparently without any evidence. R. W. Frazer, in his article on Dravidians[1], places him in the ninth century, also without any evidence. Māṇikka-vāchakar is supposed to have been born near Madura. The meaning of his name is "he whose utterances are rubies." He is supposed to have been a prodigy of intellect and was a consummate scholar in the Brahmanical learning and the *Śaivāgamas*. These Āgamas, as we have pointed out elsewhere, are written in Sanskrit verses and also in Tamil. It appears, therefore, that the background of Māṇikka-vāchakar's thought was in Sanskrit. The mythical story about Māṇikka-vāchakar, available in the *Tiru-viḷaiyāḍil* and in the *Vātavurar-purāṇa* as summarised by Pope, need not detain us here. We find that he renounced the position of a minister of the king and became a Śaiva ascetic. His mind was oppressed with the feeling of sadness for all people around him, who were passing through the cycles of birth and death, and had no passionate love for Śiva which alone could save them. This state of his mental agitation, and the confession of his ignorance and youthful folly, are specially described in some of his poems.

Later on Śiva Himself meets him, and from that time forward he becomes a disciple of Śiva. Śiva appears before him with His three eyes, His body smeared with ashes, and holding a book in His hand called *Śiva-jñāna-bodha*, the well-known work of Meykaṇḍadeva. Pope himself admits that the *Śiva-jñāna-bodha* could not have been written by the sixth century A.D., the supposed date of Māṇikka-vāchakar[2].

In the course of his career he travelled from shrine to shrine until he came to Chidambaram, where in a discussion he completely discomfited the Buddhists, partly by logic and partly by the demonstration of miraculous powers. He then returned to other devotees and set up a *liṅgam* under a tree and worshipped it day and night. It was from that time that he began his poetical compositions which are full of the glory of Śiva and His grace.

[1] In Hastings' *Encyclopaedia of Religion and Ethics*.

[2] *Śiva-jñāna-bodha* is supposed to have been written by Meykaṇḍadeva in or about A.D. 1223. See article on Dravidians by Frazer in *Encyclopaedia of Religion and Ethics*.

A study of his poems reveals the gradual evolution of his mind through various states of repentance, afflictions, sadness, and his extreme devotedness and love for Śiva. Pope, in commenting on the poetry of Māṇikka-vāchakar, says "scarcely ever has the longing of the human soul for purity and peace and divine fellowship found worthier expression[1]."

The fact of the omnipresence of God is often expressed in the Śaiva songs as the sport of Śiva. The whole universe is bright with his smile and alive with his joyous movements. This idea is so much overstressed that Śiva is often called a deceiver and a maniac, and in the Pāśupata system the Pāśupata ascetics are advised to behave like mad people, dancing about and even deceiving others into thinking of them as bad people, and making all kinds of noise and laughing in an irrelevant manner. It is also supposed that Śiva would often try the loyalty of his devotees in various forms of manifestations, trying to represent Himself in an exceedingly unfavourable light. The dancing of Śiva is particularly symbolical of his perpetual gracious actions throughout the universe and in loving hearts. He reminds one of the pre-Aryan demon dancers in the burning grounds.

We assume that the teaching of Māṇikka-vāchakar is in consonance with the teaching of the *Śiva-jñāna-bodha*, which was composed at a later date. Umāpati has a commentary on the *Śiva-jñāna-bodha* which has been translated by Hoisington in the *American Oriental Society Journal* of 1895. In this book various types of liberation are described. Distinguishing the Śaiva view from other views, one may find a number of variations in conception in the different Śaiva schools. Some of these variations have already been noted in the different sections of Southern Śaivism. There are many who think that the innate corruptions of the soul can be removed, and this may lead to a permanent release from all bonds (*pāśa*). The *Śaiva-siddhānta*, however, insists that even in this liberated state the potentiality of corruption remains, though it may not be operative. It remains there in the soul as a permanent dark spot. So the personal identity and the imperfections cling together in all finite beings, and they are never destroyed even in liberation. Other sectarian Śaivas, however, think that by the grace of Śiva the innate corruptions of the soul may be removed,

[1] Pope's translation, p. xxxiv.

from which it necessarily follows that there may be permanent release from all bonds. There are other Śaivas who think that in liberation the soul acquires miraculous powers, and that the liberated persons are partakers of divine nature and attributes, and are able to gain possession of, and exercise, miraculous powers called *siddhi*. There are others who think that in emancipation the soul becomes as insensible as a stone. This apathetic existence is the refuge of the soul from the suffering and struggle of the cycle of births and rebirths. We have already mentioned most of these ideas of liberation in a more elaborate manner in the relevant sections. But according to Māṇikka-vāchakar the soul is finally set free from the influence of threefold defilement through the grace of Śiva, and obtains divine wisdom, and so rises to live eternally in the conscious, full enjoyment of Śiva's presence and eternal bliss. This is also the idea of the Siddhānta philosophy[1].

A great pre-eminence is given to the idea of the operation of divine grace (called *aruḷ* in Tamil) in the Śaiva Siddhānta. The grace is divine or mystic wisdom, to dissipate the impurities of the *āṇava-mala* and to show the way of liberation. The souls are under the sway of accumulated *karma*, and it is by the grace of the Lord that the souls of men, in a state of bondage in the combined state, are let loose and find their place in suitable bodies for gradually working out and ultimately attaining liberation. Through all the stages, grace is the dynamic force that gradually ennobles the pilgrim towards his final destination. The grace of Śiva through the operation of His energy (*śakti*) affords light of understanding, by which people perform their actions of life and accumulate their *karma* and experience joys and sufferings. The material world is unconscious and the souls have no knowledge of their own nature. It is only by the grace of Śiva that the individuals understand their state and acquire the mystic knowledge by which they can save themselves; yet no one knows the grace of Śiva and how it envelops him, though he is endowed with all sense perceptions. From beginningless time the individuals have been receiving the grace of God, but they have seldom come under its influence, and are thus devoid of the right approach to the way to deliverance.

The grace can be observed as operative when the proper *guru* comes and advises the person to follow the right course. When the

[1] Pope, *loc. cit.* p. xliv.

opposition of sins and merits is counter-balanced, Śiva's emancipating grace begins to show its work. In order to be saved, one should know the spiritual essence of *karma* and the twofold kinds of *karma*, and the joys and sorrows which are associated with them, and the Lord Who brings the deeds to maturity at the appointed time so that the soul may experience their effects.

Just as a crystal reflects many colours under the sun's light and yet retains its own transparent character, so the energy or wisdom obtained as a grace of the Lord irradiates the soul and permeates the world. Without the mystic wisdom obtained through the grace of Śiva, no one can obtain real knowledge. The soul is unintelligent without Śiva. All the actions of souls are performed with the active guidance of Śiva, and even the perception of the senses as instruments of knowledge is owed to Śiva's grace.

In the second stage we are taught how to apply knowledge for the cleansing of the soul. Those who endure the delusive sufferings of worldly experience would naturally seek relief in the grace of God as soon as they became convinced of their impurities. To a jaundiced person even sweet milk appears bitter, but if the tongue is cleansed the bitterness is gone; so under the influence of the original impurities all religious observances are distasteful, but when these impurities are removed then the teachings of the *guru* become operative.

What cannot be perceived by the senses, supreme bliss, is known by the operation of grace in a spiritual manner. The grace of God is spontaneously revealed to us. The supreme felicity is thus a gift of grace which souls cannot obtain of themselves.

Only those who are introduced to this grace can combine with Śiva in bliss. There is a curious notion that the souls are feminine and so is the *śakti* or energy, and Śiva is the Lord with whom there is a mystic unification. Śiva is perfect bliss. If there is a mystic union between the soul and the Lord, then they should become one, leaving the duality between the soul and God unexplained; it has to be assumed, therefore, that they both become one and remain divided. When the bonds are removed the devotee becomes one with God in speechless rapture, and there is no scope for him to say that he has obtained Śiva. Those who obtain release, and those who attain the state of *samādhi*, are never torn asunder from the Lord. In that state all their physical actions are under the complete control of the Lord. There thus comes a state when the knower, the mystic knowledge, and the Śiva appear no more as distinct, but as absorbed in one another.

Though those who enter this state of *samādhi* gain omniscience and other qualities, yet while they are on this earth they know nothing whatever except the supreme Lord, the object of their mystic knowledge. All their sense-organs are restrained and sink deep into their source and do not show themselves. Within and without the divine grace stands revealed. In this mystic enlightenment the phenomenal universe is only seen in God.

In the *Vātavurār-purāṇam* as translated by Pope there is an account of the controversy of Māṇikka-vāchakar with the Buddhist teachers in Chidambaram. The controversy does not manifest any great knowledge of Buddhism on either side. The disputation hangs round this or that minor point and lacks logical co-ordination, so that it is unprofitable to follow it up. It is also extremely doubtful if that controversy were in any way responsible for the loss of prestige on the side of Buddhist thought, which must have been due, from the ninth century onwards, to the rise of various South Indian sects which quarrelled with each other, and also, mainly, to political reasons.

Māṇikka-vāchakar and Śaiva Siddhānta.

We read in Śaṅkara's commentary (II. 2. 27) that he mentions the name *Siddhānta-śāstra* written by Śiva Himself, and he gives us some specimen ideas of these which can be covered within two concepts: (1) that the Siddhāntas assume God to be the instrumental cause, against the Vedānta view that God represents the whole of reality and that there is nothing outside Him. He also (2) refers to the Śaiva doctrine which acknowledged three categories, the *pati*, *paśu*, and *pāśa*. Among the Śaivas he refers to the Mahā-kāruṇikas, Kāpālikas, etc. As I have often said, it is extremely difficult to discover with any exactitude the sort of Śaivism that Śaṅkara designates by the name Siddhānta, as also to define the characteristics of the systems that he wanted to refute. We have now before us a system of Śaivism which goes by the name of Śaiva Siddhānta and a whole lot of works regarded as the works of the Śaiva Siddhānta school. Much of it, particularly in the way of commentaries, is written in Tamil: some of it is available in Sanskrit. A sort of Śaivism very similar to this is found in the *Vāyavīya* section of the *Śiva-mahāpurāṇa*. It is said in those sections that the original doctrine of that philosophy was written in the Āgama works as composed by the successive incarnations of Śiva. The same teachings are to be found also in Tamil Āgamas, which have the same authority and content. Pope says that the Śaiva Siddhānta system is the most elaborate, influential, and undoubtedly the most intrinsically valuable of all the religions of India. This seems to me to be a wild exaggeration. The fundamental facts of Śaivism are composed of Vedāntic monism and Sāṃkhya, and sometimes the Nyāya doctrines have also been utilised. This latter refers to the Pāśupata school of Śaivism, as has been noted elsewhere. It is also doubtful if it is peculiarly South Indian and Tamil, for we have similar doctrines in the *Vāyavīya-saṃhitā* and also in a somewhat variant form in the Northern Śaivism. There are many statements by Pope which seem to have no factual value, and if the present work had any polemical intention, it would be necessary to criticise him more definitely.

Some people say that the oldest form of Śaivism is the old prehistoric religion of South India, but I have not found any evidence to show the exact nature of an existent pre-Aryan, Dravidian religion which could be identified with what we now know as Śaivism. It is as yet very doubtful whether the pre-Aryan Dravidians had any systematic form of philosophy or religion differing from that of the kindred classes of other aborigines.

In our view the *Pāśupata-sūtra* and *bhāṣya* were referred to by Śaṅkara and were probably the earliest basis of Śaivism, as can be gathered by literary evidences untrammelled by flying fancies. We are ready to believe that there were ecstatic religious dances, rites of demon-worship, and other loathsome ceremonials, and that these, though originally practised for ancestor-worship and the like, were gradually accepted by the earliest Pāśupatas, whose behaviour and conduct do not seem to affiliate them with the Brahmanic social sphere, though holders of such Śaiva doctrines had to be Brahmins. Castelessness was not a part of the earlier Pāśupata Śaivism. In a separate section we shall try to give an estimate of the evolution of the concept of Śiva from Vedic times. The affirmation that one little Christian Church on the east coast of India exerted its influence on the dominant Śaiva and Vaiṣṇava faith in the country lacks evidence. We have found that as a rule those who held the Sanskritic culture hardly ever read even Pali texts of Buddhism, though Pāli is so much akin to Sanskrit. On this account we find that the reputed disputation of Māṇikka-vāchakar with the Buddhists is uninteresting, as it does not seem that Māṇikka-vāchakar or the Ceylonese knew much of each other's faith. Pope's statement, that Kumārila Bhatta preached the doctrine of a personal deity in the South, is absolutely wrong, because the Mīmāṃsā view as expounded by Kumārila did not admit any God or creator.

Māṇikka-vāchakar, probably of the ninth century, was one of the earliest saints of the school of thought that goes by the name of Śaiva Siddhānta. Probably about a century later there arose Nāṇasambandhar and other devotees who developed the doctrine further. Their legendary tales are contained in the *Periya-purāṇa*. But it is peculiar that King Bhoja of Dhāra, who wrote a Śaiva work of great distinction called *Tattva-prakāśa*, does not take any notice of these Tamil writers. Similarly Mādhava, also in the fourteenth century, does not mention any of these Tamil writers. We are told that thereafter came fourteen sages, called *Santāna-gurus* (succession of teachers), who properly elaborated the system of philosophy known as the Śaiva Siddhānta. One of these was Umāpati, who lived in A.D. 1313. He was thus a contemporary of Mādhava, though Mādhava makes no reference to him.

The thirteenth and the fourteenth centuries were periods of great theistic enterprises in the hands of the Śaivas and the Śrīvaiṣṇavas. In interpreting *Tiru-vachakam*, Umāpati says that the real intention of all the Vedas is summed up in three mystic words: *pati*, *paśu*, and *pāśa*, the Lord, the flock, and the bond. These are the three categories of the Śaiva Siddhānta system. But we have already pointed out that there were no special peculiarities of the Śaiva Siddhānta; it was referred to by Śaṅkara in the eighth century and it formed the cardinal doctrine of the Pāśupata school of Śaivism, and also to the schools of Śaivism as we find them in the *Vāyavīya* section of the *Śiva-mahāpurāṇa*. The *pati*, *paśu* and *pāśa* are equally eternal, existing unchanged and undiminished through the ages. This *pati* is none else but Śiva, who is called by various names, such as Rudra, *paśūnām-pati*, Śiva, etc. Umāpati says that Śiva is the supreme Being, is neither permanently manifested nor unmanifested; He is without qualities or distinguishing marks, free from all impurities, absolute and eternal, the source of wisdom to innumerable souls, and not subject to any fluctuations. He is immaterial and of the nature of pure bliss. He is difficult of access to the perverse, but He is the final goal of those that truly worship Him. Śiva is thus described to be *niṣkala*, without parts, perfect in Himself, but is capable of manifestation, and in order to energise in souls the various constituents of that eternal aggregate of impurity which constitutes the bond, He assumes a *sakala* nature, that is, one composed of pieces of spiritual bodies. He is formless and has the form of wisdom. He creates, preserves, and consigns all to the power of *māyā*, but He is the ultimate refuge who never leaves us. He dwells everywhere and pervades all things as fire pervades all wood. He offers His boon only to those who approach Him for it.

Turning to the groups of animate beings called *paśu*, it is suggested that from beginningless time an infinite number of souls must have obtained their release. Generally there are three kinds of impurities—darkness, deeds (*karma*) and delusion. When delusion is removed, darkness may still continue. The souls can perceive objects through sense organs only when their functions are supplemented by some innate divine faculty. All beings are infested with original impurities. The threefold impurities which constitute the bond are directly known by Śiva.

Para-śiva or the supreme Lord and Parā-śakti are two in one. Śiva is pure intelligence (*jñāna*) and Śakti is pure energy (*kriyā*). Out of their union, evolves (1) *icchā-śakti*, which is a combination of *jñāna* and *kriyā* in equal proportion; (2) *kriyā-śakti* which is a combination of *jñāna* and *kriyā* with an excess of *kriyā*; and (3) *jñana-śakti*, which is a combination of *jñāna* and *kriyā* with an excess of *jñāna*, also called *aruḷ-śakti*. The *aruḷ-śakti* is the *jñāna-śakti* active at the time of the liberation of the souls, while as *tirodhāna-śakti* it is active at the time when the souls are fettered.

To sum up the position of the Śaiva Siddhānta as far as we can understand it from authoritative translations of Tamil works, and also authoritative studies of Tamil literature like Pope and Schomerus, we find that the souls which pervade the body are themselves inanimate, and the intellectual apparatus by which things are perceived are also unconscious. Conscious experience can only originate by the energy of Śiva. This energy, like a ray of sun, is the original *śakti* or energy which is indistinguishable from Śiva. The Śaiva Siddhānta school is in direct opposition to the Cārvāka school which denies the existence of any creator. The Śaiva Siddhānta school argues for the existence of a supreme Being who evolves, sustains, and involves the phenomenal universe. The whole universe, constituted of all beings, male and female, and those which are without life, but which come into phenomenal existence, subsists for a while and then subsides; but yet, as we have said before, this does not clarify our knowledge regarding the nature of the physical world and of the souls. It does not explain how beings became associated from the beginning with impurities called *āṇava-mala*. Even at the attainment of release the souls could not be united or become one with God. Other forms of Śaivism have attempted to follow slightly diverse lines to avoid these difficulties.

Though *śakti* is regarded as a part of Śiva—and this has led to many mystical aspects of Tantra philosophy—yet the relation of the individual devotees to God is one of servitude and entire self-surrender. It has none of the amorous sides of rapturous love that we notice among the Vaiṣṇava saints, the Ārvārs.

Tiru-vāchakam may in some sense be regarded as a spiritual biography of Māṇikka-vāchakar which records his experiences at different times of his life and explains. The work is full of his religious experiences and enthusiasm, showing different states of religious pathology. Thus he says:

What shall I do while twofold deeds' fierce flame burns still out,—
Nor doth the body melt,—nor falsehood fall to dust?
In mind no union gained with the "Red fire's honey"
    The Lord of Perun-turrai fair![1]

Shall I cry out, or wait, or dance or sing, or watch?
O Infinite, what shall I do? The Śiva who fills
With rapturous image,—great Perun-turrai's Lord
Let all with me bending adore![2]

He filled with penury; set me free from 'births,' my soul
With speechless fervours thrilled,—blest Perun-turrai's Lord,—
The Śiva in grace exceeding made me His; the balm
For all my pain, the deathless Bliss![3]

[1] *Tiru-vāchakam*, p. 334. [2] *Ibid.* [3] *Ibid.* p. 336.

Glorious, exalted over all, the Infinite,—
To me small slave, lowest of all, thou has assigned.
A place in bliss supreme, that none beside have gained or known!
Great Lord, what can I do for thee![1]

All ye His servants who've become, put far away each idle sportive thought;
Such refuge at the fort where safety dwells; hold fast unto the end the sacred sign;
Put off from you this body stained with sin; in Śiva's world He'll surely give us place!
Bhujaṇga's self, whose form the ashes wears will grant you entrance 'neath His flow'ry feet![2]

Śaiva Philosophy according to Bhoja and his commentators.

Mādhava in his *Sarva-darśana-saṃgraha* of the fourteenth century refers to a system of philosophy *Śaiva-darśana* which rejects the view that God of His own will arranges all experiences for us, but that he does so on the basis of our own *karma* and that this philosophy is based upon the *Śaivāgamas*, supposed to have been composed by Śiva, Maheśvara. In examining the philosophy of Śrīkaṇṭha and Appaya we have seen that they speak of twenty-eight Āgamas, which were all written by Śiva or His incarnations, and that, whether in Dravidian or in Sanskrit, they have the same import. Though it will not be possible for us to get hold of all the Āgamas, we have quite a number of them in complete or incomplete form. On the evidence of some of the Āgamas themselves, they were written in Sanskrit, Prākṛt, and the local country dialects[3]. We also find that, though written by Maheśvara, all the Āgamas do not seem to have the same import. This creates a good deal of confusion in the interpretation of the *Śaivāgamas*. Yet the differences are not always so marked as to define the special characteristics of the sub-schools of Śaivism.

Bhoja, probably the well-known Bhoja of the eleventh century who wrote *Sarasvatī-kaṇṭhābharaṇa* and a commentary on the *Yoga-sūtra*, wrote also a work called *Tattva-prakāśa* which has

[1] *Ibid.* p. 336.
[2] *Ibid.* p. 329.
[3] *saṃskṛtaiḥ prākṛtair yaś cāśiṣyānurūpataḥ,*
deśa-bhāṣadyupāyaiś ca bodhayet sa guruḥ smṛtaḥ.
Śiva-jñāna-siddhi (Mysore manuscript, no. 3726).

been referred to by Mādhava in his *Sarva-darśana-saṃgraha*. Mādhava also refers to Aghora-śivācārya, whose commentary on *Tattva-prakāśa* has not yet been published, but he omits Śrīkumāra, whose commentary on *Tattva-prakāśa* has been published in the Trivendrum Series along with the *Tattva-prakāśa*. Aghora-śivācārya seems to have written another commentary on the *Mṛgendrāgama* called the *Mṛgendrāgama-vṛtti-dīpikā*. In writing his commentary Aghora-śivācārya says that he was writing this commentary, because other people had tried to interpret *Tattva-prakāśa* with a monistic bias, as they were unacquainted with the Siddhānta of the Āgama-śāstras. From the refutation of the Māheśvara school by Śaṅkara in II. 2. 37, we know that he regarded the Māheśvaras as those that held God to be only the instrumental agent of the world and the material cause of the world was quite outside Him. According to the monistic Vedānta of Śaṅkara, Brahman was both the material and the instrumental cause of the world. The world was in reality nothing but Brahman, though it appeared as a manifold world through illusion, just as a rope may appear as a snake through illusion. This is called the *vivarta* view as opposed to the *pariṇāma* view, according to which there is a material transformation leading to the production of the world. The *pariṇāma* view is held by the Sāṃkhyists; the other view is that God is the instrumental agent who shapes and fashions the world out of atoms or a brute *māyā*, the material force. The Naiyāyikas hold that since the world is an effect and a product of mechanical arrangement, it must have an intelligent creator who is fully acquainted with the delimitations and the potencies of the atomic materials. God thus can be proved by inference, as any other agent can be proved by the existence of the effect. This is also the viewpoint of some of the *Śaivāgamas* such as the *Mṛgendra*, *Mātaṅga-parameśvara*, etc.

Śrīkumāra, in interpreting *Tattva-prakāśa*, seems to be in an oscillating mood; sometimes he seems to follow the Āgama view of God being the instrumental cause, and sometimes he tries to interpret on the Vedāntic pattern of *vivarta*. Aghora-śivācārya takes a more definite stand in favour of the Āgama point of view and regards God as the instrumental cause[1]. In our account of Śaivism

[1] *vivādādhyāsitaṃ viśvaṃ viśva-vit-kartṛ-pūrvakam, kāryatvād āvayoḥ siddhaṃ kāryaṃ kumbhādikaṃ yathā, iti śrīman-mātaṅge' pi, nimitta-kāraṇaṃ tu īśa iti. ayam ceśvara-vādo 'smābhiḥ mṛgendra-vṛtti-dīpikāyāṃ vistareṇāpi darśita iti.* Aghora-śivācārya's commentary on *Tattva-prakāśa* (Adyar manuscript).

as explained in the *Vāyavīya-saṃhitā*, we have seen how in the hands of the Purāṇic interpreters Śaivism had taken a rather definite course towards absolute monism, and how the Sāṃkhya conception of *prakṛti* had been utilised as being the energy of God, which is neither different from nor identical with Him. Such a conception naturally leads to some kind of oscillation and this has been noticed in the relevant places.

Mādhava sums up the content of the *Śaivāgamas* as dealing with three categories, *pati*, the Lord, *paśu*, the beings, and *pāśa*, the bonds, and the four other categories of *vidyā*, knowledge, *kriyā*, behaviour or conduct, *yoga*, concentration, and *caryā*, religious worship. Now the beings have no freedom and the bonds themselves are inanimate; the two are combined by the action of God.

Bhoja writes his book, *Tattva-prakāśa*, to explain the different kinds of metaphysical and other categories (*tattva*) as accepted by the Śaiva philosophy. The most important category is Śiva who is regarded as being *cit* by which the Śaivas understand combined knowledge and action[1]. Such a conscious God has to be admitted for explaining the superintendence and supervision of all inanimate beings. This ultimate being is all by itself; it has no body and it does not depend upon any thing; it is one and unique. It is also all-pervading and eternal. The liberated individual souls also become like it after liberation is granted to them, but God is always the same and always liberated and He is never directed by any supreme Lord. It is devoid of all passions. It is also devoid of all impurities[2].

Aghora-śivācārya follows the *Śaivāgamas* like the *Mṛgendra* or the *Mātaṅga-parameśvara* in holding that the existence of God can be inferred by arguments of the Naiyāyika pattern. It is, therefore, argued that God has created the world, maintains it, and will destroy it; He blinds our vision and also liberates us. These five actions are called *anugraha*, which we have often translated, in the absence of a better word, as grace. In reality, it means God's power that manifests itself in all worldly phenomena leading to

[1] Aghora-śivācārya quoting *Mṛgendra* in his commentary on *Tattva-prakāśa* says: *caitanyaṃ dṛk-kriyā-rūpam iti cid eva ghanaṃ deha-svarūpam yasya sa cidghanaḥ*. This *cidghana* is the attribute ascribed to Śiva in *Tattva-prakāśa*.

[2] *moho madaś ca rāgaś ca viṣādaḥ śoka eva ca, vaicittaṃ caiva harṣaś ca saptaite sahajā malāḥ*. Aghora-śivācārya's commentary (Adyar manuscript) on *Tattva-prakāśa*, *kārikā* 1.

bondage and liberation, everything depending upon the *karma* of the individual. It is quite possible that in some schools of Śaivism this dynamism of God was interpreted as His magnificent grace, and these people were called the Mahā-kāruṇikas. *Anugraha*, or grace, thus extends to the process of creation. If it were ordinary grace, then it could have been only when the world was already there[1]. This *anugraha* activity includes creation, maintenance, destruction, blinding the vision of the individuals, and finally liberating them[2]. Śrīkumāra explains the situation by holding that the act of blinding and the act of enlightening through liberation are not contradictory, as the latter applies only to those who have self-control, sense-control, fortitude, and cessation from all enjoyment, and the former to those who have not got them[3]. God thus is responsible for the enjoyable experiences and liberation of all beings through His fivefold action. His consciousness (*cit*) is integrally connected with His activity. Though God is of the nature of consciousness and in that way similar to individual souls, yet God can grant liberation to individual souls with powers which the individual souls themselves do not possess. Though God's consciousness is integrally associated with action, it is indistinguishable from it. In other words God is pure thought-activity.

The *śakti* or energy of Śiva is one, though it may often be diversely represented according to the diverse functions that it performs. Śrīkumāra points out that the original form of this energy is pure bliss which is one with pure consciousness. For the creation of the world God does not require any other instrument than His own energy, just as our own selves can perform all operations of the body by their own energy and do not require any outside help. This energy must be distinguished from *māyā*. Taking *māyā* into consideration one may think of it as an eternal energy, called *bindu-māyā* which forms the material cause of the world[4].

[1] *anugrahaś cātropalakṣaṇam. Ibid.*

[2] *Tattva-prakāśa, kārikā* 7.

[3] *Ibid.* Commentary on *Tattva-prakāśa, kārikā* 7.

[4] *kārya-bhede'pi māyādivan nāsyāḥ pariṇāma iti darśayati tasya jaḍa-dharmatvāt. adyām pradhāna-bhūtāṃ samavetām anena parigraha-śaktisvarūpam bindu-māyātmakaṃ apy asya bāhya-śakti-dvayam asti.* (Aghora-śivācārya's commentary, Adyar manuscript). Śrīkumāra, however, thinks that Śiva as

The monistic interpretation as found in Śrīkumāra's commentary is already anticipated as the Śivādvaita system in the Purāṇas, more particularly in the *Sūta-saṃhitā*[1].

Śiva arranges for the experiences and liberation of the individual souls in and through His energy alone. The fivefold action, referred to above, is to be regarded as somehow distinguishing the one energy in and through diverse functions.

The object of *Tattva-prakāśa* is to explain the Śaiva philosophy as found in the *Śaivāgamas*, describing mainly the categories of *pati*, *paśu*, and *pāśa*. The *pati* is the Lord and *paśu* is called *aṇu*, and the five objects are the five *pāśas* or bonds. The *aṇus* are dependent on God and they are regarded as belonging to different classes of bondage. The fivefold objects are those which are due to the *mala* and which belong to *bindu-māyā* in different states of evolution of purity and impurity. Śrīkumāra points out that since the souls are associated with *mala* from eternity, it comes under the sway of the *māyā*, but since the souls are of the nature of Śiva, when this *mala* is burnt, they become one with Him. The fivefold objects constituting the bondage are the *mala*, the *karma*, the *māyā*, the world which is a product of *māyā*, and the binding power[2].

It may be asked, if the energy belongs to God, how can it be attributed to the objects of bondage? The reply is that in reality the energy belongs to the Lord and the force of the *pāśa* or bondage can only be regarded as force in a distant manner, in the sense that the bondage or the power of bondage is felt in and through the individual soul who receives it from the Lord[3].

The *paśus* are those who are bound by the *pāśa*, the souls that

associated with the *māyā* forms the instrumental and material cause of the world:

nimittopādāna-bhāvena avasthānād iti brūmaḥ.

Such a view should make Śaivism identical with the Advaitism of Śaṅkara. Aghora-śivācārya wrote his commentary as a protest against this view, that it does not represent the view of the *Śaivāgamas* which regard God only as the instrumental cause.

[1] *Sūtasaṃhitā*, Book iv, verse 28 *et seq.*

[2] *malaṃ karma ca māyā ca māyottham akhilaṃ jagat, tirodhānakārī śaktir artha-pañcakam ucyate.* Śrīkumāra's commentary, p. 32.

[3] *nanu katham ekaikasyā eva śiva-śakteḥ pati-padārthe ca pāśa-padārthe ca saṃgraha ucyate. satyam, paramārthataḥ pati-padārtha eva śakter antarbhāvaḥ. pāśatvaṃ tu tasyāṃ pāśa-dharmānuvartanena upacārāt. tad uktaṃ śrīman Mṛgendre—tāsāṃ māheśvarī śaktiḥ sarvānugrāhikā śivā, dharmānu vartanād eva pāśa ity upacaryata, iti.* Aghora-śivācārya's commentary (Adyar manuscript).

go through the cycles of birth and rebirth. In this connection Śrīkumāra tries to establish the identity of the self on the basis of self-consciousness and memory, and holds that these phenomena could not be explained by the Buddhists who believed in momentary selves. These are three kinds; those which are associated with *mala* and *karma*, those which are associated only with *mala* (these two kinds are jointly called *vijñāna-kala*); the third is called *sakala*. It is associated with *mala*, *māyā* and *karma*. The first, namely the *vijñāna-kala*, may again be twofold, as associated with the impurities and as devoid of them. Those who are released from impurity are employed by God with various angelic functions, and they are called *vidyeśvara* and *mantreśvara*. Others, however, pass on to new cycles of life, being associated with a composite body of eight constituents which form the subtle body. These eight constituents are the five sensibles, *manas*, *buddhi*, and *ahaṅkāra*, and they all are called by the name of *puryaṣṭaka*, the body consisting of the eight constituents.

Those whose impurities (*mala*) get ripened may receive that power of God through proper initiation by which the impurity is removed, and they become one with God. The other beings, however, are bound by God to undergo the series of experiences at the end of which they may be emancipated.

The bonds or *pāśa* are of four kinds: first, the bond of *mala* and the *karma*. The bond of *mala* is beginningless, and it stands as a veil over our enlightenment and power of action. The *karma* also flows on, depending on the *mala* from beginningless time. The third is called *māyēya*, which means the subtle and gross bodies produced through *māyā*, which is the fourth. Aghora-śivācārya says that *māyēya* means the contingent bonds of passion, etc., which are produced in consequence of *karma*. Even those who have not the *māyēya* impurity at the time of dissolution (*pralaya*) remain by themselves but not liberated.

But what is *mala*? It is supposed to be one non-spiritual stuff, which behaves with manifold functions. It is for this reason that when the *mala* is removed in one person it may function in other persons. This *mala* being like the veiling power of God, it continues to operate on the other persons, though it may be removed in the case of some other person. As the husk covers the seed, so the *mala* covers the natural enlightenment and action of the individual; and as the husk is burnt by fire or heat, so this *mala* also may be removed when the internal soul shines forth. This *mala* is responsible for our bodies. Just as the blackness of copper can be removed by mercury, so the blackness of the soul is also removed by the power of Śiva.

Karma is beginningless and is of the nature of merit and demerit (*dharma* and *adharma*). Śrīkumāra defines *dharma* and *adharma* as that which is the special cause of happiness or unhappiness, and he tries to refute other theories and views about *dharma* and *adharma*. *Māyā* is regarded as the substantive entity which is the cause of the world. We have seen before that bondage comes out of the products of *māyā* (*māyēya*); so *māyā* is the original cause of bondage. It is not illusory, as the Vedāntists say, but it is the material cause of the world. We thus see that the power or energy of God behaving as *mala*, *māyā*, *karma*, and *māyēya*, forms the basic conception of bondage.

These are the first five pure categories arising out of Śiva. The category of Śiva is regarded as the *bindu*, and it is the original and primal cause of everything. It is as eternal as *māyā*. The other four categories spring from it, and for this reason it is regarded as *mahāmāyā*. These categories are the mythical superintending lords of different worlds called *vidyeśvara*, *mantreśvara*, etc. So, from *bindu* comes *śakti*, *sadāśiva*, *īśvara*, and *vidyeśvara*. These categories are regarded as pure categories. Again, in order to supply experiences to individuals and their scope of action, five categories are produced, namely, time (*kāla*), destiny (*niyati*), action (*kalā*), knowledge (*vidyā*), and attachment (*rāga*). Again, from *māyā* comes the *avyakta* or the unmanifested, the *guṇas*, and then *buddhi*, and *ahaṅkāra*, *manas*, the five conative senses and the five cognitive senses, and the gross matter, which make up twenty-three categories from *māyā*.

We thus see that these are in the first instance the five categories of *śiva*, *śakti*, *sadāśiva*, *īśvara*, and *vidyā*. These are all of the nature of pure consciousness (*cidrūpa*), and being of such a nature, there can be no impurity in them. We have next the seven categories which are both pure and impure (*cidacid-rūpa*), and these are *māyā*, *kāla*, *niyati*, *kalā*, *vidyā*, *rāga* and *puruṣa*. *Puruṣa*, though of the nature of pure consciousness, may appear as impure on account of its impure association. Next to these categories we have twenty-four categories of *avyakta-guṇa-tattva*, *buddhi*, *ahaṅkāra*, *manas*, the five cognitive senses, the five conative senses, the five *tanmātras*, and five *mahābhūtas*. Altogether these are the thirty-six categories.

If we attend to this division of categories, we find that the so-called impure categories are mostly the categories of Sāṃkhya philosophy. But while in the Sāṃkhya, *prakṛti* is equated with the *avyakta* as the equilibrium of the three *guṇas*, here in the Śaiva philosophy the *avyakta* is the unmanifested which comes from *māyā* and produces the *guṇas*.

To recapitulate, we find that the system of thought presented in the *Tattva-prakāśa*, as based on the *Śaivāgamas*, is a curious confusion of certain myths, together with certain doctrines of Indian philosophy. One commentator, Śrīkumāra, has tried to read the monistic philosophy of Śaṅkara into it, whereas the other commentator, Aghora-śivācārya, has tried to read some sort of duality into the system, though that duality is hardly consistent. We know from Śaṅkara's account of the philosophy of the Śaiva school that some Śaivas called Māheśvaras tried to establish in their works, the Siddhāntas, the view that God is only the instrumental cause (*nimitta-kāraṇa*) of the world, but not the material cause (*upādāna-kāraṇa*). In Śaṅkara's view God is both the material and the instrumental cause of the world and of all beings. Aghora-śivācārya's pretext for writing the commentary was that it was interpreted by people having a monistic bias, and that it was his business to show that, in accordance with the *Śaivāgamas*, God can only be the instrumental cause, as we find in the case of the Naiyāyikas. He starts with the premise that God is the sum total of the power of consciousness and the power of energy, and he says that the *māyā* is the material cause of the world, from which are produced various other material products which are similar to the Sāṃhkya categories. But he does not explain in what way God's instrumentality affects the *māyā* in the production of various categories, pure and impure and pure-and-impure. He says that even the energy of *māyā* proceeds from God and appears in the *māyā* as if undivided from it. There is thus an original illusion through which the process of the *māyā* as *bindu* and *nāda* or the desire of God for creation and the creation takes place. But he does not any further explain the nature of the illusion and the cause or the manners in which the illusion has been generated. The original text of the *Tattva-prakāśa* is also quite unilluminating regarding this vital matter. Aghora-śivācārya often refers to the *Mṛgendrāgama* for his support, but the *Mṛgendrāgama* does not follow the Sāṃkhya course of evolution as does the *Tattva-prakāśa*. There we hear of atoms constructed and arranged by the will of God, which is more in line with the Nyāya point of view.

Dealing with the nature of the soul, it is said that the souls are *aṇus* in the sense that they have only a limited knowledge. The souls are essentially of the nature of Śiva or God, but yet they have an innate impurity which in all probability is due to the influx of *māyā* into them. Nothing is definitely said regarding the nature of this impurity and how the souls came by it. Śrīkumāra explains this impurity on the Vedāntic lines as being of the nature of *avidyā*, etc. But Aghora-śivācārya does not say anything on this point. It is said that when by the fruition of action the impurity will ripen, God in the form of preceptor would give proper initiation, so that the impurity may be burnt out, and the souls so cleansed or purified may attain the nature of Śiva. Before such attainment Śiva may appoint some souls, which had had their impurities cleansed, to certain mythical superintendence of the worlds as *vidyeśvaras* or *mantreśvaras*. At the time of the cycles of rebirth, the individual souls, which have to pass through it for the ripening of their actions, do so in subtle bodies called the *puryaṣṭaka* (consisting of the subtle matter, *buddhi*, *ahaṅkāra*, and *manas*).

Turning to the categories, we see that the so-called *pāśa* is also in reality a derivative of the energy of Śiva, and for this reason the *pāśa* may be a blinding force, and may also be withdrawn at the time of liberation. The category of Śiva or *śiva-tattva*, also called *bindu*, makes itself the material for the creation of the fivefold pure *tattvas* and the other impure categories up to gross matter, earth. These fivefold pure categories are *śiva-tattva*, *śakti-tattva*, *sadāśiva-tattva*, *īśvara-tattva*, and *vidyā-tattva*. The bodies of these pure categories are derived from the pure *māyā*, called the *mahāmāyā*. Next to these we have the pure-and-impure categories of *kāla*, *niyati*, *kalā*, *vidyā*, and *rāga*, which are a sort of link between the souls and the world, so that the souls may know and work. Next from the *māyā* comes *avyakta*, the *guṇa-tattva*, and from the *guṇa-tattva*, the *buddhi-tattva*, from that, *ahaṅkāra*, from that *manas*, *buddhi*, the five conative and five cognitive senses, the five *tanmātras* and the five gross objects.

As we have hinted above, most of the Siddhānta schools of thought are committed to the view that the material cause is different from the instrumental cause. This material cause appears in diverse forms as *māyā*, *prakṛti* or the atoms and their products, and the instrumental cause is God, Śiva. But somehow or other most of these schools accept the view that Śiva, consisting of omniscience and omnipotence, is the source of all energy. If that were so, all the energy of the *māyā* and its products should belong to Śiva, and the acceptance of a material cause different from the instrumental becomes an unnecessary contradiction. Various Siddhānta schools have shifted their ground in various ways, as is evident from our study of the systems, in order to get rid of contradiction, but apparently without success. When the Naiyāyika says that the material cause, the relations, and the instrumental cause are different, and that God as the instrumental cause fashions this world, and is the moral governor of the world in accordance with *karma*, there is no contradiction. God Himself is like any other soul, only different from them in the fact that He eternally possesses omniscience and omnipotence, has no body and no organs. Everything is perceived by Him directly. Again, if one takes the *yoga* point of view, one finds that Īśvara is different from *prakṛti* or the material cause, and it is not His energy that permeates through *prakṛti*. He has an eternal will, so that the obstructions in the way of the developing of energy of *prakṛti* in diverse channels, in accordance with *karma*, may be removed to justify the order of evolution and all the laws of nature as we find them. The Īśvara or God is like any other *puruṣa*, only it had never the afflictions with which the ordinary *puruṣas* are associated, and it has no *karma* and no past impressions of *karma*. Such a view also saves the system from contradiction, but it seems difficult to say anything which can justify the position of the Siddhānta schools wavering between theism and pantheism or monism. In the case of the Śaṅkara Vedānta, Brahman also is real and he alone is the material and instrumental cause. The world appearance is only an appearance, and it has no reality apart from it. It is a sort of illusion caused by *māyā* which again is neither existent nor non-existent as it falls within the definition of illusion. The different forms of Śaiva school have to be spun out for the purpose of avoiding this contradiction between religion and philosophy.

The category of Śiva, from which spring the five pure categories spoken of above (*sadāśiva*, etc.), is called also the *bindu*, the pure energy of knowledge and action beyond all change. It is supposed that this pure *śiva* or *bindu* or *mahāmāyā* is surcharged with various powers at the time of creation and it is in and through these powers that the *māyā* and its products are activated into the production of the universe which is the basis of the bondage of the souls. This movement of the diverse energies for the production of the universe is called *anugraha* or grace. By these energies both the souls and the inanimate objects are brought into proper relation and the work of creation goes on. So the creation is not directly due to Śiva but to His energy. The difficulty is further felt when it is said that these energies are not different from God. The will and effort of God are but the manifestations of His energy[1].

The different moments of the oscillation of God's knowledge and action are represented as the different categories of *sadāśiva*, *īśvara*, *vidyā*. But these moments are only intellectual descriptions and not temporary events occurring in time and space. In reality the category of Śiva is identical all through. The different moments are only imaginary. There is only the category of Śiva, bristling with diverse powers, from which diverse distinctions can be made for intellectual appraisal[2].

In the Sāṃkhya system it was supposed that the *prakṛti*, out of its own inherent teleology, moves forward in the evolutionary process for supplying to all souls the materials of their experiences, and later on liberates them. In the Siddhānta systems the same idea is expressed by the word *anugraha* or grace. Here energy is to co-operate with grace for the production of experience and for liberation. The fact that Śiva is regarded as an unmoved and immovable reality deprives the system of the charm of a personal

[1] Thus Śrīkumāra says, quoting from the *Mātaṅga-parameśvara* (p. 79):
tad uktaṃ mātaṅge:
patyuḥ śaktiḥ parā sūkṣmā jāgrato dyotana-kṣamā,
tayā prabhuḥ prabuddhātmā svatantraḥ sa sadāśivaḥ.

[2] *tattvam vastuta ekaṃ śiva-saṃjñaṃ citra-śakti-śata-khacitaṃ,*
śakti-vyāpṛti-bhedāt tasyaite kalpitā bhedāḥ. *Tattva-prakāśa* II. 13.

God. The idea of *anugraha* or grace cannot be suitably applied to an impersonal entity.

God's energies, which we call His will or effort, are the organs or means (*kāraṇa*), and the *māyā* is the material cause out of which the world is fashioned; but this *māyā* as such is so subtle that it cannot be perceived. It is the one common stuff for all. This *māyā* produces delusion in us and makes us identify ourselves with those which are different from us. This is the delusive function of *māyā*. The illusion is thus to be regarded as being of the *anyathā-khyāti* type, the illusion that one thinks one thing to be another, just as in *Yoga*. All the *karmas* are supposed to abide in the *māyā* in a subtle form and regulate the cycles of birth and rebirth for the individual souls. *Māyā* is thus the substantial entity of everything else that we may perceive.

We have already explained the central confusion as regards the relation of the changeable *māyā* and the unchanging God or Śiva. But after this the system takes an easy step towards theism, and explains the transformations of *māyā* by the will of God, through His energies for supplying the data of experience for all individual souls. Time is also a product of *māyā*. In and through time the other categories of *niyati*, etc., are produced. Niyati means the ordering of all things. It stands for what we should call the natural law, such as the existence of the oil in the seed, of the grain in the husk, and all other natural contingencies. We have translated the word *niyati* as 'destiny' in other places, for want of a single better word. *Niyati* comes from *niyama* or law that operates in time and place. The so-called *kalā-tattva* is that function of *niyati* and *kāla* by which the impurity of the individual souls becomes contracted within them so that they are free, to a very great extent, to act and to know. *Kalā* is thus that which manifests the agency (*kartṛtva-vyañjikā*). It is through *kalā* that experiences can be associated with individuals[1]. From the functioning of *kalā* knowledge proceeds, and through knowledge all experience of worldly objects becomes possible.

In the Sāṃkhya system the *buddhi* is supposed to be in contact with objects and assume their forms. Such *buddhi* forms are

[1] Thus Śrīkumāra quoting from *Mātaṅga*, says (p. 121): *yathāgni-tapta-mṛtpātraṃ jantunā'liṅgane kṣamaṃ, tathāṇum kalayā viddhaṃ bhogaḥ śaknoti vāsituṃ, bhoga-pātrī kalā jñeya tadādharaś ca pudgalaḥ.*

illuminated by the presiding *puruṣa*. The Siddhānta system as explained in *Tattva-prakāśa* differs from this view. It holds that the *puruṣa*, being inactive, cannot produce illumination. Whatever is perceived by the *buddhi* is grasped by the category of *vidyā* or knowledge, because the *vidyā* is different from *puruṣa* and is a product of *māyā* as such. It can serve as an intermediate link between the objects, the *buddhi*, and the self. *Buddhi*, being a product of *māyā*, cannot be self-illuminating, but the *vidyā* is produced as a separate category for the production of knowledge. This is a very curious theory, which differs from Sāṃkhya, but is philosophically ineffective as an epistemological explanation. *Rāgā* means attachment in general, which is the general cause of all individual efforts. It is not a quality of *buddhi*, but an entirely different category. Even when there are no sense objects to which one may be inclined there may be *rāga* which would lead a person towards liberation[1]. The totality of *kāla*, *niyati*, *kalā*, *vidyā*, and *rāga* as associated with the *paśu* renders him a *puruṣa*, for whom the material world is evolved as *avyakta*, *guṇa*, etc. Here also the difference from the Sāṃkhya system should be noted. In Sāṃkhya the state of equilibrium of the *guṇas* forms the *avyakta*, but here the *guṇas* are derived from the *avyakta*, which is a separate category.

The Śaiva system admits three *pramāṇas*: perception, inference, and testimony of scriptures. In perception it admits both the determinate (*savikalpa*) and the indeterminate (*nirvikalpa*), which have been explained in the first two volumes of this work. As regards inference, the Śaivas admit the inference of cause from effect and of effect from cause, and the third kind of inference of general agreement from presence and absence (*sāmānyato dṛṣṭa*).

The category of *ahaṅkāra*, which proceeds from *buddhi*, expresses itself in the feeling of life and self-consciousness. The *ātman*, the basic entity, is untouched by these feelings. The system believes in the tripartite partition of *ahaṅkāra*, the *sāttvika*, *rājasa*, and *tāmasa*, after the pattern of the Sāṃkhya, and then we have virtually the same sorts of categories as the Sāṃkhya, the details of which we need not repeat.

[1] Thus Śrīkumāra says (p. 124): *asya viṣayāvabhāsena vinā puruṣa-pravṛtti-hetutvād buddhi-dharma-vailakṣaṇya-siddhiḥ, mumukṣor viṣaya-tṛṣṇasya tatsādhane viśayāvabhāsena vinā pravṛttir dṛṣṭā.*

The relation between the *māyā* and the category of Śiva is called *parigraha-śakti*, by which the mechanism of the relation is understood as being such that, simply by the very presence of Śiva, various transformations take place in the *māyā* and lead it to evolve as the world, or to be destroyed in time and again to be created. The analogy is like that of the sun and the lotus flower. The lotus flower blooms of itself in the presence of the sun, while the sun remains entirely unchanged. In the same way, iron filings move in the presence of a magnet. This phenomenon has been variously interpreted in religious terms as the will of God, the grace of God, and the bondage exerted by Him on all living beings. It is in this sense again that the whole world may be regarded as the manifestation of God's energy and will, and the theistic position confirmed. On the other hand, since Śiva is the only ultimate category without which nothing could happen, the system was interpreted on the lines of pure monism like that of Śaṅkara, wherein it appeared to be a mere appearance of multiplicity, whereas in reality Śiva alone existed. This led to the interpretation of the system of Śivādvaita that we find in the *Sūta-saṃhitā*, *Yajña-vaibhava* chapter.

The *śakti* of God is one, though it may appear as infinite and diverse in different contexts. It is this pure *śakti* which is identical with pure will and power. The changes that take place in the *māyā* are interpreted as the extension of God's grace through creation for the benefit of the individual souls. God in the aspect of pure knowledge is called *śiva* and as action is called *śakti*. When the two are balanced, we have the category of *sadā-śiva*. When there is a predominance of action it is called *maheśvara*.

The theory of *karma* in this system is generally the same as in most other systems. It generally agrees with a large part of the Sāṃkhya doctrine, but the five *śuddha-tattvas*, such as *sadā-śiva*, etc., are not found elsewhere and are only of mythological interest.

The *Śiva-jñāna-siddhiyar* not only advocates the *niyamas*, such as good behaviour, courteous reception, amity, good sense, blameless austerity, charity, respect, reverence, truthfulness, chastity, self-control, wisdom, etc., but also lays great stress on the necessity of loving God and being devoted to Him.

Śrīpati Paṇḍita's Ideas on the Vedānta Philosophy, called also the *Śrīkara-bhāṣya* which is accepted as the Fundamental Basis of Vīra-śaivism.

Śrīpati Paṇḍita lived towards the latter half of the fourteenth century and was one of the latest commentators on the *Brahma-sūtra.* Śrīpati Paṇḍita says that he got the inspiration of writing the commentary from a short treatise called the *Agastyavṛtti* on the *Brahma-sūtra* which is now not available. He also adores Revaṇa, who is regarded by him as a great saint of the sect, and also Marula who was supposed to have introduced the doctrine of six centres (*ṣaṭ-sthala*). He adores also Rāma, who flourished in the Dvāpara-yuga, and who collected the main elements from the Mīmāṃsā and the Upaniṣads for the foundation of the Śaiva philosophy as it is being traditionally carried on.

The *Śrīkara-bhāṣya* should be regarded as a definite classification of the views of the different Śrutis and Smṛtis, and for this our chief admiration should go to Rāma. But though this work keeps itself clear of the dualistic and non-dualistic views of Vedāntic interpretation, it holds fast to a doctrine which may be designated as Viśiṣādvaita, and the Śaivas, called Vīra-śaivas, would find support in the tenets of the doctrine herein propounded. It may be remembered that Śrīpati came long after Rāmānuja, and it was easy for him to derive some of his ideas from Rāmānuja.

Śaṅkara, in his interpretation of the present *sūtra* "Now then the inquiry about Brahman," lays stress on the pre-condition leading to the necessity of inquiring about Brahman, and Rāmānuja also discusses the same question, and thinks that the Pūrva-mīmāṃsā and the Vedānta form together one subject of study; but Śrīpati here avoids the question, and thinks that the *sūtra* is for introducing an inquiry as to the ultimate nature of Brahman, whether Brahman is being or non-being. According to him the *sūtra* is further interested in discovering the influence of Brahman over individuals.

He took for granted the unity of the two disciplines of Pūrva-mīmāṃsā and Vedānta as forming one science, but he fervently opposes the view of the Cārvākas that life is the product of material combinations. He explains that the Cārvākas' denial of Brahman is based on the supposition that no one has come from the other world to relate to us what happens after death. He also points out that there are other schools within the *Vaidika* fold which do not believe in the existence of God or His power over individual beings, and that the power of *karma*, technically called *apūrva*, can very well explain the sufferings and enjoyments of human beings. So, if one admits the body to be the same as the spirit, or if one thinks that there is no necessity to admit God for the proper fruition of one's deeds, the twofold reason for the study of Vedānta could be explained away.

The doubt leading to an inquiry should therefore be located somewhere else, in the nature of God, Śiva, or in the nature of the individual soul. The existence of the God Śiva as being the only reality has been declared in a number of Vedic texts. The self, which shows itself in our ego-consciousness, is also known as a different entity. As such, how can the point of doubt arise? Moreover, we cannot know the nature of Brahman by discussion, for the self being finite it is not possible to understand the nature of the infinite Brahman by understanding the nature of such a soul. Moreover, the Upaniṣads have declared that the Brahman is of two kinds, consciousness and unconsciousness. So even when there is the Brahman knowledge, the knowledge of the unconscious Brahman should remain, and as such there would be no liberation.

Now the other point may arise, that the discussion is with regard to the attainment of a certitude as to whether the Brahman is identical with the self. There are many texts to that effect, but yet the contradiction arises from our own self-consciousness manifesting us as individual personalities. To this the ordinary reply is that the individuality of our ego-consciousness will always lead us to explain away the Upaniṣad texts which speak of their identity. But the reply, on the other side, may be that the Brahman may, through *avidyā* or nescience, create the appearance of our individuality, such as "I am a man." For without such an all-pervading illusion the question of liberation cannot arise. Moreover, the pure Brahman and all the objects are as distinct from each other as light from darkness, and yet such an illusion has to be accepted. For otherwise the entire mundane behaviour would have to be stopped. So there is hardly scope for making an inquiry as to the exact nature of the Brahman, the souls and the world. For one has to accept the ultimate reality of the transcendent Brahman which cannot be described by words. Brahman is thus beyond all discussion.

In a situation like this Śrīpati first presses the question of the existence of God as being proved by the Upaniṣadic and Śruti texts, by perception and by inference. We know from experience that often people cannot attain their ends, even if they are endowed with talent, ability, riches and the like, while others may succeed, even if they have nothing. According to Śrīpati, this definitely proves the existence of an omniscient God and His relationship with human beings. In ordinary experience, when we see a temple, we can imagine that there was a builder who built it. So in the case of the world also, we can well imagine that this world must have had a builder. The Cārvāka argument, that the conglomeration of matter produces things out of itself, is untenable, because we have never seen any such conglomerations of matter capable of producing life as we find it in birds and animals. In the case of cow-dung, etc., some life may have been somehow implanted in them so that beetles and other flies may be born from them. It has also to be admitted that in accordance with one's *karma* God awards punishments or rewards, and that the fruition of deeds does not take place automatically, but in accordance with the wishes of God.

In some of the Upaniṣadic texts it is said that there was nothing in the beginning, but this nothingness should be regarded as a subtle state of existence; for otherwise all things cannot come out of nothing. This non-being referred to in the Upaniṣads also does not mean mere negation or the mere chimerical nothing, like a lotus in the sky. Bādarāyaṇa in his *Brahma-sūtra* has also refuted this idea of pure negation (II. I. 7). In fact, the Vedas and the Āgamas declare God Śiva, with infinite powers, to be the cause of the world, whether it be subtle or gross. The individuals, however, are quite different from this Brahman, as they are always afflicted with their sins and sufferings. When the Upaniṣads assert that Brahman is one with *jīva*, the individual, naturally the inquiry (*jijñāsā*) comes, how is it possible that these two which are entirely different from each other should be regarded as identical?

Śrīpati thinks that the 'identity' texts of the Upaniṣads, declaring the identity of the individual and the Brahman, can well be explained by supposition of the analogy of rivers flowing into the ocean and becoming one with it. We need not assume that there is an illusion as Śaṅkara supposes, and that without such an illusion the problem of emancipation cannot arise, because we have a direct and immediate experience of ignorance when we say "we do not know."

Śrīpati objects strongly to the view of Śaṅkara that there is a differenceless Brahman of the nature of pure consciousness, and that such a Brahman appears in manifold forms. The Brahman is of an entirely different nature from the individual souls. If such a Brahman is admitted to have *avidyā* or nescience as a quality, it would cease to be the Brahman. Moreover, no such *avidyā* could be attributed to Brahman, which is often described in the Śruti texts as pure and devoid of any thought or mind. If the *avidyā* is supposed to belong to Brahman, then one must suppose that there ought to be some other entity, by the action of which this factor of *avidyā* could be removed for liberation. Brahman cannot itself find it; being encased by the *avidyā* at one moment and free at another, it cannot then retain its absolute identity as one. It is also fallacious to think of the world as being made up of illusory perceptions like dreams, for there is a definite order and system in the world which cannot be transgressed. Bādarāyaṇa himself also refutes the idea of a non-existence of an external world (II. 2. 27, 28). Moreover, the differenceless Brahman can only be established by the authority of the scriptural texts or by inference, but as these two are included within our conceptual world of distinctions, they cannot lead us beyond them and establish a differenceless Brahman. Moreover, if the truth of the Vedas be admitted, then there will be duality, and if it is not admitted, then there is nothing to prove the one reality of the Brahman. Moreover, there is nothing that can establish the fact of world illusion. *Avidyā* itself cannot be regarded as a sufficient testimony, for the Brahman is regarded as self-illuminating. Moreover, the acceptance of such a Brahman would amount to a denial of a personal God, which is supported by so many scriptural texts including the *Gītā*.

Again, the Upaniṣad texts that speak of the world as being made up of names and forms do not necessarily lead to the view that the Brahman alone is true and that the world is false. For the same purpose can be achieved by regarding Śiva as the material cause of the world, which does not mean that the world is false.

The whole idea is that, in whatsoever form the world may appear, it is in reality nothing but Śiva[1].

When Bādarāyaṇa says that the world cannot be distinguished as different from Brahman, it naturally means that the manifold world, which has come out of Brahman, is one with Him. The world cannot be regarded as the body of Brahman, and the scriptures declare that in the beginning only pure being existed. If anything else but Brahman is admitted, then the pure monism breaks. The two being entirely opposed to each other, one cannot be admitted as being a part of the other, and the two cannot be identified in any manner. So the normal course would be to interpret the texts as asserting both the duality and the non-duality of the Brahman. Thus the Brahman is both different from the world and identical with it.

Śrīpati thinks that on the evidence of the Śruti texts a Brahmin must take initiation in Śaiva form and bear with him the Śaiva sign, the *liṅga*, as much as he should, being initiated into Vedic rites. It is then that the person in question becomes entitled to the study of the nature of Brahman, for which the *Brahma-sūtra* has been written[2]. The inquiry into the nature of Brahman necessarily introduces to us all kinds of discussions regarding the nature of Brahman.

Though Śrīpati emphasises the necessity of carrying the *liṅga* and of being initiated in the Śaiva form, yet that alone cannot bring salvation. Salvation can only come when we know the real nature of Brahman. In introducing further discussions on the nature of Brahman, Śrīpati says that wherever the scriptural texts describe Brahman as differenceless and qualityless, that always refers to the period before the creation. It is Śiva, the differenceless unity, that expands His energy and creates the world and makes it appear as it

[1] *vācārambhaṇaṃ vikāro nāmadheyaṃ mṛttikety eva satyam iti śrutau apavāda-darśanād adhyāso grāhya iti cen na vācārambhaṇa-śrutīṇāṃ śivopādānatvāt prapañcasya tattādātmya-bodhakatvaṃ vidhīyate na ca mithyātvam. Śrīkara-bhāṣya*, p. 6.

[2] *Śrīkara-bhāṣya*, p. 8. Śrīpati takes great pains to show on the evidence of scriptural texts the indispensable necessity of carrying the insignia of Śiva, the *liṅga* in a particular manner which is different from the methods of carrying the *liṅga* not approved by the Vedas, pp. 8–15.

Śrīpati points out that only the person, who is equipped with the four accessories called the *sādhana-sampad* consisting of *śama, dama, titikṣā, uparati, mumukṣutva*, etc., is fit to have the *liṅga*.

is, though He always remains the ultimate substratum. The world is thus not illusion but reality, and of the nature of Śiva Himself. This is the central idea which is most generally expanded, as we shall see. Brahman thus appears in two forms: as pure consciousness and as the unconscious material world, and this view is supported by the scriptural texts. Brahman is thus with form and without form. It is the pure Brahman that appears as this or that changing entity, as pleasure or pain, or as cause and effect. Such an explanation would fit in with our experience, and would also be perfectly reconcilable with the scriptural texts.

The suggestion of the opponents, that Īśvara or God is an illusory God, is also untenable, for no one is justified in trusting an illusory object for showing devotion to him. Such a God would seem to have the same status as any other object of illusion. Moreover, how can an illusory God bestow benefits when He is adored and worshipped by the devotee?

Śrīpati then tries to refute the idea of the pure differenceless Brahman, and summarises the arguments given by Rāmānuja as we have described them in the third volume of the present work; and we are thus introduced to the second *sūtra*, which describes Brahman as that from which the production of the world has come about.

Śrīpati, in commenting upon *Brahma-sūtra* I. I. 2, says that the pure consciousness as the identity of being and bliss is the cause of the production and dissolution of the world, as well as its fundamental substratum. The Brahman, who is formless, can create all things without the help of any external instrument, just as the formless wind can shake the forest or the self can create the dreams. It is in the interest of the devotees that God takes all the forms in which we find Him[1]. He also refers to some of the scriptural texts of the *bhedābheda* type, which considers the relation between God and the world as similar to the relation between the ocean and the waves. Only a part of God may be regarded as being transformed into the material world. In this way Śiva is both the instrumental and the material cause. A distinction has to be made between the concept that there is no difference between the instrumental and

[1] *bhaktānugrahārthaṃ ghṛta-kāṭhinyavad-divya-maṅgala-vigraha-dharasya maheśvarasya mūrtāmūrta-prapañca-kalpane apy adoṣaḥ. Śrīkara-bhāṣya,* p .30.

the material cause, and the concept that the two are the same[1]. There is no question of false imposition.

The individual souls are spoken of in the Upaniṣads as being as eternal as God. The scriptural texts often describe the world as being a part of God. It is only when the powers of God are in a contractive form before the creation, that God can be spoken of as being devoid of qualities[2]. There are many Upaniṣadic passages which describe the state of God as being engaged in the work of creation, and as the result thereof His powers seem to manifest. It is true that in many texts *māyā* is described as the material cause of the world and God the instrumental. This is well explained if we regard *māyā* as a part of God. Just as a spider weaves out of itself a whole web, so God creates out of Himself the whole world. For this reason it should be admitted that the material world and the pure consciousness have the same cause. In this connection Śrīpati takes great pains to refute the Śaṅkarite doctrine that the world is illusion or imposition. If we remember the arguments of Mādhva and his followers against the doctrine of illusion as expounded in the fourth volume of the present work, the criticisms of Śrīpati would be included in them in one form or another. We thus see that the views of Śaṅkara were challenged by Rāmānuja, Nimbārka and Mādhva.

Śrīpati says that the so-called falsity of the world cannot be explained either as indescribable (*anirvācya*) or as being liable to contradiction, for then that would apply even to the Vedas. The phrase "liable to contradiction" cannot be applied to the manifold world, for it exists and fulfils all our needs and gives scope for our actions. So far as we see, it is beginningless. It cannot therefore be asserted that at any time in the future or in the present the world will be discovered as false. It has often been said that falsehood consists in the appearance of a thing without there being any reality, just as a mirage is seen to be like water without being able to serve the purpose of water. But the world not only appears, it also serves all our purposes. All the passages in the Purāṇas and other texts where the world is described as being *māyā* are only

[1] *tasmād abhinna-nimttopādāna-kāraṇatvaṃ na tu eka-kāraṇatvaṃ. Śrīkara-bhāṣya*, p. 30.

[2] *Śakti-saṅkocatayā sṛṣṭeḥ prāk parmeśvarasya nirguṇatvāt.* *Ibid.* p. 31.

delusive statements. So God alone is both the instrumental and the substantial cause of the world, and the world as such is not false as the Śaṅkarites suppose.

In the same way, the supposition that Īśvara or the *jīva* represents a being which is nothing else but Brahman as reflected through *avidyā* or *māyā* is also untenable. The so-called reflecting medium may be conditional or natural. Such a condition may be the *māyā*, *avidyā* or the *antaḥkaraṇa*. The condition cannot be gross, for in that case transmigration to the other world would not be possible. The idea of reflection is also untenable, for the Brahman has no colour and therefore it cannot be reflected and made into Īśvara. That which is formless cannot be reflected. Again if Īśvara or *jīva* is regarded as a reflection in *māyā* or *avidyā*, then the destruction of *māyā* or *avidyā* would mean the destruction of God and of the individual soul. In the same way Śrīpati tries to refute the theory of *avaccheda* or limitations, which holds that the pure consciousness as qualified or objectively limited by the mind would constitute the individual soul; for in that case any kind of limitation of consciousness such as we find in all material objects would entitle them to the position of being treated as individual souls.

The qualities of production and destruction, etc., belong to the world and not to Brahman. How then can the production and destruction of the world, of which God is the source, be described as being a defining characteristic of Brahman? The reply is that it cannot be regarded as an essential defining characteristic (*svarūpa-lakṣaṇa*), but only as indicative of Brahman as being the source of the world, so that even if there is no world, that would not in any way affect the reality of existence of God. This is what is meant by saying that the present definition (I. I. 2), is not a *svarūpa-lakṣaṇa*, but only *taṭastha-lakṣaṇa*. Śiva alone is the creator of the world and the world is maintained in Him and it is dissolved back into Him.

In commenting upon the *Brahma-sūtra* I. I. 3, Śrīpati follows the traditional line, but holds that the Vedas were created by God, Śiva, and that all the texts of the Vedas are definitely intended for the glorification of Śiva. This is, of course, against the Mīmāṃsā view that the Vedas are eternal and uncreated, but it agrees with Śaṅkara's interpretation that the Vedas were created by Īśvara. In Śaṅkara's system Īśvara is only a super-illusion formed by the reflection of Brahman through *māyā*. We have already noticed that Śrīpati regards this view as entirely erroneous. With him Īśvara or Maheśvara means the supreme God. Śrīpati further says that the nature of Brahman cannot be understood merely by discussion or reasoning, but that He can be known only on the evidence and testimony of the Vedas. He further says that the Purāṇas were composed by Śiva even before the Vedas, and that of all the Purāṇas the *Śiva-mahāpurāṇa* is the most authentic one. Other Purāṇas which glorify Viṣṇu or Nārāyaṇa are of an inferior status.

In commenting on *Brahma-sūtra* I. I. 4, Śrīpati says that the Mīmāṃsā contention is that the Upaniṣadic descriptions of the nature of Brahman should not be interpreted as urging people to some kind of meditation. They simply describe the nature of Brahman. Knowledge of Brahman is their only end. In this interpretation Śrīpati shares more or less the view of Śaṅkara. He further says that the nature of Brahman can only be known through the Upaniṣads. No kind of inference or general agreement can prove the fact that there is one God who is the creator of the world. In all things made by human beings, such as temples, palaces, or stone structures, many people co-operate to produce the things. We cannot, therefore, argue from the fact that since certain things have been made, there is one creator who is responsible for their creations. This is a refutation of the Nyāya view or the view of many of the *Śaivāgamas*, that the existence of one God can be proved by inference.

He further says that the force that manifests itself, and has plurality or difference or oneness, is in Brahman. We cannot distinguish the force or energy from that which possesses the force. The Brahman thus may be regarded both as energy and as the repository of all energies. There cannot be any energy without there being a substance. So the Brahman works in a dual capacity as substance and as energy[1]. It cannot be said that mere knowledge cannot stir us to action; for when one hears of the good or bad news of one's son or relation, one may be stirred to action. Thus, even pure knowledge of Brahman may lead us to His meditation,

[1] *bhedābhedātmikā śaktir brahma-niṣṭhā sanātanī, iti smṛtau śakter vahni-śakter iva brahmādhiṣṭhānatvopadeśāt. niradhiṣṭhāna-śakter abhāvāt ca śakti-śaktimator abhedāc ca tatkartṛtvaṃ tadātmakatvaṃ tasyaivopapan-natvāt. Śrīkara-bhāṣya*, p. 45.

so the Mīmāṃsā contention that the description of Brahman must imply an imperative to action, and that the mere description of an existing entity is of no practical value, is false.

Śrīpati makes fresh efforts to refute the Mīmāṃsā contention that the Vedas are not expected to give any instruction regarding a merely existing thing, for that has no practical value. Śrīpati says that a pure power of consciousness is hidden from us by *avidyā*. This *avidyā* is also a power of the nature of Brahman, and by the grace of Brahman this *avidyā* will vanish away into its cause. So the apparent duality of *avidyā* is false, and the instruction as regards the nature of Brahman has a real practical value in inducing us to seek the grace of God by which alone the bondage can be removed. The intuition of Brahman (*brahma-sākṣātkāra*) cannot be made merely by the study of the Upaniṣadic texts, but with the grace of God and the grace of one's preceptor.

Śrīpati says that the *nitya* and the *naimittika karma* are obligatory, only the *kāmya karma*, that is, those actions performed for the attainment of a purpose, should be divested of any notion of the fulfilment of desire. Only then, when one listens to the Vedāntic texts and surrenders oneself entirely to Śiva, the heart becomes pure and the nature of Śiva is realised.

Śrīpati again returns to his charge against the doctrine of the falsity of the world. He says that since the Upaniṣadic texts declare that everything in the world is Brahman, the world is also Brahman and cannot be false. The entire field of bondage as we perceive it in the world before us would vanish when we know that we are one with Śiva. For in that case the appearance of the world as diverse and as consisting of this or that would vanish, for everything we perceive is Śiva. Brahman is thus both the substantial cause and the instrumental cause of the whole world, and there is nothing false anywhere. The world cannot be a mere illusion or mere nothing. It must have a substratum under it, and if the illusion is regarded as different from the substratum, one falls into the error of duality. If the so-called non-existence of the world merely meant that it was chimerical like the lotus in the sky, then anything could be regarded as the cause of the world underlying it.

It may be held that the Śaṅkarites do not think that the world is absolutely false, but that its truth has only a pragmatic value (*vyavahārika-mātra-satyatvam*). To this, however, one may relevantly ask the nature of such a character, which is merely pragmatic, for in such a case the Brahman would be beyond the pragmatic, and no one would ask a question about it or give a reply, but would remain merely dumb. If there were no substance behind the manifold appearances of the world, the world would be a mere panorama of paintings without any basic canvas. It has already been shown that the Upaniṣads cannot refer to a differenceless Brahman. If any experience that can be contradicted is called pragmatic (*vyavahārika*), then it will apply even to the ordinary illusions, such as the mirage which is called *prātibhāsika*. If it is held that to be contradicted in a pragmatic manner means that the contradiction comes only through the knowledge of Brahman, then all cases of contradiction of a first knowledge by a second knowledge would have to be regarded as being not cases of contradiction at all. The only reply that the Śaṅkarites can give is that in the case of a non-pragmatic knowledge one has the intuition of the differenceless Brahman and along with it there dawns the knowledge of the falsity of the world. But such an answer would be unacceptable, because to know Brahman as differenceless must necessarily imply the knowledge of that from which it is different. The notion of difference is a constituent of the notion of differencelessness.

Neither can the conception of the *vyavahārika* be made on the supposition that that which is not contradicted in three or four successive moments could be regarded as uncontradicted, for that supposition might apply to even an illusory perception. Brahman is that which is not contradicted at all, and this non-contradiction is not limited by time.

Again it is sometimes held that the world is false because it is knowable (*dṛśya*), but if that were so, Brahman must be either knowable or unknowable. In the first case it becomes false, in the second case one cannot talk about it or ask questions. In this way Śrīpati continues his criticism against the Śaṅkarite theory of the falsity of the world, more or less on the same lines which were followed by Vyāsatīrtha in his *Nyāyā-mṛta*. It is, therefore, unprofitable to repeat these, as they have already been discussed in the fourth volume of the present work. Śrīpati also continues his criticism against the view that Brahman is differenceless on the same lines as was done by Rāmānuja in the introductory portion of his *bhāṣya* on the *Brahma-sūtra*, and these have been fairly elaborately dealt with in the third volume of the present work.

To declare Brahman as differenceless and then to attempt to describe its characteristics, saying, for example, that the world comes into being from it and is ultimately dissolved in it, would be meaningless. According to the opponents, all that which is regarded as existent would be false, which under the supposition would be inadmissible. If the world as such is false, then it is meaningless to ascribe to it any pragmatic value.

The question may be raised, whether the Brahman is knowledge or absence of knowledge. In the first case it will be difficult for the opponent to describe the nature of the content of this knowledge. The other question is, whether the opponent is prepared to regard the distinction between the false objects (the appearance of the world) and the Brahman as real or not. If the distinction is real, then the theory of monism fails. There is no way of escape by affirming that both the ideas of difference and identity are false, for there is no alternative. Moreover, if Brahman was of the nature of knowledge, then we should be able to know the content of such knowledge, and this would be contradictory to the idea of Brahman as differenceless. There cannot be knowledge without a content; if there is a content, that content is as external as Brahman Himself, which means that the manifold world of appearance before us is as external as Brahman. There cannot be any knowledge without a definite content. Moreover, if the world appearance is regarded as having a pragmatic value, the real value must be in that something which is the ground of the appearance of the manifold world. In such a case that ground reality would be a rival to the Brahman and would challenge His oneness. In this way, Śrīpati refutes the interpretation of Śaṅkara that the Brahman is differenceless and that the world-appearance is false. He also asserts that human beings are inferior to God's reality, and can have a glimpse of Him through His grace and by adoring Him.

The central idea of the Vīra-śaiva philosophy as propounded by Śrīpati is that God is indistinguishable from His energies, just as the sun cannot be distinguished from the rays of the sun. In the original state, when there was no world, God alone existed, and all the manifold world of matter and life existed in Him in a subtle form wholly indistinguishable from Him. Later on, when the idea of creation moved Him, He separated the living beings and made them different and associated them with different kinds of *karma*. He also manifested the material world in all the variety of forms. In most of the philosophies the material world has been a questionable reality. Thus, according to Śaṅkara, the world-appearance is false and has only a pragmatic value. In reality it does not exist, but only appears to do so. According to Rāmānuja the world is inseparably connected with God and is entirely dependent upon Him. According to Śrīkaṇṭha the world has been created by the energy of God and in that sense it is an emanation from Him, but Śrīpati refers to certain texts of the Upaniṣads in which it is said that the Brahman is both conscious and unconscious. Thus Śrīpati holds that everything we see in the world is real, and has Śiva or God as its substratum. It is only by His energy that He makes the world appear in so many diverse forms. He denounces the idea of any separation between the energy (*śakti*) and the possessor of it (*śaktimān*). Thus, if the world is a manifestation of the energy of God, that does not preclude it from being regarded as of the nature of Śiva Himself. Thus Śrīpati says that liberation can only come when God is worshipped in His twofold form, the physical and the spiritual. This makes him introduce the idea of a compulsory visible insignia of God, called the *liṅga*. Śrīpati also advocates the idea of gradation of liberation as held by Mādhva and his followers.

It must, however, be noted that, though God transforms Himself into the manifold world, He does not exhaust Himself in the creation, but the greater part of Him is transcendent. Thus, in some aspect God is immanent, forming the stuff of the world, and in another aspect he is transcendent and far beyond the range of this world. The so-called *māyā* is nothing but the energy of God, and God Himself is an identity of pure consciousness and will, or the energy of action and power.

Though, originally, all beings were associated with particular kinds of *karma*, yet when they were born into the material world and were expected to carry out their duties and actions, they were made to enjoy and to suffer in accordance to their deeds. God is neither partial nor cruel, but awards joy and suffering to man's own *karma* in revolving cycles, though the original responsibility of association with *karma* belongs to God. In this Śrīpati thinks that he has been able to bridge the gulf between the almighty powers of God and the distribution of fruits of *karma* according to individual deeds, thus justifying the accepted theory of *karma* and reconciling it with the supreme powers of the Lord. He does not seem to realise that this is no solution, as at the time of original association the individuals were associated with various kinds of *karma*, and were thus placed in a state of inequality.

Śrīpati's position is pantheistic and idealistically realistic. That being so, the status of dream experiences cannot be mere illusion. Śaṅkara had argued that the experiences of life are as illusory as the experiences of dreams. In reply to this Śrīpati tries to stress the view that the dream-experiences also are not illusory but real. It is true, indeed, that they cannot be originated by an individual by his personal effort of will. But all the same, Śrīpati thinks that they are created by God, and this is further substantiated by the fact that the dreams are not wholly unrelated to actual objects of life, for we know that they often indicate various types of lucky and unlucky things in actual life. This shows that the dreams are somehow interconnected with the actual life of our waking experiences. Further, this fact demolishes the argument of Śaṅkara that the experiences of waking life are as illusory as the experiences of dreams.

In speaking of dreamless sleep, Śrīpati says that in that state our mind enters into the network of nerves inside the heart, particularly staying in the *purītat*, being covered by the quality of *tamas*, and this state is produced also by the will of God, so that when the individual returns to waking life by the will of God, this *tamas* quality is removed. This explains the state of *suṣupti*, which is distinguished from the stage of final liberation, when an individual becomes attuned to God and becomes free of all associations with the threefold *guṇas* of Prakṛti. He then finally enters into the transcendent reality of Śiva and does not return to any waking consciousness. So it must be noted that, according to Śrīpati, both the dream state and the dreamless state are produced by God. Śrīpati's description of *suṣupti* is thus entirely different from that of Śaṅkara, according to whom the soul is in Brahma-consciousness at the time of dreamless sleep.

Śrīpati supports his thesis that in dreamless sleep we, with all our mental functions, pass into the network of nerves in the heart, and do not become merged in Brahman, as Śaṅkara might lead us to suppose. For this reason, when we wake the next day, we have revived in our memory the experiences of the life before the sleep. This explains the continuity of our consciousness, punctuated by dreamless sleep every night. Otherwise if we had at any time merged into Brahman, it could not be possible for us to remember all our duties and responsibilities, as if there were no dreamless sleep and no break in our consciousness.

In discoursing on the nature of difference between swoon (*mūrcchā*) and death, Śrīpati says that in the state of unconsciousness in swoon, the mind becomes partially paralysed so far as its different functions are concerned. But in death the mind is wholly dissociated from the external world. It is well to remember the definition of death as given in the *Bhāgavata Purāṇa* as being absolute forgetfulness (*mṛtyur atyanta-vismṛti*).

According to the view of Śaṅkara, the Brahman is formless. Such a view does not suit the position of Vīrā-śaivism as propounded by Śrīpati. So he raises the question as to whether the Śiva, the formless, is the same as the Śiva with the form as found in many *Śiva-liṅgas*, and in reply Śrīpati emphasises the fact that Śiva exists in two states, as the formless and as being endowed with form. It is the business of the devotee to realise that Śiva is one identical being in and through all His forms and His formless aspect. It is in this way that the devotee merges himself into Śiva, as rivers merge into the sea. The individual or the *jīva* is not in any sense illusory or a limitation of the infinite and formless nature into an apparent entity as the Śaṅkarites would try to hold. The individual is real and the Brahman is real in both the aspects of form and formlessness. Through knowledge and devotion the individual merges into God, as rivers merge into the sea, into the reality which is both formless and endowed with manifold forms.

Vīra-śaivism indeed is a kind of *bhedābheda* interpretation of the *Brahma-sūtra*. We have, in the other volumes of the present work, dealt with the *bhedābheda* interpretation, as made by Rāmānuja and Bhāskara from different angles. In the *bhedābheda* interpretation Rāmānuja regards the world and the souls as being organically dependent on God, who transcends the world of our experience. According to Bhāskara, the reality is like the ocean of which the world of experience is a part, just as the waves are parts of the ocean. They are neither absolutely one with it nor different from it. The Vīra-śaivism is also a type of *bhedābheda* interpretation, and it regards the absolute reality of the world of experience and the transcendent being, which is beyond all experience. Śrīpati sometimes adduces the illustration of a coiled snake which, in one state remains as a heap, and in another state appears as a long thick cord. So the world is, from one point of view different from God, and from another point of view one with God. This example has also been utilised by Vallabha for explaining the relationship between God and the world. The individual beings or *jīvas* may, through knowledge and devotion, purge themselves of all impurities, and with the grace of God ultimately return to the transcendent being and become merged with it. So things that appeared as different may ultimately show themselves to be one with Brahman.

Śrīpati points out that by the due performance of caste duties and the Vedic rites, the mind may become purified, so that the person may be fit for performing *yoga* concentration on Śiva, and offer his deep devotion to Him, and may thus ultimately receive the grace of God, which alone can bring salvation.

There has been a long discussion among the various commentators of the *Brahma-sūtra* as to whether the Vedic duties, caste-duties, and occasional duties form any necessary part of the true knowledge that leads to liberation. There have been some who had emphasised the necessity of the Vedic duties as being required as an indispensable element of the rise of the true knowledge. Others like Śaṅkara and his followers had totally denied the usefulness of Vedic duties for the acquisition of true knowledge. Śrīpati had all along stressed the importance of Vedic duties as an important means for purifying the mind, for making it fit for the highest knowledge attainable by devotion and thought. It may be noted in this connection that the present practice of the Liṅgāyats is wholly the concept of an extraneous social group and this anti-caste attitude has been supported by some authors by misinterpretation of some Vīra-śaiva texts[1]. But in commenting on the first topic of *Brahma-sūtra* III. 4, Śrīpati emphasises the independent claims of the knowledge of God and devotion to Him as leading

[1] See Professor Sakhare's *Liṅga-dhāraṇa-candrikā* (Introduction, pp. 666 *et seq.*) and also *Vīra-śaivānanda-candrikā* (*Vādakāṇḍa*, ch. 24, pp. 442 *et seq.*).

to liberation, though he does not disallow the idea that the Vedic duties may have a contributory effect in cleansing the mind and purifying it, when the person performs Vedic duties by surrendering all his fruits to God. Śrīpati, however, denounces the action of any householder who leaves off his Vedic duties just out of his personal whim.

In commenting on *Brahma-sūtra* III. 4. 2, Śrīpati quotes many scriptural texts to show that the Vedic duties are compulsory even in the last stage of life, so that in no stage of life should these duties be regarded as optional. In this connection he also introduces incidentally the necessity of *liṅga-dhāraṇa.* Though the Vedic duties are generally regarded as accessories for the attainment of right knowledge, they are not obligatory for the householder, who may perform the obligatory and occasional duties and yet attain a vision of God by his meditation and devotion.

The essential virtues, such as *śama* (inner control), *dama* (external control), *titikṣā* (endurance), *uparati* (cessation from all worldly pleasures), *mumukṣutva* (strong desire for liberation), etc., are indispensable for all, and as such the householders who have these qualities may expect to proceed forward for the vision of God. All injunctions and obligations are to be suspended for the preservation of life in times of danger. The Upaniṣads stress the necessity of the various virtues including concentration of mind leading to *Brahma-vidyā.* Śrīpati points out that every person has a right to pursue these virtues and attain *Brahma-vidyā.* This is done in the very best way by accepting the creed of Pāśupata Yoga.

The duties of a Śiva-yogin consist of his knowledge, disinclination, the possession of inner and outer control of passions, and cessation from egotism, pride, attachment and enmity to all persons. He should engage himself in listening to Vedāntic texts, in meditation, in thinking and all that goes with it in the *yoga* process, like *dhyāna*, *dhāraṇā*, and also in deep devotion to Śiva. But though he may be so elevated in his mind, he will not show or demonstrate any of these great qualities. He will behave like a child. Those that have become entirely one with Śiva need not waste time in listening to Vedāntic texts. That is only prescribed for those who are not very advanced. When a man is so advanced that he need not perform the *Varṇāśrama* duties or enter into *samādhi*, he is called *jīvan-mukta* in such a state; it depends upon the will of such a man whether he should enter into the *jīvan-mukta* state with or without his body. When a person's mind is pure, he may obtain an intuitive knowledge of Śiva by devotion. A truly wise man may be liberated in the present life. Unlike the system of Śaṅkara, Śrīpati introduces the necessity of *bhakti* along with knowledge. He holds that with the rise of knowledge, all old bonds of *karma* are dissolved and no further *karma* would be attached to him.

INDEX[1]

[1] The words are arranged in the order of the English alphabet. Sanskrit and Pāli technical terms and words are in small italics; names of books are in italics with a capital. English words and other names are in roman with a capital. Letters with diacritical marks come after ordinary ones.

Kāmin, 141
kāmya karma, 182
Kāṇāda, 6, 70*n*.
Kāṇādas, 15
Kānphāṭā Yogis, 58
Kāpāleśvara, temple of, near Nasik, 2–3
Kāpālikas, 1, 2–3, 9*n*., 50, 70, 72, 91, 97, 154
Kāpālika-vrata, 2
kāraṇa, 1, 15, 131, 133, 137, 170
Kāravaṇa-māhātmya, 7, 13, 14
kārikā, 115, 146
Kāruṇika-siddhāntins, 1, 2, 4, 50, 70
kārya, 1, 131, 132, 133
Kārikā, 11
Kāśikā-vṛtti, 12*n*.
Kāśmīr form of Śaivism, 98, 101–2
Kāyārohaṇa (Kāravaṇa), Bhṛgu-kṣetra, 7
kāya-siddhi, 59
Kena Upaniṣad, 119
kevalin, 141
Knowledge, 35, 48, 55, 63, 75, 165, 170–1, 174, 181; identical in essence with activity, 30–1; wrong knowledge, 32, 100; in the stage of *ahaṅkāra*, 34; as pure consciousness, 37, 57, 58, 93; special quality of knowledge possessed by the soul, 92–3; an aspect of Śiva, 100–1, 153–4; devotion identified with knowledge, 102, 103, 105; sorrow removed through knowledge, 108, 117; mediate and immediate knowledge, 118; leads to *yoga*, 122, 125; revealed through awareness, 133; Pāśupata view of, 141–2, 146–7; pragmatic and non-pragmatic knowledge, 182–3; whether Brahman is of the nature of knowledge, 184; acquisition of knowledge assisted by performance of Vedic duties, 188–9; intuitive knowledge of Śiva, 189–90
Koluttunga I, Chola king, 45
kriyā, 33, 123, 148, 157, 161
kriyā-śakti, 62, 100, 147, 157
kriyākhyā śakti, 120
kṣara, 109
kula, 58
Kumāra, 6
Kumārila Bhatta, 156
kuṇḍalinī, 59
Kuṇi, 6
Kureśa, 45
Kuśika, 6, 13, 131*n*., 144
Kūrma-purāṇa, 6*n*., 66, 72, 73

Lakulīśa, 5, 6 *and n*., 7
lakulīśa, 7
Lākulas, 50–1
Lākulīśa-pāśupatas, 1, 51, 72, 142
Lākulīśa-pāśupata-darśana, 7
Liberation, 22, 67, 69, 70, 73, 76–7, 142, 145, 162, 171, 174, 186; although attainable by personal action, such action is due to the grace of God, 78–9, 88–9, 105, 115; and the enjoyment of pure bliss, 82, 86–7; soul becomes omniscient in liberation, 93, 141, 161, and one with Brahman, 94; four types of liberation, 102–3; attained through true knowledge, 105, 115, 118, 189–90, through meditation, 108, 147, through suffering, 117, through the will of God, 119, 136, through non-attachment to virtue and vice, 122, through yogic processes, 122–8, 152, through the grace of God, 131–2, 152–3, through strength or power (*bala*), 146, through the dispersal of the non-spiritual, 164–5, through the worship of God in the physical and spiritual form, 185; assisted by performance of Vedic duties, 188–9
liṅga, 42, 52, 61–2, 119*n*., 133–4, 177 *and n*., 185
liṅga-dhāraṇa, 38, 42, 44, 46, 53, 189
Liṅga-dhāraṇa-candrikā of Nandikeśvara, 52, 188*n*.
liṅga-sthala, 61–2
Liṅgāyats, 42
Logos, 121
Lokākṣī, 6

Mādhva, 65, 179, 185
mahat, 119*n*.
Mahābhārata, 5, 7, 67, 91, 97
mahābhūtas, 166
Mahādeva, 141
mahādeva, 120
Mahādevī, 53
mahādevī, 120
Mahā-guru Kaleśvara, 61
Mahā-kāruṇikas, 121*n*., 154, 162